Praise for *Bullying Beyond the Schoolyard*

"Sameer Hinduja and Justin Patchin seamlessly weave the latest research with riveting examples from the frontlines of cyberbullying. This is the definitive work on cyberbullying, rich with practical tools for teachers, school personnel, parents, and students to prevent and respond to cyberbullying."

Suzanne Peck, President, Peck Consultants,
Author, *Stand Tall*

"The authors of *Bullying Beyond the Schoolyard* have written the manual on how to recognize, prevent, and respond to cyberbullying. I recommend that every educator and parent take the time to read and understand the important issue of cyberbullying. This book offers the answers educators and parents have been looking for when it comes to cyberbullying!"

Dr. Jolene Dockstader, Seventh-Grade
Language Arts Teacher, Jerome Middle School, ID

"The original text has become the seminal and authoritative text on the topic of cyberbullying. I am confident that the second edition will continue to be an essential resource for school districts, administrators, educators, parents, and policymakers."

Jude A. Huntz, Chancellor,
Diocese of Kansas City–St. Joseph, MO

"*Bullying Beyond the Schoolyard* is one of the most honest books I have read about the realities of childhood bullying and cyberbullying. I am recommending it to all my colleagues at my school for a book study. It should be required reading for anyone involved in educating children."

Donna Eurich, Middle School Teacher,
St. Clare Catholic School, North Palm Beach, FL

"Drs. Hinduja and Patchin answer questions about cyberbullying that we all have. As an educator and a parent, I appreciate the candor and informative nature of their book. I feel my home and school benefit from the topics we can now discuss to make our battle better prepared."

Dr. Frank Rudnesky, Principal,
Belhaven Middle School, Linwood, NJ

Praise for the First Edition

"School leaders need information about cyberbullying and resources on how to protect the children in their care. This book provides timely research, best practices, and personal voices from students that will go a long way toward improving student safety."

Gail Connelly, Executive Director,
National Association of Elementary School Principals

"Hinduja and Patchin are two of the most respected researchers on cyberbullying, and their in-depth research lays the foundation for this book. This book contains the best practices that principals can implement at their schools to prevent and respond to acts of cyberbullying."

Gerald N. Tirozzi, Executive Director,
National Association of Secondary School Principals

"Cyberbullying can have the same debilitating effects on a young person as face-to-face bullying: depression, a drop in school grades, loss of self-esteem, suicide, and other violent acts. We simply must do all we can to stop this devastating problem. This book is an excellent resource that clearly presents the relevant issues and provides many practical strategies to help readers address cyberbullying."

Alfonso E. Lenhardt, President and CEO,
National Crime Prevention Council

"An important contribution to the burgeoning literature on cyberbullying and a valuable tool for concerned adults that will enhance the safety and well-being of young people as they navigate their increasingly technological worlds. Backed by years of research and enhanced by the authors' perspectives from the worlds of criminology, juvenile justice, and computer science, this book offers educators, families, and youth service providers an array of useful information, ranging from the social and legal context to concrete strategies for responding to cyberbullying."

Scott Hirschfeld, Director of Curriculum, Anti-Defamation League

"Cyberbullying is a significant concern for teens and tweens in the 21st century. This timely and informative book brings adults up to speed on how kids are using technology to harm their peers."

Tina Meier, Cyberbullying Activist, Founder,
The Megan Meier Foundation

"Sameer Hinduja and Justin Patchin get it! There are only a few researchers and others who are focusing on this growing problem, and these two are pioneers in the field. While there is a lot of press about Internet safety issues such as predators and pedophiles, cyberbullying—using 21st century technologies as tools of peer abuse—tends to get lost in the shuffle. As professors of criminal justice, they get the fact that cyberbullying is not fundamentally a technology problem. Rather, it is a social and educational problem involving youth and their use of a variety of new technologies. The first responders should be parents and educators. From the table of contents and the preface, through each chapter, and throughout the wealth of immediately usable tools, this book is both an eye-opener and a hands-on text for classroom and support program educators and parents. It also puts things into practical perspective for professionals in law enforcement and the technology industry. It will take all of us to keep our young people safe in this new technological world. This is a much-needed resource."

Mike Donlin, Senior Program Consultant,
Seattle Public Schools, WA

"An exemplary volume, providing information, tools, and resources that can be used in every school."

Teaching Tolerance magazine, Fall 2010

To the teens who struggle with cyberbullying every day and to the adults who work to make their lives better. This book is for you.

Bullying
Beyond the Schoolyard

PREVENTING AND RESPONDING TO CYBERBULLYING

Second Edition

Sameer Hinduja • Justin W. Patchin

CORWIN
A SAGE Company

FOR INFORMATION:

Corwin
A SAGE Company
2455 Teller Road
Thousand Oaks, California 91320
(800) 233-9936
www.corwin.com

SAGE Publications Ltd.
1 Oliver's Yard
55 City Road
London EC1Y 1SP
United Kingdom

SAGE Publications India Pvt. Ltd.
B 1/I 1 Mohan Cooperative Industrial Area
Mathura Road, New Delhi 110 044
India

SAGE Publications Asia-Pacific Pte. Ltd.
3 Church Street
#10-04 Samsung Hub
Singapore 049483

Executive Editor: Arnis Burvikovs
Associate Editor: Desirée A. Bartlett
Editorial Assistants: Ariel Price and
                        Andrew Olson
Production Editor: Melanie Birdsall
Copy Editor: Diane DiMura
Typesetter: C&M Digitals (P) Ltd.
Proofreader: Susan Schon
Indexer: Molly Hall
Cover Designer: Michael Dubowe
Marketing Manager: Amanda Boudria

Printed in the United States of America

Library of Congress Cataloging-in-Publication Data

Hinduja, Sameer
Bullying beyond the schoolyard : preventing and responding to cyberbullying / Sameer Hinduja, Justin W. Patchin. — Second edition.

pages cm
Includes bibliographical references and index.

ISBN 978-1-4833-4993-0 (pbk.)

1. Cyberbullying. 2. Bullying. 3. Computer crimes. 4. Internet and teenagers. I. Patchin, Justin W. II. Title.

LB3013.3.H566 2014
302.34′302854678—dc23   2014025191

This book is printed on acid-free paper.

SFI   Certified Sourcing
       www.sfiprogram.org
       SFI-00453

14 15 16 17 18 10 9 8 7 6 5 4 3 2 1

Contents

Preface

Fifteen-year-old Phoebe Prince moved to South Hadley, Massachusetts, from Ireland at the beginning of the 2009–2010 school year. As a new, pretty, interesting girl from another country, she had attracted the attention of some of the local boys, which led to growing resentment from some of the girls at the school. As a result, several students began relentlessly bullying her until she couldn't take it anymore and chose to end her life. Media reports exclusively zeroed in on bullying and cyberbullying as the cause of Phoebe's suicide; some of the teens involved were even criminally charged. Actions taken by the school prior to the suicide were scrutinized, the community and nation clamored for justice, and the family and loved ones of Phoebe were left to face the incredibly painful fallout of what happened.

Like many of the previous cases of teen suicide tied to bullying that we are familiar with, there is more to the story than the simple sound bite explanation that bullying and cyberbullying led to Phoebe's death (more on this in Chapter 4). Emily Bazelon, bestselling author of Sticks and Stones, *detailed the emotional and psychological struggles and interpersonal conflict that Phoebe was dealing with in her coverage of the tragedy for Slate magazine. For example, she cut herself. She was prescribed medication to help with mood swings. Her parents and the school say they were on watch for signs of depression, but she first attempted suicide the day after Thanksgiving that year by swallowing a bottle of her pills. During this time, she also had dated at least two of the popular boys at her new school who had recently been in relationships with other girls. These girls apparently became jealous and, along with others, targeted Phoebe incessantly both at school and online. When taking into account everything that Phoebe had going on in her life, it appears that the bullying she experienced was the straw that broke the proverbial camel's back.*

Phoebe did not deserve to be bullied—no one does. Without a doubt, adolescence is an incredibly difficult developmental stage of life, fraught with numerous struggles and complexities. Some teens are better able than others to deal with the challenges of it all, including the stress and harm that stems from peer harassment. To be sure, some demonstrate remarkable resilience and can cope positively and persevere. Others, unfortunately, cannot and are very much affected, feeling angry, frustrated, depressed, and even suicidal.

Would Phoebe have committed suicide if she hadn't been bullied? Of course there is no way anyone can answer that question. There is little doubt she was tormented at great lengths by some of her classmates and that it persisted for a long time. Those experiences, coupled with the other challenges she was working through, were a recipe for disaster. A lot of seemingly little things related to bullying can quickly add up to something humongous in the eyes and lives of adolescents and can be overwhelming—making it feel like the walls surrounding them are slowly but surely closing in. Indeed, technology can magnify these so-called "little things" by exposing the target to a wider audience and by creating a perception in the victim that the whole world is against them. It also makes it harder to escape because of the ubiquitous nature of technology and how teens seem perpetually tethered to their devices and their online social world, which for the most part, mirrors many realities of their offline world.

The purpose of *Bullying Beyond the Schoolyard* is to bring you up to speed about the kinds of hurtful behaviors youth are experiencing and perpetrating online and to equip you with the knowledge and resources necessary to do something about them. Despite significant advances, many adults still lack basic knowledge when it comes to electronic devices, social media, smartphone apps, and the seemingly ever-changing online venues. Or at least they are often behind when compared with their kids. This book will help you catch up by describing the technology that youth are using, and in some cases misusing, every single day. The point is not to scare you into a negative perception of devices, sites, and apps—because they are amazing and here to stay! Instead, we want to educate and empower you to take certain proactive steps to protect youth and prevent and respond to inappropriate behaviors that involve technology.

While this book is primarily concerned with cyberbullying among students, we also touch on what should be done in situations where students employ electronic devices to harass educators. In fact, many of the lessons learned about how a school can and should respond to cyberbullying come from several cases where students were disciplined for cyber-harassing staff (Chapter 5 covers these issues in depth). Given the similarities, the methods discussed in this book for preventing and responding to cyberbullying among adolescents can also be applied to incidents of staff harassment.

APPROACH

Rather than acting solely on what is heard in the popular media concerning a new phenomenon, educators, parents, and others concerned about kids need to examine the problem of cyberbullying responsibly to learn how best to address it. The alarmist and sensationalistic headlines in the national news may grab our attention, but they do little to inform or teach us about the actual scope, prevalence, frequency, causes, and consequences of electronic aggression among teenagers. Research does.

Much of the information reported throughout this book stems from our own original research conducted since 2002. We have surveyed nearly 15,000 students from dozens of schools in the United States through eight separate surveys. Most recently (spring of 2014), we gathered and analyzed data from a random sample of 650 middle school students from a school in the northeastern United States. In all of our surveys, we ask youth about their experiences with traditional schoolyard bullying and cyberbullying as well as a number of other related factors (e.g., computer proficiency, stressful life events, self-esteem, and suicidal ideation). Our goal is to systematically and scientifically illuminate the problem of cyberbullying to better inform those who work most closely with youth.

Moreover, these data are supplemented by information collected from thousands of youth who have formally and informally corresponded with us over the years. We wanted them to tell us about their cyberbullying experiences *in their own words*. We found out that many targets of cyberbullying were scared to talk about it with their parents because they didn't want to be blamed or lose their computer privileges. We learned that some incidents lasted for years and that youth felt helpless and didn't know where to go for help. Adolescents in our research had a great deal to say about cyberbullying and wanted their voices to be heard. We wrote this book in part for that purpose: to tell their stories. And, as you will see, these stories are rich, colorful, eye opening, and even heartrending as they provide a very personal, vulnerable perspective.

The chapters that follow also include accounts from adults who are at the forefront of Internet-based behavioral issues. We have spoken to teachers, school administrators, counselors, law enforcement officers, parents, and many other youth-serving professionals who have been grappling with the complications that arise from cyberbullying incidents. Most of these folks simply improvised and did their best because not much was known about how to handle these unique cases properly. Since there are so many gray areas in terms of responding to cyberbullying, their interpretations and actions are important to consider because they contribute toward building a body of knowledge over time that can consistently provide meaningful guidance. It is hoped that the best practices we have collected and now share in this book can inform the actions of those of you who are in the trenches so that your prevention and response strategies have utility and value.

TARGET POPULATION

It is important in this introduction that we define the age range of youth to whom we are referring in this book. In short, we focus our discussion on adolescents. That said, we realize that the terms *adolescent* and *adolescence* mean different things to different people. Most researchers identify three distinct developmental periods: early adolescence (usually between ages 10–13), middle adolescence (ages 14–17), and late adolescence (18 through the early 20s).[1] We are most concerned with school-age youth—those under eighteen and in their early and middle developmental stages—so the majority of stories and data in this book originate from this population. While this is not to suggest that the cyberbullying experiences of older adolescents and adults (or even very young children) should be ignored, we have chosen to focus on an age group that is most susceptible to cyberbullying and least likely (comparatively speaking) to have acquired the skills to cope positively with it. In addition, we believe that it is easier to identify and intervene in experiences of online aggression among this population, which is still under the watch and care of parents and educators.

TERMINOLOGY

Throughout this book, we use terms like *cyberbully, aggressor,* and *offender* to refer to the one who has engaged in bullying behaviors. Similarly we use *victim* and *target* to refer to those who experience bullying. We want to acknowledge up front that we would have preferred not to use some of these terms in specific ways. For example, we generally don't like using any of the above as nouns (e.g., referring to the "bully" or the "victim") and try to avoid doing so wherever possible both in this book and when speaking with others. Unfortunately, we were compelled in some cases to use these as shorthand ways to refer to those involved in various roles. It would have been awkward to repeatedly write "the one who was targeted" or "the one who participated in bullying behaviors" over and over again throughout the book. Also, since both boys and girls are involved in bullying and in order to avoid the equally awkward use of *him or her* and *she and he,* we alternate between these gender-specific pronouns throughout.

THE IMPORTANT ROLE OF EDUCATORS

When considering our audience, we decided specifically to target educators with this information, since they are often the first contact when adolescent aggression occurs. In many cases, kids are spending more direct time each school day with their teachers than they are with their parents. As a result, educators may notice when something isn't quite right by picking up on subtle cues. Administrators, counselors, teachers, and others who work with teens on a daily basis also tend to be more proactive in informing themselves about issues facing youth today. In addition, schools that participate in the e-Rate program or are otherwise mandated by their state bullying law (discussed in more depth in Chapter 5) have an obligation to educate their students about responsible technology usage, including cyberbullying specifically. Educators are also required to respond to all forms of bullying that disrupt the learning environment at school, no matter where they occur. Finally, we believe educators can also serve as the conduit through which this important information reaches the parents of their students, as well as others in the community who need to learn about this problem.

Even though the vast majority of cyberbullying behaviors take place off school grounds, they very often make their way back into the school. In fact, many adolescent problems these days either begin at school and progress online or are initiated online and continue at school. Like it or not, educators will frequently have to deal with repercussions of disagreements or issues that began or escalated a great distance from the schoolhouse doors. Thankfully, you will see that there is much educators can and should do with respect to the online behaviors of their students—even if most of those actions and interactions occur outside of the confines of the school.

IMPORTANT FEATURES OF THE BOOK

Bullying Beyond the Schoolyard includes a number of special features that will help you identify, prevent, and respond to cyberbullying incidents. In addition to incorporating personal voices and viewpoints from youth affected by or involved in cyberbullying incidents, as well as educators and parents who are responsible for their safety and well-being, the book also contains several valuable in-text features to help reinforce the key concepts, including the following:

> *Bullying Beyond the Schoolyard* includes a number of special features that will help you identify, prevent, and respond to cyberbullying incidents.

- Breakout boxes highlighting important strategies to deal with cyberbullying

- Review of the latest research in this emerging area
- Summary of important legal rulings and what they mean to you
- Warning signs to help identify cyberbullies and their targets
- Practical ideas for you to implement to make a difference this school year
- Questions for reflection after each chapter
- Chapter summaries
- Index

Along with the special features in the text, the book also includes a number of tools in the Resources section that can assist you in understanding and addressing cyberbullying. These resources can be reproduced and distributed to others to help inform and educate your community about cyberbullying. They include the following:

- Cyberbullying Scenarios for Discussion
- Technology Use Contract
- Cyberbullying and Online Aggression Survey Instrument (2014 version)
- Cyberbullying Incident Tracking Form
- Cyberbullying Report Card for Schools
- Cyberbullying Trustee Designation
- Supplemental Staff Development Questions

ORGANIZATION OF THE BOOK

This book has been organized in such a way that will allow for easy access of important information, depending on the issues you currently face. We do not expect you to remember everything you read, so we structured the book to serve as a handy reference or resource. While there is some necessary overlap between chapters, each part is largely distinct in its examination of a particular topic relating to cyberbullying.

> This book has been organized in such a way that will allow for easy access of important information, depending on the issues you currently face.

Chapter 1 frames the problem of cyberbullying by first summarizing one of the most noteworthy stories from the last few years, and one that powerfully highlights the harm that can result when we ignore the misuse of electronic devices, social media, and the Internet. It continues by breaking down what we know about traditional forms of bullying in terms of its definition, prevalence, associated factors, and consequences. Cyberbullying is then defined and the important elements are discussed in a way that can inform the remainder of the book.

Chapter 2 provides background on the evolution of smartphones and social media and outlines the benefits they provide for their users. We then summarize the most popular cell phone applications and social media platforms that teens are (currently) using and highlight their attractive qualities, unique features, and societal impact. You may very well know and use some of these but may be unfamiliar or even unaware of others. And hopefully, this foundational information helps in promoting a more robust understanding of what kids like to do online.

Chapter 3 explains why cyberbullying stands on its own as a form of peer harassment by clarifying six key facets to consider: anonymity and pseudonymity, disinhibition, deindividuation, lack of supervision, virality, and limitless victimization risk. These characteristics, simply put, enable individuals to harass, humiliate, and threaten others more easily and readily than in the real world. Here, a number of quotes and real-life examples are presented to highlight the relevance of each facet.

Chapter 4 summarizes our research and that of others who have systematically studied the problem. The findings from these studies can help depict the scope and gravity of cyberbullying and be used to inform policy and programming as we move forward. Also, we are often asked, "Why exactly do kids bully other kids online?" While there is no simple answer to this question, a number of developmental, behavioral, psychological, and sociological explanations can help us understand the possible causes of this problem.

Chapter 5 presents a comprehensive discussion of the legal issues confronting school administrators who are attempting to understand the parameters of their role in responding to cyberbullying incidents. School officials are in a difficult position because they don't want to overstep their legal authority in disciplining student behavior that occurs off campus. We argue, however, that they can (and should) intervene in specific situations—in incidents that ultimately impact students or the learning environment at school. We review a number of court cases that support this perspective and detail the essential components of a well-developed and structured cyberbullying policy for schools.

Chapter 6 provides a number of practical recommendations for preventing cyberbullying. These include the following: formally assessing the frequency and scope of the problem among students; educating staff and youth through information sharing, assemblies, and rule setting; galvanizing teens to spread the message through peer mentoring programs; creating and maintaining a positive school climate; using blocking or filtering mechanisms; implementing formal anti-bullying prevention programming; and educating parents so they can do their part. The remainder of the chapter focuses on what parents and students can specifically do to reduce the chances of victimization, and to increase the positive and productive use of technology among adolescents. Our discussion of prevention wraps up with a summary of warning signs that may signal that a child is being cyberbullied, or is bullying someone else online.

Finally, Chapter 7 explores constructive ways in which to respond to cyberbullying. When appropriate, educators must step up quickly to identify and then discipline harmful behaviors in cyberspace by their students. We argue that informal response strategies will prove most useful for the majority of cyberbullying behaviors but also discuss when and how formal disciplinary action must be pursued. Also covered are ancillary but helpful strategies such as creative discipline ideas, aggravating circumstances where enhanced punitive measures are merited, how to reach and work with service and content providers to delete harmful material and accounts, and how to work with law enforcement. Informed and practical advice for parents of both those bullied and those who bully online is also provided, along with guidance for teens who are victimized or witness it happening. Overall, we convey that the role of each is critical to present a united front against cyberbullying and attempt to ensure that everyone knows all possible and optimal courses of action when dealing with incidents.

> Bullying is pressing in on us partly because the rise of the Internet forced us to see it up close, in printouts and screen shots or video clips, and partly because of the stubborn nature of the problem, across cultures and centuries. And it merits serious and sustained attention, because awareness is the first step to preventing bullying and to helping kids through it.
>
> —Emily Bazelon, *Sticks and Stones*[2]

NOTES

1. Judith G. Smetana, Nicole Campione-Barr, and Aaron Metzger. "Adolescent Development in Interpersonal and Societal Contexts." *Annual Review of Psychology* 57 (2006): 255–284.
2. Emily Bazelon. *Sticks and Stones: Defeating the Culture of Bullying and Rediscovering the Power of Character and Empathy,* p. 298. New York: Random House, 2013.

Acknowledgments

This book would not have been possible without the assistance of a number of important individuals in our personal and professional lives. First, we are both grateful to have supportive families who have cared for, encouraged, and inspired us over the years. Their love and affirmation has sustained us through the long hours of research and writing. We gratefully acknowledge the support of the Office of Research and Sponsored Programs at the University of Wisconsin-Eau Claire and the Division of Research at Florida Atlantic University for their support of our research presented throughout this book.

We would also like to convey appreciation to our professional colleagues who stand alongside us at the forefront of online safety issues among youth. We are most indebted to those who routinely take the time to dialog with us about these important issues, including Emily Bazelon, Michele Borba, Anne Collier, Darren Laur, Trudy Ludwig, Amanda Lenhart, Larry Magid, Sue Scheff, Rachel Simmons, Deb Temkin, Nancy Willard, and Rosalind Wiseman. For them, and for all who have been affected by cyberbullying, we offer this book as well as our commitment to continue this vital work. Finally, we would like to thank God for giving us the opportunities and abilities to study this problem and contribute to its understanding.

We would also like to extend our gratitude toward the staff at Corwin and SAGE Publications for their expert guidance throughout this process. Thanks especially to Arnis Burvikovs, Desirée Bartlett, Melanie Birdsall, and Ariel Price for helping us to bring this project to fruition. We also thank Diane DiMura for clarifying the meaning of our words while keeping our respective voices. In addition, we were fortunate to have several blind reviewers whose suggestions contributed to a tighter and more comprehensive work.

PUBLISHER'S ACKNOWLEDGMENTS

Corwin gratefully acknowledges the following reviewers for their editorial insight and guidance:

Dr. Jolene Dockstader, Seventh-Grade Language Arts Teacher
Jerome Middle School
Jerome, ID

Donna Eurich, Middle School Teacher
St. Clare Catholic School
North Palm Beach, FL

Dr. Carol S. Holzberg, Technology Coordinator
Greenfield Public Schools
Greenfield, MA

Jude A. Huntz, Chancellor
Diocese of Kansas City–St. Joseph
Kansas City, MO

About the Authors

 **Sameer Hinduja, PhD,** is a professor of criminology and criminal justice at Florida Atlantic University.

 **Justin W. Patchin, PhD,** is a professor of criminal justice at the University of Wisconsin-Eau Claire.

Since 2002, Dr. Hinduja and Dr. Patchin have been exploring the online behaviors of adolescents, including cyberbullying, social networking, and sexting. They are the authors of five books on the topic of cyberbullying, including *School Climate 2.0: Preventing Cyberbullying and Sexting One Classroom at a Time* (also from Corwin). They travel across the United States and abroad training educators, parents, teens, and others on how to keep youth safe online. They co-direct the Cyberbullying Research Center (www .cyberbullying.us) that serves as an information clearinghouse for those interested in learning more about cyberbullying and what they can do about it.

CHAPTER ONE

Bullying: Past, Present, and Future

The New Adolescent Aggression

> All I saw on Facebook was: "she deserved it . . . I hope she's dead . . . I hope she dies this time and isn't so stupid." I'm constantly crying now. Every day I think "why am I still here?" I'm stuck . . . what's left of me now . . . nothing stops. I have nobody . . . I need someone.
>
> —Amanda, 15, British Columbia*

AMANDA'S STORY

Many girls look forward to their sixteenth birthday with a great deal of anticipation and joy. It is supposed to be such a special day of celebration and even life-long memories. Unfortunately, young Amanda Todd from Port Coquitlam, British Columbia, never got to have this experience—in part because of the hate and harassment she experienced online, in school, and in her community. Amanda was a typical seventh-grader who, along with her friends, started using her webcam to meet new people across the nation and world. However, her life turned upside down when she met a guy online who sweet-talked her into taking off her top. Without really considering the implications of

---

Authors'Note: *All of the quotes used in this book are real stories shared by real people. Some of them have been edited for spelling and distracting grammatical errors. The substance of the quotes, however, has not changed.

her shortsighted action, Amanda naively went along with it. This decision ended up drastically affecting the course and outcome of her life.

Approximately one year after exposing herself via webcam, Amanda received a message on Facebook from the guy she had flashed. He threatened to distribute her topless picture unless she revealed more of herself to him. This did not seem like an empty threat as her blackmailer told her he knew her address and the names of her family and friends. When Amanda didn't comply, he did as promised—and Amanda and her family were awakened at 4 a.m. by local police officers who informed them that the picture was being distributed across the Internet. Soon after, it made its way around her school, and she had to deal with malicious taunts and tremendous cruelty from her peers (e.g., "porn star," "whore," "slut"). As a result, Amanda developed anxiety, major depression, and panic disorder and started abusing drugs and alcohol. Things didn't seem like they could get any worse, and so she decided it would be best to switch to a different school in the hopes of moving on with her life.

Sadly, the nightmare was far from over. Her blackmailer (and now stalker) tracked her to her new school, created a Facebook profile with Amanda's exposed breasts as the main profile picture, and then contacted her new classmates. This led to continued bullying and cyberbullying from school-mates, which took its toll as Amanda fell into a deep depression. To help cope and to try to escape the endless harassment and persecution, she changed schools yet again.

For a little while, it seemed like Amanda's situation was finally starting to turn around at the third school. She even met a boy who expressed an interest in her, which lifted her spirits and gave her a new sense of hope. Unfortunately, though, he took advantage of her while his girlfriend was away on vacation. This led to the girlfriend and her friends coming to school to find Amanda to exact revenge. She was mercilessly beaten by some while others stood around cheering, yelling vicious insults, and video recording the incident. In severe mental and emotional anguish, Amanda attempted suicide that afternoon by drinking bleach. Thankfully, though, she was rushed to the hospital where her stomach was pumped to save her in time.

In yet another effort to flee from the source of her pain and start over, Amanda moved to a new city. However, social media and smartphones made it easy for the harassment to follow her wherever she went. Her mom Carol has shared that "every time she moved schools [her stalker] would go undercover and become a Facebook friend. What the guy did was he went online to the kids who went to (the new school) and said that he was going to be a new student—that he was starting school the following week and that he wanted some friends and could they friend him on Facebook. He eventually gathered people's names and sent [the nude content] to her new school" (which included students, teachers, and parents). Such extreme and unrelenting torment led to continued substance abuse and self-harm and ultimately contributed to a decision by Amanda to overdose on her antidepressants—resulting in another hospital stay.

All of this, of course, gave her peers even more reasons to bully, reject, and humiliate her. In response and perhaps as a last-ditch cry for help, Amanda created a nine-minute YouTube video in September 2012 to share her anguish with the world. In it, she candidly told her story through the use of flashcards which conveyed how alone she felt. Unfortunately, her situation did not improve, and any help or support she did receive was simply not enough as the bullying and cyberbullying continued. In fact, individuals left vicious and hateful comments on her video saying that she should have used a different kind of bleach, and tried harder to kill herself. About a month after creating the YouTube video, Amanda decided that there was just no escape for her from the incessant abuse and pain. On October 10, 2012, just weeks before her sixteenth birthday, she successfully took her own life in her bedroom.

This story might seem sensationalistic, but it is true. We remember the first time we saw Amanda Todd's video and how our hearts started to race and our lungs started to tighten because we could empathize with her pain and struggle and yet we felt completely helpless to do anything about it. But in this story, we recognized how a perfect storm of elements came together: a teen desperate to find herself and feel accepted and loved; extensive social cruelty, exclusion, and bullying; and the widespread use of social media as a vehicle for communications and, in this case, a medium to harm instead of help. And so the incidents and outcome—extreme and tragic when compared to most cases of cyberbullying—can serve as both a cautionary tale and a case study depicting how teens can exploit their access to various devices, networks, and apps to hurt others if not educated and equipped with the knowledge they need to responsibly and wisely use them.

Amanda's story raises a number of important questions. Obviously, we wonder what could have been done to prevent this tragedy. Why are some teens so cruel to initiate the hate and harassment but then continue even as Amanda tried to escape it? What could have been done by Amanda's friends? How could the school have intervened and dealt with the problem and the aggressors? Would it have mattered? How could they have supported and protected Amanda? What could her family have done to help Amanda cope and outlast the harassment? What about at the neighborhood, community, and even societal level?

Amanda could have been our little sister, our daughter, or one of our kids' best friends. She could have been someone whose parents are friends of ours, who we barbecue with during the summer. She could have been on the same sports teams as other kids we know and love. It is devastating to think about the loss in this case—how a young, bright, beautiful girl will not be able to live up to her potential because of the way she was treated, and how the world was prematurely robbed of someone who could have contributed to it in amazing ways. But this is our reality. While the details of Amanda's story are extreme, and the vast, vast majority of peer harassment situations do not lead to such horrific outcomes, it vividly illustrates what *can* happen. And every incident we see or hear about involving kids traumatized at the hands of others—regardless of the severity—motivates us in the same way to do all we can about this problem. Because it is not right, and no one deserves to be mistreated. Ever. We are sure you feel the same way.

The primary goal of this book is to illuminate the best ways you can help the students you care for in your school and the children you have in your household. More than providing important information to understand cyberbullying, though, we want to give you the knowledge, skills, and tools necessary to address it. If you have previously faced some of these issues, you know how difficult it is to navigate this complex and challenging terrain. If you haven't encountered any instances of online aggression among the youth you serve, sooner or later you will. Regardless, we hope this book becomes your favorite resource when dealing with cyberbullying among youth.

> No one deserves to be mistreated. Ever.

Before we can dive into the details about what exactly cyberbullying looks like (and what you can do about it), first we need to take a step back and provide a basic foundation by reviewing what we know about traditional schoolyard bullying. This backdrop should help you fully appreciate the harm that often stems from bullying and clarify how cyberbullying can do the same. Perhaps you have a conception of bullying based on your personal experiences, news headlines or stories, television and movie scenes, or other sources. However, those are all largely anecdotal, high-profile, or isolated examples that may not represent the majority of bullying experiences. Over the last few decades, a number of scholars have actively researched bullying to identify trends and patterns across the personal experiences of thousands of youth. We now summarize what you need to know from this body of knowledge.

TRADITIONAL (SCHOOLYARD) BULLYING

The specific impact of bullying on young people has been studied at great length in the disciplines of counseling, education, sociology, psychology, psychiatry, and criminology. Most generally, the term *bullying* is equated to the concept of harassment, which is a form of unprovoked aggression often directed repeatedly toward another individual or group of individuals.[1] However, bullying tends to become more insidious as it continues over time and may be better equated to *violence* rather than *harassment*. Accordingly, Erling Roland states that bullying is "longstanding violence, physical or psychological, conducted by an individual or a group directed against an individual who is not able to defend himself in the actual situation."[2] Scandinavian researcher Dan Olweus, who is arguably most responsible for the current academic interest in the topic, defines bullying as "aggressive behavior that is intentional and that involves an imbalance of power. Most often, it is repeated over time."[3] Tonja Nansel, a senior investigator at the National Institutes of Health, and her colleagues define bullying as aggressive behavior or intentional "harm doing" by one person or a group, generally carried out repeatedly and over time and involving a power differential.[4] Finally, the Minnesota Department of Education states that "definitions of bullying vary, but most agree that bullying includes the intent to harm, repetition, and a power imbalance between the student targeted and the student who bullies."[5]

In January of 2014, the Centers for Disease Control and Prevention, the Department of Education, and the Health Resources and Services Administration, worked with a number of bullying experts across various fields to develop a uniform definition of bullying:

> Bullying is any unwanted aggressive behavior(s) by another youth or group of youths who are not siblings or current dating partners that involves an observed or perceived power imbalance and is repeated multiple times or is highly likely to be repeated. Bullying may inflict harm or distress on the targeted youth including physical, psychological, social, or educational harm.[6]

This is as good a definition as is currently available yet still likely falls short. Despite the variation across different perspectives, certain dominant themes are pretty obvious. First, the behavior is intentional and purposed rather than accidental or inadvertent. Accidents happen all of the time on the playground, and some of these result in physical harm. Still, most people recognize that accidental or unintentional behaviors do not constitute bullying. Most state bullying laws explicitly include an element of intent. For example, Delaware law characterizes bullying as an "intentional written, electronic, verbal or physical act."[7] Louisiana defines cyberbullying as "the transmission of any electronic textual, visual, written, or oral communication with the malicious and willful intent to coerce, abuse, torment, or intimidate a person."[8] Indeed, intent is generally a fundamental component of criminal law. In order to hold someone criminally responsible, not only must we establish that the person engaged in a wrongful act, but that he or she did so with *mens rea*, that is, a guilty mind. When it comes to law there are always exceptions, and we believe that the vast majority of bullying incidents can and should be handled outside of the formal law. The point is that most academic and legal definitions of bullying include intent.

Second, bullying necessarily involves maliciousness on the part of the aggressor, and that maliciousness is one type of *violence*. Researchers have attempted to categorize various types of bullying violence in multiple ways. Some have focused on differentiating between direct aggression and indirect aggression.[9] Direct aggression involves physical violence (hitting, kicking, taking items by force) and verbal violence (taunting, teasing, threatening).[10] Indirect aggression includes more subtle, manipulative acts such as ostracizing, intimidating, or controlling another person.[11] Others have focused on distinguishing between overt and covert (relational) forms of aggression. Overt aggression might involve name-calling, pushing, or hitting, while relational aggression includes gossip, rumor spreading, social sabotage, exclusion, and other behaviors destructive to interpersonal relationships.[12]

Third, one instance of aggression is not sufficient to qualify as bullying; to be considered bullying, behavior must occur, or present the threat of occurring, on a repetitive basis. This is one of the features that distinguishes bullying from other forms of peer harassment. We should clarify that just because a hurtful behavior only happens once doesn't mean that it should be ignored. It just means that it isn't accurate to refer to it as bullying. But part of the reason bullying can be so emotionally or psychologically damaging is *because* it is repetitive. The repetitive nature of bullying creates a dynamic where the victim continuously worries about what the bully will do next. Indeed, the target often alters his or her daily behaviors to avoid personal contact with the bully because it is assumed that something bad will happen if they interact. Do you personally remember choosing to go down different hallways or to show up to class right when it began instead of early to avoid spending unnecessary "quality time" with someone who always hassled you? We vividly recall instances from our middle school days that taught us the art of skillfully dodging any run-ins with the bullies in our respective lives.

> I just want to end this problem. I don't want to fight anymore with anyone. I've been trying to mind my own business but nobody seems to leave me alone. They always ask for a fight. I always try to ignore it but it's just too impossible for me to just let it go. I never fought with anyone till this year. This has been the worst year yet. My life is falling apart and I just don't know what to do anymore.
>
> —Scarlett, 15, Virginia

Fourth, inherent in any conception of bullying is the demonstration (or interpretation) of power by the offender over the target. If both parties were equal (socially, physically, or otherwise), one might think that neither has the proverbial upper hand. With differential levels of power, though, bullying can occur. Many characteristics can give a bully perceived or actual power over a victim, including popularity, physical strength or stature, social competence, quick wit, extroversion, confidence, intelligence, age, sex, race, ethnicity, or socioeconomic status.[13] And even more relevant to the primary topic of this text, technological proficiency can imbue a person with power over another. Youth who are able to skillfully navigate online environments or who know how to cover their virtual tracks have a leg up on a newbie who doesn't fully understand how to set up their accounts properly, or how to identify the authors of hurtful content.

To summarize, there appear to be four distinct components of bullying, which are listed in Box 1.1.

Box 1.1

Characteristics of Bullying

- Intentional behavior
- Repetition
- Violence or aggression
- Power differential

While the harassment associated with bullying can occur anywhere, the term *bullying* often concerns the behavior as it occurs between adolescent peers in some proximity to school. This includes at or around school bus stops, in school hallways and bathrooms, on the playground, or otherwise close to or inside the school setting. Bullies can also follow their targets to other venues, such as shopping malls, restaurants, or neighborhood hangouts, to continue the mistreatment.

> *Bullying* often concerns the behavior as it occurs between adolescent peers in some proximity to school.

Nevertheless, because of the prominence of the school in the lives of youth, these behaviors and interactions often reveal themselves at or near that environment. Of course, this means that teachers, school counselors, and other school officials are among the most important when it comes to bullying prevention, identification, and response.

The Definitional Debate: What Exactly Is *Bullying*?

As is probably clear based on the discussion above, there's been much debate between and among researchers, legislators, policymakers, and school administrators about the best way to define bullying. Each seems to conceptualize it differently, largely due to the constraints placed on them by their constituents. For example, researchers need to define it in a way that is measureable; legislators need to state it unambiguously so that it can withstand legal scrutiny; policymakers need to convert laws into practical and understandable guidelines for educators; and school administrators see variations of the behaviors every day and probably best understand the varied nature of experiences.

For years, we deliberately remained on the sideline when it came to debates like this. For us, whether some behavior was bullying or not was really beside the point. We advocated for identifying and focusing on the *specific problematic behavior* and addressing it reasonably and appropriately for what it was. Unfortunately, this is no longer an option as some states have passed laws that mandate specific actions when it comes to behaviors defined as bullying. For example, New Jersey law requires principals to investigate every incident of bullying within one school day and complete a formal report within ten school days that must be submitted to the superintendent within two days of completion.[14] Results of the investigation must be presented to the school board at the next regularly scheduled meeting. Students in Georgia who are found to have bullied others for a third time are sent to an alternative school.[15] Furthermore, labeling a particular behavior as bullying can complicate and inflame a situation—especially if the label is being misapplied. So it has become imperative to clearly articulate what is meant by bullying.

Trudy Ludwig, author of *My Secret Bully*[16] and many other outstanding children's books, also recognizes that not all hurtful peer-to-peer behavior can be accurately defined as bullying. She shares how one school she visited helped its community differentiate bullying from other forms of hurtful behavior:

- When someone says or does something unintentionally hurtful and they do it once, that's **RUDE**.
- When someone says or does something intentionally hurtful and they do it once, that's **MEAN**.
- When someone says or does something intentionally hurtful and they keep doing it—even when you tell them to stop or show them that you're upset—that's **BULLYING**.

And again, just because something doesn't necessarily qualify as bullying doesn't mean that it isn't hurtful or important to stop.

We don't expect to resolve this decades-long debate in this book, but we do hope to encourage researchers, policymakers, legislators, educators, and others who are charged with putting students in particular categories (e.g., the "bully") to think carefully about the criteria they use to make these decisions. Defining a person's behavior as bullying or labeling someone a bully can set that person on a particular trajectory, and it is best not to do this capriciously or haphazardly.

Prevalence of Traditional Bullying

Now that we've outlined some of the foundational features and characteristics of bullying, we'd like to take some time to highlight what is known about the extent of the problem. In recent years, a number of rigorous research studies have clarified the proportion of youth who have had experiences with bullying. As an example, a notable international study involving 202,056 students found that an average 26 percent of adolescents were involved as a bully, a victim, or as both (with rates varying by country and other demographic variables).[17] One nationally representative (US) study of 15,686 students in Grades 6 through 10 identified that approximately 11 percent of respondents were victims of bullying each year, while 13 percent were bullies and another 6 percent were both victims and bullies.[4] Similarly, the US Department of Justice's Bureau of Justice Statistics reported that of those youth between the ages of twelve and eighteen, 8 percent had been victims of bullying in the previous six months.[18] Other studies have suggested that the prevalence of bullying in American elementary schools is between 14 and 19 percent,[19] while the secondary school rate is between 3 and 10 percent.[20] Overall, conservative estimates maintain that *at least* 5 percent of those in primary and secondary schools (ages 7–16) are victimized by bullies *each day*—but the percentage may well be much higher.[21]

In addition, the National Crime Victimization Survey in the United States has been tracking bullying experiences through its nationally representative School Crime Supplement since 1989.[22] Surveys were administered in 1989, 1995, 1999, and biennially ever since. Researchers in this study changed how they measure bullying between 2003 and 2005, moving from a single question, "During the last 6 months, have you been bullied at school," to a series of questions that focus on specific bullying experiences (e.g., being made fun of, rumors spread, threats, etc.). As a result, it is difficult to compare rates from earlier studies to more recent ones. In 2005, however, 28.5 percent of students ages twelve to eighteen said they were bullied. In 2011, the latest year available, 27.8 percent (over 6.8 million youth) reported that they had been bullied at school. So, essentially, the proportion of teens who have experienced bullying at school has remained largely unchanged over the last decade or so.

Emotional and Psychological Consequences of Bullying

Consequences of bullying victimization identified in previous research include psychological and psychosomatic distress and problematic emotional and social responses.[23] For example, eating disorders and chronic illnesses have affected many of those who have been tormented by bullies, while other victims have run away from home.[24] According to an Office of Juvenile Justice and Delinquency Prevention fact sheet on juvenile bullying, victims of bullying often felt lonely, humiliated, insecure, and fearful going to school; experienced poor relationships and had difficulty making friends; and struggled with emotional and social adjustments.[25]

It has also been discovered that victims also regularly experience feelings of vengefulness, anger, and self-pity.[26] Indeed, depression has been a frequently cited consequence of bullying and seems to continue into adulthood—demonstrating the potentially long-term implications of peer mistreatment during adolescence.[27] Bullying victims have generally demonstrated more depression and distress than nonvictims.[28]

> The proportion of teens who have experienced bullying at school has remained largely unchanged over the last decade.

Finally, research based in the United States has found that being a victim of traditional bullying frequently increases the likelihood of experiencing suicidal thoughts by 10 percent in boys and by more than 20 percent in girls.[11] Generally speaking, victims tend to consider suicide and attempt suicide more often than nonvictims.[29] We'll discuss this very important relationship more in Chapter 4.

Academic and Behavioral Consequences of Bullying

The relationship between bullying and academic difficulties is a complicated one. There is no question that youth who are being bullied have a tough time concentrating on learning and therefore may struggle in their studies.[30] But at least one study has also found that those who struggle at school make for good targets of bullying.[31] So it is hard to know whether bad students make good targets or if being bullied contributes to bad school performance. We do know that some students who are bullied at school may attempt to avoid that environment as much as possible—which may worsen academic difficulties and lead to tardiness or truancy.[32] While missing school may not seem too alarming, it has been identified as often leading to delinquency, dropping out, and other undesirable outcomes.[33] Research has also linked bullying victimization to behaviors such as vandalism, shoplifting, dropping out of school, drug use, fighting, and school violence.[34]

As a final cautionary tale, consider the Columbine High School tragedy in Littleton, Colorado, in 1999. The educational system was challenged to address bullying because Eric Harris (age 18) and Dylan Klebold (age 17)—the two teenagers who carried out the massacre of twelve students and a teacher, while wounding twenty-four others, before committing suicide—were reported to have been ostracized and bullied by their classmates. Additional research of thirty-seven school shooting incidents involving forty-one attackers from 1974 through 2000 discovered that 71 percent of the attackers "felt bullied, persecuted, or injured by others prior to the attack."[35] It was determined that being bullied played at least some role in their later violent outburst.

> Research has linked bullying victimization to behaviors such as vandalism, shoplifting, dropping out of school, drug use, fighting, and school violence.

To review, the consequences of bullying victimization identified in previous research are both subtle (emotional and psychological) as well as tangible (physical and behavioral). We have felt it crucial to detail and group together these findings because traditional bullying has been studied for many years, while cyberbullying has only recently begun to be explored.

> Though I know life has its challenges, it seems this new generation is faced with a whole new challenge brought about via cyberbullying and related technology-based assaults.
>
> —Mother of a 14-year-old victim of cyberbullying, Hawaii

WHAT EXACTLY IS *CYBERBULLYING*?

In general, we define *cyberbullying* as "willful and repeated harm inflicted through the use of computers, cell phones, and other electronic devices" (see Box 1.2 for cyberbullying synonyms). We developed this definition because it is simple, concise, and reasonably comprehensive and it captures the most important elements. These elements include the following:

- **Willful:** The behavior has to be deliberate, not accidental.
- **Repeated:** Bullying reflects a pattern of behavior, not just one isolated incident.
- **Harm:** The target must perceive that harm was inflicted.
- **Computers, cell phones, and other electronic devices:** This, of course, is what differentiates cyberbullying from traditional bullying.

Box 1.2

Cyberbullying Synonyms

- cyber-bullying
- cyber bullying
- electronic bullying
- e-bullying
- cyber harassment

- text bullying
- SMS bullying
- mobile bullying
- digital bullying
- Internet bullying

Based on the research we have reviewed, the constructs of *malicious intent, violence,* and *repetition* are highly relevant when constructing a comprehensive definition of traditional bullying and are similarly appropriate when attempting to understand cyberbullying. To be sure, cyberbullies seek pleasure or perceived social benefits through the mistreatment of another. Violence is often associated with aggression and corresponds with actions intended to inflict injury or harm (of any type). Through electronic means, cyberbullies commonly convey direct threats of physical violence ("I am going to pound you at school tomorrow!!!") and manifest indirect psychological, emotional, or relational aggression ("UR gay and smelly and nobody likes you."). All of this is carried out with some measure of maliciousness, even if it is subtle and not patently visible.

Just like with traditional bullying, it is also important to remember that one instance of mistreatment cannot accurately be equated to bullying; it must involve harmful behavior of a repetitive nature. We believe that the nature of cyberbullying makes it very likely that repetitive harm will occur. For example, imagine someone posts a particularly embarrassing picture of another person online in such a way that others can see it, link to it, and leave public comments in reference to it. While the action of uploading the picture is a one-time behavior, others can view it or otherwise refer to it repeatedly, thereby resulting in recurring humiliation and shame to the target. One person might see it or millions of people might see it. And even if only one person actually saw the photo, the perception of the target is that everyone did.

Though not explicit in our definition, there is usually an imbalance of power in cyberbullying situations. We chose not to include it as a definitional component because the type of power being exerted in cyberspace is somewhat amorphous and often shifting. While power in traditional bullying might be physical (stature) or social (wit or popularity), online power may simply stem from proficiency with or the knowledge or possession of some content (information, pictures, or video) that can be used to inflict harm. Anyone with any of these characteristics or possessions within a certain online context has power, which can be wielded through some form

> *Cyberbullying* is defined as "willful and repeated harm inflicted through the use of computers, cell phones, and other electronic devices."

of cyberbullying. Indeed, anyone who can utilize technology in a way that allows them to mistreat others is in a position of power—at least at that moment—relative to the target of the attack. In addition, it can be difficult to measure this differential. As researchers we want to focus on the characteristics that are at least somewhat quantifiable. Suffice it to say that if one is being targeted for harassment in a way that doesn't allow him to capably respond, he lacks power in that dynamic and it is right to say that he is being bullied.

Also, we must mention that we tend to explicitly focus our attention on adolescents when we refer to cyberbullying. Many people use the term *bullying* to refer to a wide variety of behaviors between individuals of varying ages. We feel, though, that it is more appropriate to reserve the term *bullying,* and therefore also *cyberbullying,* for the kinds of behaviors we describe below as they occur between adolescent peers. While these behaviors often occur among adults as well, it is not usually proper to call the incidents bullying. We acknowledge that there is some debate about this distinction, but we want to be clear who and what *we are discussing* in this book.

One of the reasons why cyberbullying is sometimes not taken seriously is that there remains a subset of adults who continue to perceive traditional bullying as simply "a rite of passage among adolescents," as "boys being boys," or as an inevitable and even instructive element of growing up. If you experienced bullying during your formative years, perhaps you share those beliefs. We believe, however, that if emotional, psychological, and potentially even physical harm stemming from online aggression can be reduced or prevented, it is definitely worth the effort. Our conversations with bullied youth around the world corroborate that notion. This book represents our effort to educate school personnel and other adults about cyberbullying so that they are better equipped to address, prevent, and respond to electronic harassment in meaningful and productive ways.

> Well I get bullied a lot. In school, girls and boys even stare at me and laugh. They talk about me as if I'm not there. They make me feel worthless. Just today I logged onto my Instagram and I saw a girl who wrote "ew" on one of my pictures and started saying a lot of negative things. I just hate this. I feel so suicidal I don't understand why people hate me so much. I hate myself too. I can't even cope with life anymore. It's all too much especially when it's been going on for 5 years but it's only recently getting worse.
>
> —Corrinne, 16, England

Accidental Cyberbullying

Earlier in this chapter, we presented the fundamental characteristics of bullying (e.g., harm, repetition, power differential) and pointed out that to be accurately classified as bullying, a behavior needs to be intentional. Parenting advocate Sue Scheff wrote an article for the *Huffington Post* describing what she referred to as "accidental" bullying and cyberbullying. She pointed to examples of incidents where teens say things to others, usually online, that aren't intended to be hurtful but are experienced as such. "Even though it wasn't your objective," Scheff writes, "your words can be taken out of context by others when they're read and regurgitated, amplifying your digital footprint."[36] This can happen offline as well, of course, but technology certainly does more easily obscure actual intent. Many know from experience that it often leads to more frequent misunderstandings as communication occurs without important facial expressions, vocal intonations, or other interpretive behavioral cues that provide color and context to what is conveyed.

Scheff credits digital safety expert Katie Greer for first alerting her to these types of behaviors. In Scheff's article, Greer explains accidental bullying in this way: "Oftentimes, kids described trying to be nice or positive to one friend or cause via various social networking sites, and unintentionally hurting someone's feelings, or leaving someone out in the process."[68] It is true that it is common for teens to say things to classmates or even to their best friends, without malice or intent to cause harm, but yet the comments are misinterpreted or otherwise result in harm. But is this bullying?

The concept of an accidental bully is not new. Internet lawyer Parry Aftab has included the "inadvertent cyberbully" in her taxonomy for years (since at least 2006). "They do it for the fun of it. They may also do it to one of their friends, joking around. But their friend may not recognize that it is another friend or may take it seriously." According to Aftab, inadvertent cyberbullies "don't lash out intentionally," which is curious because she defines cyberbullying as "when a minor uses technology as a weapon to *intentionally* target and hurt another minor" [emphasis added].[37] Like Greer, Aftab describes a situation where teens do or say something to be funny or even helpful, but it is misinterpreted or, for one reason or another, results in hurt feelings.

Greer offers an example in which the friends of a teen girl set up an online profile on Instagram where people are asked to comment or vote for the prettiest girl among four shown. The idea is to show their friend that she is very pretty. The profile creators stuff the virtual ballot box so that their friend emerges victorious, not realizing that by doing so the other three girls involved in the vote have had their feelings hurt (because, after all, they aren't the prettiest). Were the less pretty girls in this example bullied? If the teens who created the site genuinely and honestly did not do so to cause harm to the girls who did not win, then we do not believe it is accurate to classify the incident as bullying.

Of course, the key to this is determining intent. It is possible that the girls responsible in Greer's example could have intended all along to take particular classmates down a notch by setting it up so they would emerge as losers. Or rig the vote in a way that one specific girl received significantly fewer votes than all of the rest, thereby securing her spot as the "least prettiest." It would be correct to classify those cases as bullying, though definitely not accidental. But if the girls are sincere and authentic in stating that they really didn't mean to cause harm to those who were not voted the prettiest, then it isn't bullying. It should not be ignored, however, and the girls responsible should be informed about the unintended consequences of their actions so that they will refrain from similar behaviors in the future. Hopefully that will be the end of the issue. If not, then subsequent intervention would be necessary.

Because it is impossible to know for certain what was going on in the mind of a teen when she behaved in a particular way, it is important to gather as much information as possible with which to determine whether or not the behavior in question could have been intentional. For example, is this the first time the particular student has been accused of bullying? Have there been behavioral problems with the student in the past? Were the students involved previously friends? Was there a falling out? Did anyone else (other students or staff) notice previous problems between the students?

Of course, we need to keep in mind that just because a teen has never misbehaved in the past, doesn't mean they didn't do so deliberately this time. And former friends often mistreat each other, especially if there was a recent issue that led to the breakup. The problematic behavior itself is only one piece of the puzzle. The more information you are able to gather about the nature of the relationships among all involved, the easier it will be to figure out what happened and why—and whether it is appropriate to categorize the incident as bullying.

SUMMARY

By now, we have set the stage by providing some background on traditional bullying and its newer variant: cyberbullying. Regardless of the form, bullying involves intentional and repeated harmful behaviors targeted at someone who cannot easily defend himself. There is so much yet to discuss: from the range of emotional, psychological, social, and behavioral consequences; to the legal issues that are implicated when considering if and when educators can discipline online behaviors of students; to exactly what we can do to prevent and respond to the problem. First, though, we must make sure we are all on the same page regarding the *cyber* aspect of cyberbullying. In Chapter 2, we dive deep into a discussion of the various mediums and venues that have gained widespread adoption and use among youth. Here, we cover and clarify the benefits of social media and associated smartphone apps, while also pointing out the ways in which these marvels of the modern world can be used to harm others.

QUESTIONS FOR REFLECTION

1. How does your school define *bullying*? Is it similar to the examples provided in this book? Does it include cyberbullying?

2. How do we define *cyberbullying*? Is this definition comprehensive enough?

3. How does cyberbullying differ from traditional schoolyard bullying? How are the two forms similar?

4. What are some of the consequences of experience with bullying or cyberbullying?

5. Do you think someone could be an "unintentional" or "accidental" bully or cyberbully?

NOTES

1. M. Manning, J. Heron, and T. Marshal. "Style of Hostility and Social Interactions at Nursery, at School, and at Home: An Extended Study of Children." In *Aggression*

and Antisocial Behavior in Childhood and Adolescence, edited by Lionel A. Hersov, M. Berger, and David R. Shaffer, 29–58. Oxford: Pergamon, 1978.

2. Erling Roland. "Bullying: The Scandinavian Research Tradition." In *Bullying in Schools,* edited by Delwyn P. Tattum and David A. Lane, 21–32. Stoke-on-Trent, UK: Trentham, 1989.

3. Dan Olweus. *Bullying at School.* Oxford, UK: Blackwell, 1993; Dan Olweus. "Bullying Among School Children." In *Health Hazards in Adolescence*, 259–297. Berlin: De Gruyter, 1990; Dan Olweus. *Aggression in the Schools. Bullies and Whipping Boys*. Washington, DC: Hemisphere Press, 1978.

4. Tonja R. Nansel, Mary Overpeck, Ramani S. Pilla, W. June Ruan, Bruce Simons-Morton, and Peter Scheidt. "Bullying Behaviors Among U.S. Youth: Prevalence and Association With Psychosocial Adjustment." *Journal of the American Medical Association* 285, no. 16 (2001): 2094–2100.

5. Minnesota Department of Education. "Bullying and Cyber-Bullying." *Safe and Healthy Learners* (2014). http://education.state.mn.us/MDE/StuSuc/SafeSch/BullyiCyberBullyPrev/index.html.

6. Matthew R. Gladden, Alana M. Vivolo-Kantor, Merle E. Hamburger, and Corey D. Lumpkin. *Bullying Surveillance Among Youths: Uniform Definitions for Public Health and Recommended Data Elements, Version 1.0* (2014). http://www.cdc.gov/violenceprevention/pdf/bullying-definitions-final-a.pdf.

7. Delaware State Code. Title 14: Education, Free Public Schools, § 4112D School Bullying Prevention (2014).

8. Louisiana State Legislature. La. Rev. Stat. § 14:40.7 Cyberbullying (2014).

9. Delwyn P. Tattum. "Violence and Aggression in Schools." In *Bullying in Schools,* edited by Delwyn P. Tattum and David A. Lane, 17–19. Stoke-on-Trent, UK: Trentham, 1989; Dan Olweus. *Aggression in the Schools. Bullies and Whipping Boys*. Washington, DC: Hemisphere Press, 1978; Valerie E. Besag. *Bullies and Victims in Schools.* Milton Keynes, UK: Open University Press, 1989; Susan P. Limber and Maury N. Nation. "Bullying Among Children and Youth." In *Combating Fear and Restoring Safety in Schools,* edited by June L. Arnette and Marjorie C. Walsleben. Office of Juvenile Justice and Delinquency Prevention (1998). http://www.ojjdp.gov/jjbulletin/9804/bullying2.html; Barbara Leckie. "Girls, Bully Behaviours and Peer Relationships: The Double Edged Sword of Exclusion and Rejection." Presented at Annual Conference of Australian Association for Research in Education, Brisbane, Australia, 1997; Nels Ericson. "Addressing the Problem of Juvenile Bullying." *OJJDP Fact Sheet, 27*. Washington, DC: US Department of Justice, Office of Justice Programs, Office of Juvenile Justice and Delinquency Prevention, 2001.

10. David S. J. Hawker and Michael J. Boulton. "Twenty Years' Research on Peer Victimization and Psychosocial Maladjustment: A Meta-Analytic Review of Cross-Sectional Studies." *Journal of Child Psychology and Psychiatry* 41, no. 4 (2000): 441–445.

11. Marcel F. van der Wal, Cees A. M. de Wit, and Remy A. Hirasing. "Psychosocial Health Among Young Victims and Offenders of Direct and Indirect Bullying." *Pediatrics* 111 (2003): 1312–1317.

12. Mitchell J. Prinstein, Julie Boergers, and Eric M. Vernberg. "Overt and Relational Aggression in Adolescents: Social-Psychological Adjustment of Aggressors and Victims." *Journal of Clinical Psychology* 30 (2001): 479–491; Nicki R. Crick and Jennifer K. Grotpeter. "Relational Aggression, Gender, and Social-Psychological Adjustment." *Child Development* 66 (1995): 710–722; Nicki R. Crick. "The Role of Relational Aggression, Overt Aggression, and Prosocial Behavior in the Prediction of Children's Future Social Adjustment." *Child Development* 67 (1996): 2317–2327; S. Sharp. "How Much Does Bullying Hurt? The Effects of Bullying on the Personal Well-Being and Educational Progress of Secondary Aged Students." *Educational and Child Psychology* 12 (1995): 81–88; Dieter Wolke, Sarah Woods, Linda Bloomfield, and Lyn Karstadt. "The Association Between Direct and Relational Bullying and Behaviour Problems Among Primary School Children." *Journal of Child Psychology and Psychiatry* 41, no. 8 (2000): 989–1002.

13. Dan Olweus, Susan P. Limber, and Sharon Mihalic. "Bullying Prevention Program." In *Fight Crime: Invest in Kids. Blueprints for Violence Prevention: Book Nine*, edited by Delbert S. Elliott. Boulder, CO: Center for the Study and Prevention of Violence, 1999; Dan Olweus. *Aggression in the Schools. Bullies and Whipping Boys*. Washington, DC: Hemisphere Press, 1978; Ken Rigby and Phillip T. Slee. "Dimensions of Interpersonal Relating Among Australian School Children and Their Implications for Psychological Well-Being." *The Journal of Social Psychology* 133, no. 1 (1993): 33–42; Erling Roland, *Terror i skolen*. Stavanger, Norway: Rogaland Research Institute, 1980; Phillip T. Slee and Ken Rigby. "The Relationship of Eysenck's Personality Factors and Self-Esteem to Bully-Victim Behaviour in Australian School Boys." *Personality and Individual Differences* 14 (1993): 371–373.

14. New Jersey Legislature Anti-Bullying Bill of Rights Act. P.L. 2010, Chapter 122 (2011).

15. Georgia Department of Education. O.C.G.A. 20–2–751.4 (2014).

16. Trudy Ludwig. *My Secret Bully*. Berkeley, CA: Tricycle Press, 2005.

17. Wendy Craig, Yossi Harel-Fisch, Haya Fogel-Grinvald, Suzanne Dostaler, Jorn Hetland, Bruce Simons-Morton, Michal Molcho, Margarida Gaspar de Mato, Mary Overpeck, Pernille Due, William Pickett. "A Cross-National Profile of Bullying and Victimization Among Adolescents in 40 Countries." *International Journal of Public Health* 54 (2009): 216–224.

18. Jill F. DeVoe, Katharin Peter, Philip Kaufman, Sally A. Ruddy, Amanda K. Miller, Mike Planty, Thomas D. Snyder, Detis T. Duhart, and Michael R. Rand. *Indicators of School Crime and Safety 2002*. NCES 2003–009. Washington, DC: US Department of Education, National Center for Education Statistics, and US Department of Justice, Bureau of Justice Statistics, 2002.

19. Joseph A. Dake, James H. Price, and Susan K. Telljohann. "The Nature and Extent of Bullying at School." *Journal of School Health* 73, no. 5 (2003):173–180.

20. Riittakerttu Kaltiala-Heino, Matti Rimpelä, Päivi Rantanen, and Arja Rimpelä. "Bullying at School—An Indicator of Adolescents at Risk for Mental Disorders." *Journal of Adolescence* 23 (2000): 661–674.

21. Dan Olweus. *Aggression in the Schools. Bullies and Whipping Boys*. Washington, DC: Hemisphere Press, 1978; Erling Roland, *Terror i skolen*. Stavanger, Norway: Rogaland Research Institute, 1980; Kirsti M. Lagerspetz, Kaj Björkqvist, Marianne Berts, and Elisabeth King. "Group Aggression Among School Children in Three Schools." *Scandinavian Journal of Psychology* 23 (1982): 45–52; Kaj Björkqvist, Kerstin Ekman, and Kirsti M. Lagerspetz. "Bullies and Victims: Their Ego Picture, Ideal Ego Picture, and Normative Ego Picture." *Scandinavian Journal of Psychology* 23 (1982): 307–313.

22. National Center for Educational Statistics. *Student Reports of Bullying and Cyber-Bullying: Results From the 2009 School Crime Supplement to the National Crime Victimization Survey* (2011). http://nces.ed.gov/pubs2011/2011336.pdf.

23. Anat Brunstein Klomek, Frank Marracco, Marjorie Kleinman, Irvin S. Schonfeld, and Madelyn S. Gould. "Bullying, Depression, and Suicidality in Adolescents." *Journal of the American Academy of Child and Adolescent Psychiatry* 46 (2007): 40–49; Robin M. Kowalski and Susan P. Limber. "Psychological, Physical, and Academic Correlates of Cyberbullying and Traditional Bullying. " *Journal of Adolescent Health* 53, no. 1 (2013): S13–S20. doi:10.1016/j.jadohealth.2012.09.018; Sheri Bauman, Russell B. Toomey, and Jenny L. Walker. "Associations Among Bullying, Cyberbullying, and Suicide in High School Students." *Journal of Adolescence* 36, no. 2 (2013): 341–350. doi: 10.1016/j .adolescence.2012.12.001; Dorothy Seals and Jerry Young. "Bullying and Victimization: Prevalence and Relationship to Gender, Grade Level, Ethnicity, Self-Esteem and Depression." *Adolescence* 38 (2003): 735–747; Helen Cowie and Lucia Berdondini. "The Expression of Emotion in Response to Bullying." *Emotional and Behavioural Difficulties* 7, no. 4 (2002): 207–214; Gerd Karin Natvig, Grethe Albrektsen, and Ulla Quarnstrøm. "Psychosomatic Symptoms Among Victims of School Bullying." *Journal of Health Psychology* 6 (2001): 365–377; Ryu Takizawa, Barbara Maughan, and Louise Arseneault. "Adult Health Outcomes of Childhood Bullying Victimization: Evidence From a Five-Decade Longitudinal British Birth Cohort." *American Journal of Psychiatry* 171 (2014): 777–784. doi:10.1176/appi.ajp.2014.13101401.

24. Mark G. Borg. "The Emotional Reaction of School Bullies and Their Victims." *Educational Psychology* 18, no. 4 (1998): 433–444. doi: 10.1080/01443419 80180405; Riittakerttu Kaltiala-Heino, Matti Rimpelä, Mauri Marttunen, Arja Rimpelä, and Päivi Rantanen. "Bullying, Depression, and Suicidal Ideation in Finnish Adolescents: School Survey." *British Medical Journal* 319, no. 7206 (1999): 348–351; Ruth H. Striegel-Moore, Faith-Anne Dohm, Kathleen M. Pike, Denise E. Wilfley, and Christopher G. Fairburn. "Abuse, Bullying, and Discrimination as Risk Factors for Binge Eating Disorder." *The American Journal of Psychiatry* 159, no. 11 (2002): 1902–1907.

25. Nels Ericson. "Addressing the Problem of Juvenile Bullying." *OJJDP Fact Sheet, 27*. Washington, DC: US Department of Justice, Office of Justice Programs, Office of Juvenile Justice and Delinquency Prevention, 2001.

26. Mark G. Borg. "The Emotional Reaction of School Bullies and Their Victims." *Educational Psychology* 18, no. 4 (1998): 433–444. doi: 10.1080/0144341 980180405; Marina Camodeca and Frits A. Goossens. "Aggression, Social

Cognitions, Anger and Sadness in Bullies and Their Victims." *Journal of Child Psychology and Psychiatry* 46 (2005): 186–197; Minne Fekkes, Frans I. M. Pijpers, and S. Pauline Verloove-Vanhorick. "Bullying Behavior and Associations With Psychosomatic Complaints and Depression in Victims." *Journal of Pediatrics* 144, no. 1 (2004): 17–22. doi: 10.1016/j.jpeds.2003.09.025.

27. David S. J. Hawker and Michael J. Boulton. "Twenty Years' Research on Peer Victimization and Psychosocial Maladjustment: A Meta-Analytic Review of Cross-Sectional Studies." *Journal of Child Psychology and Psychiatry* 41, no. 4 (2000): 441–445; Manuel Gámez-Guadix, Izaskun Orue, Peter K. Smith, and Esther Calvete. "Longitudinal and Reciprocal Relations of Cyberbullying With Depression, Substance Use, and Problematic Internet Use Among Adolescents." *Journal of Adolescent Health* 53, no. 4 (2013): 446–452; Dan Olweus. "Bullying at School: Long-Term Outcomes for Victims and an Effective School-Based Intervention Program." In *Aggressive Behavior: Current Perspectives,* edited by L. Rowell Huesmann. New York: Plenum Press, 1994.

28. David S. J. Hawker and Michael J. Boulton. "Twenty Years' Research on Peer Victimization and Psychosocial Maladjustment: A Meta-Analytic Review of Cross-Sectional Studies." *Journal of Child Psychology and Psychiatry* 41, no. 4 (2000): 441–445; Marcel F. van der Wal, Cees A. M. de Wit, and Remy A. Hirasing. "Psychosocial Health Among Young Victims and Offenders of Direct and Indirect Bullying." *Pediatrics* 111 (2003): 1312–1317; Ryu Takizawa, Barbara Maughan, and Louise Arseneault. "Adult Health Outcomes of Childhood Bullying Victimization: Evidence From a Five-Decade Longitudinal British Birth Cohort." *American Journal of Psychiatry* 171 (2014): 777–784. doi:10.1176/appi.ajp.2014.13101401; Carla Mills, Suzanne Guerin, Fionnuala Lynch, Irenee Daly, and Carol Fitzpatrick. "The Relationship Between Bullying, Depression and Suicidal Thoughts/Behavior in Irish Adolescents." *Irish Journal of Psychological Medicine* 21, no. 4 (2004): 112–116; Kirsti Kumpulainen and Eila Räsänen. "Children Involved in Bullying at Elementary School Age: Their Psychiatric Symptoms and Deviance in Adolescence." *Child Abuse and Neglect* 24 (2000): 1567–1577; Kirsti Kumpulainen, Eila Räsänen, Irmeli Henttonen, Fredrik Almqvist, Kaija Kresanov, Sirkka-Liisa Linna, Irma Moilanen, Jorma Piha, Kaija Puura, and Tuula Tamminen. "Bullying and Psychiatric Symptoms Among Elementary School-Age Children." *Child Abuse & Neglect* 22, no. 7 (1998): 705–717; Katrina Williams, Mike Chambers, Stuart Logan, and Derek Robinson. "Association of Common Health Symptoms With Bullying in Primary School Children." *British Medical Journal* 313, no. 7048 (1996): 17–19.

29. Anat Brunstein Klomek, Frank Marracco, Marjorie Kleinman, Irvin S. Schonfeld, and Madelyn S. Gould. "Bullying, Depression, and Suicidality in Adolescents." *Journal of the American Academy of Child and Adolescent Psychiatry* 46 (2007): 40–49; Sheri Bauman, Russell B. Toomey, and Jenny L. Walker. "Associations Among Bullying, Cyberbullying, and Suicide in High School Students." *Journal of Adolescence* 36, no. 2 (2013): 341–350. doi: 10.1016/j .adolescence.2012.12.001; Manuel Gámez-Guadix, Izaskun Orue, Peter K.

Smith, and Esther Calvete. "Longitudinal and Reciprocal Relations of Cyberbullying With Depression, Substance Use, and Problematic Internet Use Among Adolescents." *Journal of Adolescent Health* 53, no. 4 (2013): 446–452; Carla Mills, Suzanne Guerin, Fionnuala Lynch, Irenee Daly, and Carol Fitzpatrick. "The Relationship Between Bullying, Depression and Suicidal Thoughts/ Behavior in Irish Adolescents." *Irish Journal of Psychological Medicine* 21, no. 4 (2004): 112–116; Marla E. Eisenberg, Dianne Neumark-Sztainer, and Mary Story. "Association of Weight-Based Teasing and Emotional Well-Being Among Adolescents." *Archives of Pediatrics and Adolescent Medicine* 157 (2003): 733–738; Sean D. Cleary. "Adolescent Victimization and Associated Suicidal and Violent Behaviors." *Adolescence* 35 (2000): 671–682.

30. Jonathan Nakamoto and David Schwartz. "Is Peer Victimization Associated With Academic Achievement? A Meta-Analytic Review." *Social Development* 19 (2009): 221–242.

31. David Schwartz, JoAnn M. Farver, Lei Chang, and Yoolim Lee-Shin. "Victimization in South Korean Children's Peer Groups." *Journal of Abnormal Child Psychology* 30 (2002): 113–125.

32. Ken Rigby and Phillip T. Slee. "Dimensions of Interpersonal Relating Among Australian School Children and Their Implications for Psychological Well-Being." *The Journal of Social Psychology* 133, no. 1 (1993): 33–42; BBC-News. "Girl Tormented by Phone Bullies." http://news.bbc.co.uk/1/hi/ education/1120597.stm.

33. Tonja R. Nansel, Mary Overpeck, Ramani S. Pilla, W. June Ruan, Bruce Simons-Morton, and Peter Scheidt. "Bullying Behaviors Among U.S. Youth: Prevalence and Association With Psychosocial Adjustment." *Journal of the American Medical Association* 285, no. 16 (2001): 2094–2100; David P. Farrington. "Truancy, Delinquency, the Home, and the School." In *Out of School: Modern Perspectives in Truancy and School Refusal*, edited by Lionel A. Hersov and Ian Berg, 49–63. New York: Wiley, 1980; Eileen M. Garry. "Truancy: First Step to a Lifetime of Problems." *Juvenile Justice Bulletin* (NCJ161958). Washington, DC: US Department of Justice, Office of Justice Programs, Office of Juvenile Justice and Delinquency Prevention, 1996; Tom Gavin. "Truancy: Not Just Kids' Stuff Anymore." In *FBI Law Enforcement Bulletin 66*. Washington DC: US Department of Justice, Federal Bureau of Investigation, 1997.

34. Nels Ericson. "Addressing the Problem of Juvenile Bullying." *OJJDP Fact Sheet, 27*. Washington, DC: US Department of Justice, Office of Justice Programs, Office of Juvenile Justice and Delinquency Prevention, 2001; Marcel F. van der Wal, Cees A. M. de Wit, and Remy A. Hirasing. "Psychosocial Health Among Young Victims and Offenders of Direct and Indirect Bullying." *Pediatrics* 111 (2003): 1312–1317; Manuel Gámez-Guadix, Izaskun Orue, Peter K. Smith, and Esther Calvete. "Longitudinal and Reciprocal Relations of Cyberbullying With Depression, Substance Use, and Problematic Internet Use Among Adolescents." *Journal of Adolescent Health* 53, no. 4 (2013): 446–452; Ken Rigby. "Consequences of Bullying in Schools." *Canadian Journal of Psychiatry* 48 (2003): 583–590; Justin W. Patchin. "Bullied Youths Lash Out: Strain as an

Explanation of Extreme School Violence." *Caribbean Journal of Criminology and Social Psychology* 7, no. 1/2 (2002): 22–43; Michelle L. Ybarra, Marie Diener-West, and Philip J. Leaf. "Examining the Overlap in Internet Harassment and School Bullying: Implications for School Intervention." *Journal of Adolescent Health* 41 (2007): S42–S50. doi: 10.1016/j.jadohealth.2007.09.004; Loraine Townsend, Alan J. Flisher, Perpetual Chikobvu, Carl Lombard, and Gary King. "The Relationship Between Bullying Behaviours and High School Dropout in Cape Town, South Africa." *South African Journal of Psychology* 38, no. 1 (2008): 21–32.

35. Bryan Vossekuil, Robert A. Fein, Marisa Reddy, Randy Borum, and William Modzeleski. "The Final Report and Findings of the Safe School Initiative: Implications for the Prevention of School Attacks in the United States." Washington, DC: US Secret Service and US Department of Education, 2002. http://www.secretservice.gov/ntac/ssi_final_report.pdf.

36. Sue Scheff. "Accidental Bullying and Cyberbullying." http://www.huffingtonpost.com/sue-scheff/accidental-bullying-and-c_b_3843092.html.

37. Parry Aftab. "How Do You Handle a Cyberbully?" http://stopcyberbullying.org/educators/howdoyouhandleacyberbully.html.

CHAPTER TWO

Teens Online Today

Where and Why

On a Thursday afternoon in early December, 2005, Musselman High School (West Virginia) senior Kara Kowalski came home from school and logged onto MySpace to create a group page titled "S.A.S.H.," which she said was an acronym for "Students Against Sluts Herpes." Included on the page was the quote, "No No Herpes, We don't want no herpes." She invited approximately 100 of her classmates to join the group and participate in what she later described as an effort to "make other students actively aware of STDs," which was a "hot topic" at her school.[1]

Soon after its creation, around two dozen other Musselman students joined the group and subsequently began posting comments and photos to the page, most of which included references to Shay N., another Musselman student. For example, Ray Parsons—the first to join the group—posted a photo of himself holding a sign that read "Shay Has Herpes" from a school computer during an after-hours class. Kara quickly responded by posting "Ray you are soo funny!=)" and "the best picture [I]'ve seen on myspace so far!!!!" Another student posted a photo of Shay that was labeled "portrait of a whore." Another student posted a photo of Shay with red dots drawn all over her face to simulate herpes. Shay learned about the page within just a few hours of the photos being posted and told her father, who phoned Ray to express his anger over the photo and comments. Ray immediately called Kara who tried to delete the page but couldn't. Instead, she changed the title to "Students Against Angry People." The next day Shay and her parents filed a formal report at school, and Kara was subsequently suspended for ten days (which was later reduced to five days) for creating a "hate website" and consequently violating the school's harassment, bullying, and intimidation policy.

J ust as the telephone revolutionized interpersonal interaction in the 20th century by enhancing our ability to "reach out and touch" others, and as the automobile provided us the means to transcend space and time constraints previously insurmountable, information technology has dramatically altered and expanded the way in which individuals interact. At the time of this writing, there are 7.2 billion people on earth, and 3 billion Internet users. This means that around 40 percent of the world is online.[2] Here in America, we have an approximate population of 325 million people, and 85 percent of us are online. We shake our heads in astonishment when considering how fortunate we are to be living during this era of monumental change and progress, the likes of which we may never see again in our lifetimes. And while adults have led the way in creating these new technologies, teenagers have often been the driving force behind their growth, especially as it relates to novel online methods of communication.

> I'd rather give up, like, a kidney than my phone. How did you manage before? Carrier pigeons? Letters? Going round each others' houses on BIKES?[3]
>
> —Philippa, 16, UK

Based on the latest available data from the Pew Internet & American Life Project in 2012, over 95 percent of teens are online, with 74 percent accessing the Internet via their mobile devices. Eighty-one percent have a phone (over half of those are smartphones) and 23 percent have a tablet. At least four out of five (81 percent) twelve- to seventeen-year-olds use social networking sites, with many accessing them and the rest of the web via their smartphones as well as from laptops, desktops, or tablet computers.[4] In many ways, proficiency with these devices and applications (apps) has become absolutely critical for personal and professional success, and it is largely demanded that adolescents in the current generation have an adequate level of expertise with a vast array of Internet technologies before they enter college or the workforce.

Most teenagers do not struggle with being technologically proficient—it almost seems to come naturally for them. Rather, it is the adult population that has had some difficulty keeping up with the profound transformations that technological advances have introduced into our culture. The terms *digital natives* and *digital immigrants* have been used in the past to describe how youth (the "natives") have grown up with electronic devices, social media, and the Internet and therefore use them as seamless, complementing extensions of their "real-world" behaviors (most teens would tell you that there is nothing "unreal" about their interactions online).[5] Adolescents today have not known a

period of their lives when they were not able
to search the Internet or communicate with
others electronically from anywhere and at
any time. Being raised in the Information
Age has given adolescents an apparent
intrinsic ability to understand how electronic

Most teenagers do not struggle
with being technologically
proficient—it almost seems to
come naturally for them.

devices can and must be used for a vast number of purposes. And many youth
are completely embedded in an online culture that is largely inseparable and
indistinct from their offline world, even though many adults struggle to comprehend this lifestyle practice.

Most adults (the "immigrants"), on the other hand, haven't grown up
with technology and therefore have to work extra hard to learn how to use
and best exploit the benefits that it has to offer.[5] To be sure, many are jump-
ing right in, as evidenced by the fact that older adults are the fastest growing
segment on Facebook.[6] Nevertheless, differences in experiences tend to
shape adults' perceptions and perspectives when it comes to technology. For
example, since adults have lived a period of time without these communications tools, they don't tend to get as upset when there is a brief disruption to
their access. Sure, if e-mail goes down or we don't have a good cell phone
signal, we are inconvenienced and annoyed. But we will live.

For teens, these experiences can be much more distressing. They have
come to take technology for granted and when something happens that inter-
rupts this access, they sometimes freak out. This is one reason why it can be
difficult for teens to completely walk away from an online environment in
which they are being mistreated. They feel the need to be a part of that
community—even if they are being bullied. Now, though, we need to
remember that these technologies are not just *part* of adolescents' lives. They
are their lives, and if we think about things that way we will more readily
understand what is going on, and what to do about it. First, let's discuss how
mobile devices have revolutionized how people communicate and interact.

OUR SMARTPHONE SOCIETY

As we pointed out above, the majority of teens have smartphones, and many
of them (and us, to be honest) seem inextricably connected to these marve-
lous devices. Demonstrating this growing dependence, we sometimes find
ourselves checking our phone for messages, alerts, or calls—even when we
don't notice it ringing or vibrating. Many sleep with their phone next to
their bed because they want to make sure they don't miss any calls, messages, or other updates during the night. And many teens have told us that
their phone is something they *can't live without*! Of course, most of us love
our devices because they help us keep in touch with people. We can also

organize our daily schedules, priorities, and routines and be productive or entertained while waiting for whatever is next in our lives. We just take it for granted to have connectivity to all sorts of people and information in the palm of our hands.

We have witnessed the transition of mobile phones from devices that could only make and receive voice calls to ones that send and receive texts, pictures, and short videos to those with the capacity to receive e-mails and browse the Internet. What we were previously able to do only on bulky desktops and laptops, we do in our hands. But then the industry took everything to an entirely new level by providing the ability for individuals and companies to create self-contained pieces of software that could run on phones. And look where it has brought us—to a time where most of us love and constantly use a variety of social media apps. Some individuals can't pick up and use their phone for a specific task without also, almost unconsciously, checking Instagram, Snapchat, Twitter, or Facebook to see if they have any new notifications or content to go through (can you relate?). In fact, it's been one tremendous reciprocal relationship to behold: the proliferation of smartphones has been a primary cause of the expansion of the types and utilization of social media, and the desire for people to constantly be connected online has been a boon to the purchase and ubiquity of the devices.

> I posted a picture of my guy friend on Instagram for his birthday. After I got a couple of likes, I went on Twitter. Four girls there were saying hurtful things about me for posting the picture. I don't know why they felt so offended. They posted tweets calling me names. I wanted to turn my phone off, but when other people started to like and retweet, those awful things I just couldn't!
>
> —Sara, 15, New Jersey

TECHNOLOGY BECOMES MORE SOCIAL

As we've mentioned, instant messaging and e-mail have historically been the primary mediums through which interaction took place. However, the last decade has borne witness to an explosion in the use of social media for communications, where individuals set up accounts and create profiles to represent themselves and then link them together with others in some capacity.

Depending on the specific platform, social networking websites and apps enable individuals to create digital representations of themselves—and share biographical information, personal anecdotes or ramblings, affiliations, likes and dislikes, interests, thoughts, quotes, ideas, and—of course—multimedia (pictures, video, and audio). Youth especially have embraced this way of communication and interaction and have been the engine behind the success of most (if not all) social media spaces. According to communications professor Susannah Stern, creating an online persona (e.g., a profile on a social media website) allows teens to "display the selves they are, the selves they wish to become, and the

> Social media allows youth to participate in a full-time, always-on community.

selves they wish others to see."[7] This then allows them to participate in a full-time, always-on, community in which they can feel emotionally close and connected to others even when they are physically apart.[8]

WHERE ARE TEENS ONLINE TODAY?

Against this backdrop, a number of social networking sites have surfaced in the last decade which have gained and held some measure of popularity (and there have been countless others that haven't). The social media landscape is constantly shifting, and we've lived long enough to know that what is all the rage one year is often supplanted by something new the next. To note, our first edition of this book—which we wrote in 2007 and published in 2008—featured expansive and almost exclusive coverage of MySpace (remember that site?). In case you're wondering, it is currently owned by Specific Media LLC and Justin Timberlake and has been repurposed to feature musical artists and bring together the listening community. Just as the book was gaining increased readership, Facebook skyrocketed past MySpace as the most popular social networking site—and we had barely even mentioned it! Thankfully, our discussion of the important issues were presented broadly enough where they still clearly applied, no matter what social media environment was hot, and we'll take that same tack with this second edition. Before getting into these issues, though, we begin with a brief summary of the *current* popular places teens are congregating (and we'll see which ones are still around for the third edition of this book!).

Facebook

Facebook still boasts by far the largest population of users overall (upwards of 1.4 billion as of the summer of 2014), and is the third most popular website overall in both the United States and the world (right behind Google and YouTube).[9] Over the years, Facebook has developed a variety of features that has allowed it to stand above and apart from the rest. Those of us who do use it benefit from the chat (private/public) functionality; picture, video, and file sharing; and the posts we make and receive on each other's Wall (a visible space within each profile where users can share anything and everything with those to whom they are connected). Various popular websites outside of the social media sphere (such as CNN, MSN, ESPN, Bleacher Report) allow users to comment (and interact with others) on their articles while logged into Facebook (and Twitter and Google+, in many cases). Finally, Facebook's detailed Privacy settings allow users to share as much or as little about their lives as they want. Content can be completely locked down, visible only to friends, or publicly viewed by other users. And like most popular sites, users can block others, making themselves inaccessible through the site.

Stories have surfaced in recent months that suggest a decline in enthusiasm and even participation by teens and young adults on Facebook.[10] According to teens, it's because there are other simpler alternatives available (primarily Instagram, Snapchat, Twitter, Vine, Ask.fm, and WhatsApp) and because Facebook has lost "cool" points because of all the adults on it, the advertisements and marketing ads throughout, and some the new features that make things complicated and therefore annoying.[11] In recent years, Facebook appears to be gearing content more toward what older consumers want, as compared to teens (perhaps in their interest to monetize their services). Indeed, the average Facebook user is now a twenty-five-year-old female college graduate with a modest income.[12] All of this said, though, Facebook has been the king of social media innovation for over a decade and it is hard to imagine an online world without them.

Twitter

While Facebook tries to position itself as being able to offer all things to all people, other social media sites have had to specialize in order to thrive (or survive). For example, Twitter is currently one of the largest of the social network platforms and is unique, in part, because of its self-defined limits to the length of posts. Messages posted on the site (called *tweets*) are restricted to no more than 140 characters. This limitation stemmed from the worldwide standard length of text messages and because users (originally) posted to their Twitter accounts by sending a cell phone text message to the service. At the time they launched, phones were limited to sending messages of 160 characters or less and, while phones and messaging have advanced to allow for more characters, Twitter has maintained the 140 character limit (originally, 20 characters were reserved for the username of the recipient). The short messages enable their network to function as a way for quick, succinct bursts of information to circulate between and among people across schoolyards, nations, and even continents.

The 140-character restriction limits Twitter's functionality when compared to Facebook, but its purpose is not to compete with Facebook. Rather, it has occupied a niche as a pure and robust communications tool for users to quickly find and connect with others (and always be updated with what they post) and broadcast information quickly and powerfully to hundreds, thousands, or millions of others who "follow" them. It also allows individuals to send short and to-the-point direct messages and replies (which can include pictures and web links) to specific people and to follow "trending" (or currently popular) topics and stories on a second by second basis. Hashtags (#) are also used on Twitter (and now Instagram and Facebook) to highlight particular keywords for search purposes across everyone's accounts on the social media site and to label tweets as related to specific content (e.g., #cyberbullying for information on cyberbullying, #ISTE2014 for the International Society for Technology in Education 2014 conference, or #edchat for information on educational issues). Hashtags can also be a fun way to describe a person or experience (e.g., #rockstar, #fail). Of course like anything, these can be abused, as we will discuss in Chapter 3.

Instagram

Instagram has distinguished itself by providing an easy-to-use and elegant platform for individuals to take, manipulate, and post pictures and videos to share with their followers. Of course, it also allows others to "like" and post comments on the images posted. That is really it—you can't do much else—and that's the beauty of it. Latest statistics indicate that it has well over 200 million monthly users and is growing faster than any other major social media app or site.[13] Instagram's popularity burgeoned in the last few years, and it's perhaps no coincidence that Facebook purchased it in early 2012.[14] "Facebook realized it needed not just a mobile future, but also a future for this younger or teen audience" and that "teenagers use [Instagram] to share pictures of themselves . . . the more you share, the greater the reaction, and the more you push outside comfort zones, the more people react."[15]

I have always been kind to people, ALWAYS! But in the seventh grade, my attitude changed. There was a girl who kept bullying me calling me fat, stupid, little white girl. That really hurt my feelings. Then the girl did a TBH (to be honest) video about me and posted it on Instagram. When I saw the video I just stood at my desk crying. I was so upset that I just walked to my parents and cried and told them everything. My parents called the school about the video and the girl got in trouble and suspended. I am still to this day so hurt. To everyone out there who may have had this happen to them, it's always a good idea to go tell your parents or teacher. It sucks but I got through it. Just always be nice online.

—Deni, 13, undisclosed US location

Snapchat

Snapchat allows users to send messages, drawings, photos, or videos from their phone to someone else's that will display on the recipient's screen from one to ten seconds. After the time has elapsed, the content disappears and is seemingly gone forever. Most teens realize that even though the image may no longer be visible on the 5-inch screen in front of them, it doesn't mean it is really completely gone (despite implicit promises from the app itself). Latest statistics show that 70 million active users send over 400 million *snaps* each day,[16] and teens enjoy the service because it is simple, seemingly secret, and fun. Snapchat may also appeal to youth because they simply want to be connected with their friends and "do life" together, and one of the ways this connection is maintained and strengthened is by sharing as many moments as possible with each other. Many times, though, these moments are banal, represent an inside joke, provide a short quick laugh, or are just a token to let someone else know they are thinking about them. Increasingly, teens don't want messages, photos, or videos representing these moments preserved forever online through Twitter or Facebook.[17] They just want to quickly connect, feel gratified, and move on.

> Someone made a fake Snapchat and sent a picture of someone's butt to them. Now I'm being made fun of, when I didn't do it. Parents are even harassing me. I'm scared.
>
> —James, 14, Illinois

Vine

Vine is Twitter's entrée into the world of video sharing. Its unique nature stems from the requirements that users post looping videos no longer than six seconds in length. Teens love it because it allows for creativity and cuteness—they can make clips of literally anything that comes across their minds, and there is no pressure to create a masterpiece.[18] The services are easy to use and millions of Vines are posted to Twitter every single day. A recent Twitter survey showed that top users posted around thirty to fifty Vines each week.[19]

Ask.fm

As of the end of the 2013–2014 school year, Ask.fm was perhaps *the most controversial* social media platform used by teens and is used by 123 million individuals across the world as of the summer of 2014.[20] Still, it is really no different from the other anonymous question-and-answer websites that preceded it (like the less popular Spillit.me and now defunct Formspring.me). Typically, users create a profile and then open themselves up to anonymous and pseudonymous inquiries and statements from others who visit that profile. Ostensibly, the environment is meant to encourage fun, flirtatious conversation and open, honest dialog between individuals. In reality, though, allowing others to post whatever they want on one's profile behind the cloak of a screen name leaves one incredibly vulnerable to hate and harassment. Recently, Ask.fm has created some new features that will allow users to quickly report cyberbullying and are implementing limitations for users that do not register in order to bring about more accountability on the site.[21] These changes have been introduced as ownership of the platform has shifted from a company in Latvia to American-based IAC (owners of Ask.com). The new owners have vowed to clean up the social media site, or shut it down. Despite the optimism, the negatives of sites like these (which encourage anonymity and trash-talking without accountability) currently outweigh the positives.

> Since ask.fm is becoming the "it" thing, I decided to make an account as well. But little did I know, that my ex's friends will send so much hate to me. Because anonymity is an option, I can't even blame a specific person. I get things such as "bitch u are so ugly." or "your parents deserve to die for giving birth to such an ugly daughter." It came to a point where I just wanted to ask my ex what problem he has with me, but I can't just blame him without being 100% sure it was him and his friends who were sending me this. I still have a lot of questions that are full of hatred and unanswered. Even disabling my account doesn't help much!
>
> —Dali, 16, Thailand

Yik Yak, Secret, and Whisper

Yik Yak combines the public short-form posting of Twitter with the anonymity of Ask.fm and location-based boundaries. Specifically, it allows users to anonymously post comments that can be viewed by anyone who is within 1.5 miles of the person who posted it—or at least the 500 who are closest. When installing the app, the user gets a warning message stating that the app contains mature material and is therefore only appropriate for users seventeen years of age and older. But that didn't stopped high school students in some cities from signing up in droves. One can easily see the attraction for students here: They can post nameless comments that others in their immediate vicinity can see. As such, it is perfectly tailored for a school environment. Often the comments are mundane observations for their classmates about what is going on around them. But they could include harassing messages, answers to tests, sexually explicit comments, hate speech, or bomb threats. The anonymous nature of the posts may embolden users to let down their guard and post things they normally wouldn't say in a face-to-face interaction. Thankfully, most teens are savvy enough at this point to realize that eventually it could come back around to them. In fact, there was at least one example of a student being arrested for what was posted on the app. Moreover, because the app is location based, company officials have agreed to block it in the vicinity of primary and secondary schools which has helped stem the tide of is impact.

> This app [Yik Yak] is TERRIBLE! Several girls at my school have wound up in the counselor's office crying due to the extreme cyberbullying this app allows for. In addition, negative comments have been posted about many people (including myself) at my school: teachers, friends, and acquaintances. The worst thing is that there isn't much the school can do about it because it's anonymous.
>
> —Katie, unknown location

Secret is an app launched in January 2014 and has been described as an anonymous "community with no names, profiles or photographs."[22] When you make a post, it sends it to you and also to a select subset of your friends (i.e., the contacts in your phone) and possibly friends of those friends—all of whom (of course) must have the app (or they are not involved at all). The more people like it within the app, the further it will spread. More secrets are shown to a user when they have more friends (based on unique algorithms), with the primary goal being to ensure secrecy and prevent people from finding out who truly said what. According to its creators, "We built Secret for people to be themselves and share anything they're thinking and feeling with their friends without judgment. We did this by eliminating profile photos and names and by putting the emphasis entirely on the words and images being shared. This way, people are free to express themselves without holding back."[23] They also mention that the anonymous nature of Secret allows for people to like, comment, and re-share other people's posts that may be considered controversial, giving them the freedom to endorse anything without shame.

Similar to Secret is Whisper, which allows users to post anonymous comments written on different images and is available for Android devices as well.[24] Basically, users create a username and PIN, upload or select a picture from their vast library, add a custom filter, and then add custom text (whatever you want to whisper to the world). Then, you can decide to share your location, post it with hashtags to enable others to find it, and share it on other social media platforms. People who see it can like it and leave comments just as we have grown accustomed to on Facebook and Instagram and can also share it across other platforms. Whisper never knows who you are, doesn't access your phone's contacts, and shows anonymous posts from all over the world (instead of just from your friends).

Other Messaging Apps

There are a few more apps that are pretty popular right now among adolescent populations, including Kik, WhatsApp, Viber, and Voxer. These are simply messaging apps that allow for text, audio, and video to be easily exchanged in a chat-like interface among users regardless of the operating system software on their phone.[25] Their adoption really depends on where one lives; they are more popular in some countries than others and also differentially used in various regions and pockets and communities of America. It is not known how large a user base these apps will attain, or if they have already reached their peak.

One reason apps like these are popular among teens is because they give them a way to obscure some of their communications with others. Some parents routinely check the text messages that their children send and receive. Unaware parents may miss a large majority of the messages being sent and received if they only review the phone's default messaging app and fail to examine what is being typed using these newer apps. Moreover, some parents put restrictions on the number of messages their children can send in a given month. These apps circumvent such restrictions by using Wi-Fi so the messaging does not count toward one's cell phone plan limitations.

This guy is posting stuff on Kik, and he's saying I love him and I'm stalking him and blah, but in the non-joking way. I've lost so many friends, and now I'm alone, I haven't even met him, I don't even have a phone, I'm a sixth grader trying to be me . . . I'm too scared to talk to the office, in fear he might not leave me alone, or do worse. It's not just cyberbullying, it's harassment, and now I barely have any friends, and people glare at me in the halls, constantly whispering when they see me. They ignore me, not even acknowledging my existence, but I'm too scared and alone to do anything about it.

—Kelsey, 11, New Jersey

Gaming Networks

Increasing numbers of youth use their portable device or console (e.g., Nintendo DS, DSi, or 3DS; Wii or Wii U; Microsoft Xbox 360 or Xbox One; Sony PlayStation 3 or 4, or PlayStation Portable) to connect to an online gaming network and play various action (Grand Theft Auto), first-person-shooter (Call of Duty, Battlefield, BioShock, Killzone), third-person-shooter (Gears of War, Red Dead Redemption), role-playing (Dark Souls, Skyrim, Diablo), adventure (Journey, The Walking Dead, The Wolf Among Us), or driving (Need for Speed, Gran Turismo, Forza), sports (FIFA14, Madden NFL 25, NBA Live 14) games against opponents from other cities, states, and even countries. For some, it is incredibly fun, entertaining, and a huge part of their lives.

To add to the experience, many enjoy the private message or group chat functionality built into many of these networks (depending on the game) and often also use headsets with microphones, which allow them to speak to (and hear from) others as if they were together in the same room. These technologies then allow players to express excitement, displeasure, or anger vocally to others involved in the game. As such, they have the opportunity to verbalize or type out malicious statements or insults, which can inflict emotional or psychological harm on the target. For some youth, their participation and interaction with online gaming is their window and connection to the world. It is how they most often and most comfortably socialize and grow in their ability to communicate and relate with one another because they don't (yet) feel confident. Therefore, it is devastating when a member (or members) of a community to which they long to belong rejects them through cruel comments or harmful actions. The popularity of online gaming coupled with a relative ignorance of the parents as to the interactive features makes this environment rife with the possibility of cyberbullying regularly occurring.

IT'S NOT ALL BAD

Even though you've likely heard of many incidents where the apps and social media sites discussed above have been used to cause significant harm (such as Shay's experience described at the beginning of the chapter), we don't want you to focus only on the risks and negatives and thereby throw the proverbial baby out with the bathwater. In fact, we know from more than a decade's worth of research that *most teens are not misusing technology or mistreating others while online*. To put this in perspective, if we focused on all of the people who are killed or seriously injured every year in automobile accidents, we would probably never get in a car. Yet most of us do and we remain safe. Likewise, if used responsibly, participation in social media provides a number of potential benefits for adolescents.

Personal Benefits

Research has shown that online interaction provides a venue to learn and refine the ability to exercise self-control, to relate with tolerance and respect to others' viewpoints, to express sentiments in a healthy and appropriate manner, to engage in critical thinking and decision making, and to give and receive social support.[27] It also allows youth to shape their reputation while promoting self-discovery and identity management among an age group whose self-worth stems largely from peer perceptions, popularity dynamics, and current cultural trends.[28] Additionally, online

> Most teens are not misusing technology or mistreating others while online.

interaction provides a virtual venue in which to share web-based cultural artifacts like links, pictures, videos, and stories (anything that could go viral!) and remain closely connected with friends or relatives regardless of geographical location.

In addition, social networking platforms serve as a largely uncontrolled, unregulated, unconstrained public space in which adolescents can "see and be seen" in ways that support youth socialization and the assimilation of cultural knowledge.[29] For generations, teenagers have sought out places where they can hang out without being constantly supervised by adults. It used to be at the malt shop, the skating rink, the neighborhood basketball court, or the local mall. Because of cultural changes and safety concerns in some cities and neighborhoods, these opportunities have gradually disappeared, and public spaces have become largely unwelcoming to adolescents who just want to spend time with friends outside of the home.[30] Many kids these days are only involved in activities that are directly supervised by adults, but they long for time alone with friends. As a result, many youth flock to social networking sites because they are perceived to be relatively free from direct adult supervision and control. And when a particular platform appears to become popular among the adults in their lives (e.g., Facebook recently), teens pull back and find somewhere else to interact (e.g., Snapchat or Kik). This pattern is likely to continue as long as new websites and apps are invented and adults continue to lag behind in using them.

BREAKOUT BOX

Location Sharing

You probably know by now that Facebook, Twitter, and Instagram allow for users to share their location with any and every post they make, if they so desire. Growing in popularity are location-based "social discovery" apps like Tinder, Blendr, and Grindr, which allow users who share some sort of mutual interest (e.g., seeking a romantic partner or simply desiring to meet another like-minded individual for business or recreation) and are somewhat nearby in proximity to connect and interact. Platforms like Foursquare allow individuals to use their phone to "check-in" at various locations by running an application that scans for and identifies where that person is and what is around them. The app then "rewards" individuals who check in with points, badges, hierarchical titles (such as *Mayor* and *Superuser*), tips from other users who have checked in, and special deals. As an example, a teacher could use Foursquare to check in at her local Starbucks and, when doing so, might receive a coffee coupon on her iPhone to use during her beverage purchase.

As you can see, this landscape is rife with some really cool potential to bring people together and facilitate new personal and professional friends and relationships. It feels awesome to let others know where you are, particularly if it's interesting and fun and may lead to them leaving more likes or comments on your post. And it's powerful to have the ability to connect with strangers and turn them into friends or even boyfriends or girlfriends. That said, we generally advise people to avoid using these location-sharing features or location-centric apps because it is our opinion that the potential risks outweigh the benefits. These apps provide the opportunity for many others who you have no desire to know or meet to find you. Research has shown that the risk of victimization by strangers is much smaller as compared to your risk of being victimized by those you know at least a little bit.[26] This is because victimization is typically not completely random and sometimes stems from the fact that some people share some information about themselves that someone with malicious motives saw and took advantage of. By using social media, users invite others into their lives to some degree, based on what is shared and posted online. This can provide the opportunity and sometimes even a basic level of trust to exploit a situation and cause harm.

It also bears mentioning that apps on phones and tablets use GPS or cellular tower triangulation to pinpoint the location of users. We personally recommend that all users disable these services on their electronic device (even if they disable it, 911 services can still identify where they are in case of an emergency) to make sure they are not opening themselves up for victimization based on the apps they have. At the very least, they should ensure that these locations are not tied to their identity in any way and "pushed" to public profiles and sites for others to see.

In addition, current digital cameras, phones, and other devices allow for automatic geotagging. This is the process of tying location-based metadata to photos, videos, and even text messages. This metadata is hidden but often includes longitude and latitude data, the name of the phone's user or the name given to the phone, and date and time stamps for when the content was created. This feature can be beneficial if you need to remember exactly what beach you were on when you took that picture of a sunset years ago. However, a photo of a teen's beautiful girlfriend in her backyard may also have the exact location of her house attached to it. Geotagging tends to be enabled by default on most smartphones.

It is important to discuss these issues with students and encourage them to avoid using these services. If students want others to know where they are—so they can come over or meet up for a party, study session, coffee, or beach day—they should just send out text messages directly to specific individuals. This keeps the uninvited from showing up. They should also take a few seconds and disable geotagging on their phone, camera, and laptop so that all of the pictures and video they take and then upload do not have GPS coordinates or other location-based information embedded in their metadata. Finally, they should disable all location sharing on their Facebook, Twitter, Instagram, and other social media activity. Youth shouldn't always feel the need to tell people on social media exactly where they are while they are there. Instead, and as mentioned, it's a lot safer for them to just send individual texts to let them know.

Educational Benefits

Many schools (perhaps even your own!) are embracing social networking websites as instructional tools. Quite a number of teachers have created virtual classrooms, which include supplementary information about the topics discussed in the brick-and-mortar environment. For example, an English teacher could have students post their writings online for other students (or complete strangers) to read and critique. A photography class might post their pictures on sites that allow for expeditious review and evaluation by others. One ninth-grade science teacher in Atlanta has even used the popular game Angry Birds to teach complicated physics principles.[31]

Additionally, many schools now use a Facebook page or Twitter feed to send messages, newsletters, or other important information very quickly to all members of their community.[32] Coaches regularly utilize social media sites and apps to get information quickly to their players. Some administrators are even taking advantage of the benefits of social networking websites to *build* a strong school community and facilitate connections among students across campus.[33]

Finally, some schools have set up walled-garden (nonpublic) online social networking platforms, limiting content and access to include only their school communities.

> The myth about social media in the classroom is that if you use it, kids will be Tweeting, Facebooking and Snapchatting while you're trying to teach. We still have to focus on the task at hand. Don't mistake *social media* for *socializing.*[34]
>
> —Vicki Davis, teacher and IT integrator (@coolcatteacher)

SUMMARY

After reading this chapter, we hope that you now have a deeper understanding of the attractiveness, benefits, and variety of online platforms that exist and have been embraced by so many individuals (especially teens!). In all of these settings, adolescents have found their socialization needs can be met—and perhaps even augmented because of the positives that accompany communicating with each other online. However, the negatives of online interaction are real and tend to surface in time. Though we've really only scratched the surface, you can also probably envision how the various features (and ubiquity) of these communications technologies can lead to opportunities to harass and mistreat others. Thankfully most teens are using the apps and environments discussed safely and responsibly. But some aren't. The remainder of the book will focus on their behaviors because, even though they are in the minority, their impact is often deeply felt.

> The benefits of social media outweigh its negative effects, even though it's the negative incidents that get the media's attention. Students are able to connect with others in ways they never could before, exposing them to different worldviews and perspectives that may not be prevalent in their schools. Social media also provides a venue to allow youth to express themselves through the written word and receive support and affirmation when going through difficult times. Instead of the easy solution of banning adolescents from social media, we need to do the hard work of teaching teenagers about how to properly use these outlets so that cyberbullying does not occur.
>
> —Tiffany, undisclosed location

In the next chapter, we start this discussion by zeroing in on the unique qualities that contribute to cyberbullying being the problem that it is. We also break down and illustrate some of the leading ways in which it takes place and provide true and relatable stories from youth we know, which should serve to reinforce and bring to life exactly what we are talking about. These depictions should serve as a compelling backdrop upon which we can discuss the best ways to promote safe participation and reduce victimization online.

QUESTIONS FOR REFLECTION

1. Why are adolescents (and many adults) attracted to social networking websites?

2. Why is Facebook such a popular social media site today? Do you think that is changing? What is the most popular site at your school today?

3. Do you think the benefits of social media outweigh the risks? Why or why not?

4. What characteristics of social media sites make them potentially a popular environment for cyberbullies?

5. What advice would you give a younger student who is setting up a social media profile for the first time?

NOTES

1. Kowalski v. Berkeley County Schools. 652 F.3d 565 (4th Cir. 2011).
2. Internet Live Stats. http://www.internetlivestats.com/.
3. Jon Henley. "Teenagers and Technology: 'I'd Rather Give Up My Kidney Than My Phone.'" http://www.theguardian.com/lifeandstyle/2010/jul/16/teenagers-mobiles-facebook-social-networking.
4. Mary Madden, Amanda Lenhart, Maeve Duggan, Sandra Cortesi, and Urs Gasser. "Teens and Technology 2013." http://www.pewinternet.org/2013/03/13/teens-and-technology-2013/.
5. Marc Prensky. "Digital Natives, Digital Immigrants." In *On the Horizon* 9, no. 5 (2001): 1–2.
6. Stephanie Dressler. "Retirees Are the Fastest-Growing Age Group on Social Media: Financial Firms Should Adjust Accordingly." http://www.dukaspr.com/?blog=retirees-are-the-fastest-growing-age-group-on-social-media-financial-firms-should-adjust-accordingly.
7. Susannah R. Stern. "Adolescent Girls' Expression on Web Home Pages: Spirited, Sombre and Self-Conscious Sites." *Convergence* 5, no. 4 (1999): 22–41.
8. danah boyd. "Why Youth (Heart) Social Network Sites: The Role of Networked Publics in Teenage Social Life." In *Youth, Identity, and Digital Media,* edited by David Buckingham, 119–142. Cambridge: MIT Press, 2007; danah boyd. *It's Complicated: The Social Lives of Networked Teens.* New Haven, CT: Yale University Press, 2014.
9. Alexa.com. "Facebook.com." http://www.alexa.com/data/details/traffic_details/facebook.com.
10. Richard Davies. "Facebook May Be Losing Its Cool With Teens." http://abcnews.go.com/blogs/business/2013/10/facebook-may-be-losing-its-cool-with-teens/; Josh Constine. "Kids Love Snapchat Because They See Facebook Like Adults See LinkedIn." http://techcrunch.com/2013/10/28/why-ephemeral-tech-is-here-to-stay/.
11. Vignesh Ramachandran. "Teens Getting Tired of Facebook Drama, Pew Survey Finds." http://mashable.com/2013/05/22/teen-pew-study-social-media/; Ruby Karp. "I'm 13 and None of My Friends Use Facebook." http://mashable.com/2013/08/11/teens-facebook/.
12. Leo Widrich. "Social Media in 2013: User Demographics for Twitter, Facebook, Pinterest and Instagram." http://blog.bufferapp.com/social-media-in-2013-user-demographics-for-twitter-facebook-pinterest-and-instagram.
13. Brian O'Keefe. "Instagram CEO: We're Growing Fast. So What If I Left a Lot of Money on the Table?" http://fortune.com/2014/07/15/brainstorm-tech-instagram-kevin-systrom/.

14. Vindu Goel. "Is Instagram Another Path to Riches for Facebook?" http://bits
    .blogs.nytimes.com/2014/02/18/is-instagram-another-path-to-riches-for-face-
    book/?_php=true&_type=blogs&_r=0.

15. Jennifer Van Grove. "Why Teens Are Tiring of Facebook." http://www.cnet
    .com/news/why-teens-are-tiring-of-facebook/.

16. Business Insider. "Snapchat's Monthly Average Users." https://intellegence
    .businessinsider.com/we-estimate-that-snapchat-has-upwards-of-70-million-
    users-globally-2014-4.

17. Josh Constine. "Kids Love Snapchat Because They See Facebook Like Adults
    See LinkedIn." http://techcrunch.com/2013/10/28/why-ephemeral-tech-is-here-
    to-stay/.

18. Jenna Wortham. "Vine, Twitter's New Video Tool, Hits 13 Million Users."
    http://bits.blogs.nytimes.com/2013/06/03/vine-twitters-new-video-tool-hits-
    13-million-users/?_php=true&_type=blogs&_r=0.

19. Paresh Dave. "Busiest Vine Users Send Out More Than 14 Short Videos a Day."
    http://articles.latimes.com/2013/jun/20/business/la-fi-tn-mostactive-vine-users-
    share-more-than-14-vines-a-day-on-twitter-20130620.

20. Ask.fm. "Safety Center." http://ask.fm/about/safety/about-company.

21. Heather Saul. "Ask.fm 'Will Be Safer From Online Bullying' as Owners Intro-
    duce New Features." http://www.independent.co.uk/news/uk/home-news/askfm-
    will-be-safer-from-online-bullying-as-owners-introduce-new-features-8774234
    .html.

22. Harry McCracken."'Secret' iPhone App Is Silicon Valley's Newest Obsession."
    http://time.com/6015/secret-app/.

23. Secret, Inc. "Speak Freely: Introducing a New Way to Connect With Friends."
    https://itunes.apple.com/us/app/secret-speak-freely/id775307543?mt=8.

24. Dann Berg. "Secret vs. Whisper: What's the Best Anonymous Sharing App?"
    http://blog.laptopmag.com/secret-vs-whisper.

25. Joanne Doubtfire. "What Is WhatsApp and Why Is It So Popular?" http://
    joannedoubtfire.hubpages.com/hub/WhatsAppiPad.

26. David Finkelhor and Richard K. Ormrod. "Characteristics of Crimes Against
    Juveniles." *Juvenile Justice Bulletin* (NCJ179034). https://www.ncjrs.gov/pdf-
    files1/ojjdp/179034.pdf.

27. Ilene R. Berson, Michael J. Berson, and John M. Ferron. "Emerging Risks of
    Violence in the Digital Age: Lessons for Educators From an Online Study of
    Adolescent Girls in the United States." *Journal of School Violence* 1, no. 2
    (2002): 51–71; Mitzuko Ito, Heather A. Horst, Matteo Bittani, danah boyd,
    Becky Herr-Stephenson, Patricia G. Lange, C. J. Pascoe, and Laura Robinson.
    "Living and Learning With New Media: Summary of Findings From the Digital
    Youth Project." *The John D. and Catherine T. MacArthur Foundation Reports
    on Digital Media and Learning*, 2008. http://digitalyouth.ischool.berkeley.edu/
    files/report/digitalyouth-WhitePaper.pdf; Amanda Lenhart, Kristin Purcell,
    Aaron Smith, and Kathryn Zickuhr. "Social Media and Young Adults." *Pew
    Internet & American Life Project.* http://www.pewinternet.org/2010/02/03/

social-media-and-young-adults/; Gwenn Schurgin O'Keeffe and Kathleen Clark-Pearson. "Clinical Report—The Impact of Social Media on Children, Adolescents, and Families." *Pediatrics* 127 (2011): 800–804. doi: 10.1542/peds.2011-0054.

28. Mary Madden, Amanda Lenhart, Maeve Duggan, Sandra Cortesi, and Urs Gasser. "Teens and Technology 2013." http://www.pewinternet.org/2013/03/13/teens-and-technology-2013/; Mitzuko Ito, Heather A. Horst, Matteo Bittani, danah boyd, Becky Herr-Stephenson, Patricia G. Lange, C. J. Pascoe, and Laura Robinson. "Living and Learning With New Media: Summary of Findings From the Digital Youth Project." *The John D. and Catherine T. MacArthur Foundation Reports on Digital Media and Learning*, 2008. http://digitalyouth.ischool.berkeley.edu/files/report/digitalyouth-WhitePaper.pdf; Erik H. Erikson. *Childhood and Society.* New York: Norton, 1950; danah boyd. "Identity Production in a Networked Culture: Why Youth Heart MySpace." Speech at American Association for the Advancement of Science, St. Louis, MO, February 19, 2006; Mark R. Leary, Alison L. Haupt, Kristine S. Strausser, and Jason T. Chokel. "Calibrating the Sociometer: The Relationship Between Interpersonal Appraisals and State Self-Esteem." *Journal of Personality and Social Psychology* 74 (1998): 1290–1299; Mark R. Leary, Ellen S. Tambor, Sonja K. Terdal, and Deborah L. Downs. "Self-Esteem as an Interpersonal Monitor. The Sociometer Hypothesis." *Journal of Personality and Social Psychology* 68 (1995): 518–530; Sandra L. Calvert. "Identity Construction on the Internet." In *Children in the Digital Age: Influences of Electronic Media on Development,* edited by Sandra L. Calvert, Amy B. Jordan, and Rodney R. Cocking, 57–70. Westport, CT: Praeger, 2002; Sherry Turkle. *Life on the Screen: Identity in the Age of the Internet.* New York: Simon and Schuster, 1995; danah boyd. "Taken Out of Context: American Teen Sociality in Networked Publics" (2008). http://www.danah.org/papers/TakenOutOfContext.pdf; Mary Madden, Amanda Lenhart, Sandra Cortesi, Urs Gasser, Maeve Duggan, and Aaron Smith. "Teens, Social Media, and Privacy." http://www.pewinternet.org/2013/05/21/teens-social-media-and-privacy/.

29. danah boyd. *It's Complicated: The Social Lives of Networked Teens.* New Haven, CT: Yale University Press, 2014.

30. danah boyd. "Why Youth (Heart) Social Network Sites: The Role of Networked Publics in Teenage Social Life." In *Youth, Identity, and Digital Media,* edited by David Buckingham, 119–142. Cambridge: MIT Press, 2007.

31. John Burk. "Why You Should Wait to Teach Projectile Motion Part 2: Introducing Projectile Motion Using Angry Birds." http://quantumprogress.wordpress.com/2011/02/16/why-you-should-wait-to-teach-projectile-motion-part-1-the-problem/.

32. Justin Appel. "Report Identifies Ed-Tech Trends to Watch: Emerging Forms of Publication, Massively Multiplayer Educational Gaming Among Trends on the Horizon Expected to Have a Huge Impact on Schools." *eSchool News.* http://www.lmtsd.org/cms/lib/PA01000427/Centricity/Domain/91/Top%20News%20-%20Report%20identifies%20ed-tech%20trends%20to%20watch.pdf.

33. Nancy Hass. "In Your Facebook.com." *New York Times*. http://www.nytimes .com/2006/01/08/education/edlife/facebooks.html; Kelly Walsh. "Facebook in the Classroom. Seriously." *EmergingEdTech*. http://www.emergingedtech .com/2011/03/facebook-in-the-classroom-seriously/.

34. Vicki Davis. "A Guidebook for Social Media in the Classroom." *Education Trends*. http://www.edutopia.org/blog/guidebook-social-media-in-classroom- vicki-davis?page=7.

CHAPTER THREE

The Nature and Forms
of Cyberbullying

Described as "intelligent, bright, clever and bubbly" and a "personable, pleasant young lady and very grounded for her age," Hannah Smith was a typical teenager in many ways. She also, like many youth, longed to be noticed, recognized, accepted, and to belong. And like others, she was bullied in a number of ways by peers (in part because she had eczema, according to her father). According to her older sister, Hannah had been a target of the cruelty of others for years. For example, she was attacked at a party. And before that, her coat was glued to a chair at school.[1] She even received messages online that told her that she should just take her own life, and eventually the torment became too much to handle as the fourteen-year-old from Leicestershire, England, hanged herself on August 2, 2013. Days before her death she hauntingly posted, "You think you want to die, but in reality you just want to be saved" and left a suicide note found by her sister that read "As I sit here day by day I wonder if it's going to get better. I want to die, I want to be free. I can't live like this any more. I'm not happy."[2]

Based on findings from the subsequent police investigation, messages received principally on the social media site Ask.fm were cited as a primary cause of the suicide.[1] However, we know that the root of such tragedies is rarely that clear cut. As we will cover in more detail in the following chapter, research makes clear that peer harassment is just one of many factors that contributes to increased risk of suicide. And, as you'll soon learn, this story took an unexpected and disturbing turn.

Many teens are mistreated online at some point in their adolescence. And a lot of the negative behaviors are occurring through the social media websites and cell phone apps we described in the previous chapter. We now

● 45

turn our attention to the many different forms of cyberbullying and some of the unique factors that make these behaviors potentially more problematic than traditional types of bullying. While there are many similarities when comparing bullying as it often occurs at school versus online, it will become clear that technology does create new, additional challenges (and opportunities).

THE NATURE OF CYBERBULLYING

Before diving into the practical details of how cyberbullying is typically carried out, it is instructive to reflect on the nuances and subtleties associated with cyberbullying that make it an attractive behavioral choice. Why not just bully and mistreat others in real life—using face-to-face interactions? Why use technological devices to manifest hate and aggression? The answer to these questions, as you will see, is quite intuitive. Simply put, the technology makes bullying (and the harm the aggressor desires to cause) much *easier*—in every sense of that word. This is largely because of the following key elements:

- Anonymity and pseudonymity
- Disinhibition
- Deindividuation
- Lack of supervision
- Virality
- Limitless victimization risk

Each of these is discussed in more detail below.

Anonymity and Pseudonymity

One of the contributing factors to the cyberbullying problem is that those who seek to cause harm to others can remain "virtually" anonymous. Pseudonyms in social media platforms, online gaming networks, e-mail, instant messaging, and other Internet venues can make it difficult for adolescents to determine the identity of their aggressors. And those aggressors can express sentiments of malice behind that cloak of anonymity while on their device, which aids in freeing them from traditionally constraining pressures of society, conscience, morality, and ethics to behave in a kind or respectful manner. Jami, fourteen, from an undisclosed location in the United States, acknowledged the anonymous but harmful nature of these online interactions:

> Just because you say it doesn't hurt you because they are online, it does. They call you names because everyone online is anonymous. So they think they can do whatever they want to you. But honestly it annoys me that everyone thinks they can do whatever they want because you don't know who they are.

Further, it seems that bullies might be emboldened when using electronic means to carry out their antagonistic agenda because it takes less courage to express hurtful comments using a keyboard or keypad than one's voice. It is actually quite difficult for most people to be mean to others when they are face-to-face with them because shame and guilt readily kick in. However, hateful words and statements that an individual might be ashamed or embarrassed to use when face-to-face are no longer off-limits (or even tempered!) when that person is physically distant from the target. Anecdotal accounts from victims studied in our research point to extreme viciousness and unconscionable textual violence expressed by cyberbullies who exploit the anonymity of their actions. For example, Toni, seventeen, from Washington told us:

> The last time I was bullied online was when I got an e-mail from some anonymous person who said they went to my school, telling me that I was going to go to hell for dating girls. I have no idea who the messenger was.

Even though it appears that cyberbullies can hide behind a virtual veil to protect their identities, it is important to understand that individuals are almost never completely anonymous when interacting in cyberspace. This is because a unique identifying set of numbers (Internet Protocol [IP] address) is assigned to every device when it is connected to the Internet. All data and communications sent from it include that address and are marked with a specific and exact date and time stamp. As such, the origination of any message from any account logged into any device at any time can—with some effort—be identified. This becomes one's digital footprint that is much more durable than many people think. The IP address leads you to an Internet service provider or cell phone service provider who would have the account information for whoever is registered to that IP address. The primary limitations to tracking someone down are resources and authority. It can take a lot of time (or money, if you hire someone to do it) to obtain identifying information from websites or Internet service providers. Plus, law enforcement or another form of government typically need to be involved, along with a court order for the requested identifying information.

When investigating a traditional bullying incident, you are often confronted with conflicting stories about what actually happened. It can be a "he said, she said" type of situation that you need to disentangle. With cyberbullying, however, there is *always* evidence of the behavior and almost always some indication of its origin (that digital footprint we just talked about). Even though bullies may feel anonymous or think they cannot be detected, it is often much easier to investigate incidents of cyberbullying than traditional bullying because some evidence *always* exists. It can be found on the sender's or recipient's device; on the devices of friends, bystanders, or witnesses; on social media sites; on the intermediary computer systems through which the message or posting or picture traveled en route; in electronic activity logs; or in the form of screenshots and printouts.

Finally, despite the potential for anonymous attacks, in our research we find that the vast majority of students who are being cyberbullied know, or at least think they know, who is responsible for cyberbullying them. In most cases, it is someone from their social circle—someone they know—like a former friend, a former romantic partner, or even the new romantic partner of the former romantic partner. Very rarely is it some stranger trolling the Internet randomly looking to cause harm to someone else. That does happen, but it doesn't seem to affect youth as much as when they know it is someone from their school. Generally students can determine who is behind the harassment based on what is being said or because of references to particular others.

> Individuals are almost never completely anonymous when interacting in cyberspace.

Disinhibition

Related to anonymity and pseudonymity online is the concept of *disinhibition*. To be disinhibited is to be freed from restraints on your behavior. In some venues, disinhibition can be a positive thing. For example, someone who tends to be socially restrained may be disinhibited, and as a result more outgoing, when attending a costume party. Hiding behind the safety of a mask, they can interact more boldly with others without fear of social missteps. Alcohol also serves as a common disinhibitor: People who are inebriated often act out in very atypical ways. However, disinhibition makes it more difficult to control impulsive behavior because the consequences of inappropriate behavior are not instant or immediately clear to the actor.

Relatedly, bullies online do not have to deal with the immediate emotional, psychological, or physical effects of face-to-face bullying on their victim. When a person expresses hurtful words to another in real life, there is likely to be some consequence. Maybe a fight breaks out. Even if that doesn't happen, verbal violence will likely be volleyed back and forth between the two parties (and their respective entourages). Maybe the target of the comments becomes visibly upset and the person who expressed them is forced to see the results of their cruelty. Frequently when we talk with youth who admit to us that they have cyberbullied others, they tell us they didn't mean any harm and they were just joking around. Messages conveyed in cyberspace, however, lack the vocal or visual cues that would communicate disappointment, concern, and misunderstanding (such as facial expressions or body language) and can therefore be easily misinterpreted. Such feedback in real life tends to induce most aggressors (unless they are sociopathic) to temper or qualify their words and to realize when "enough is enough."

> I wasn't taking into consideration the fact that they might not think that my jokes were too funny. If they ask me to stop or showed signs of wanting me to stop, I do immediately. I was online and they didn't say for me to stop, so I had no way of knowing what mood they were in. I told them something that I regret now.
>
> —Collin, 17, Missouri

Deindividuation

Deindividuation is a sociopsychological concept that can also help shed some light on why some youth engage in cyberbullying. In general, the concept illustrates how individuals become extricated from responsibility for their actions simply because they don't have an acute awareness of themselves, others, or of the social environment that provides the context for the behavior.[3] In short, *deindividuation* has been defined as a "subjective state in which people lose their self-consciousness."[4] Basically, a person's behavior is influenced more by the online setting than by what they know from real-world social norms, or potential consequences.[5] Essentially, interacting online releases people from traditional constraints on their behavior by deindividuating them—by reducing their awareness of themselves and their ability to self-regulate what they do.

Youth who congregate in a particular Internet-based space may feel "hidden" among the others and more a part of a group than alone and therefore may feel freer to act in a deviant manner. In this group setting, they would be much more responsive to situational factors and their own emotions and attitudes as the driving force for behavior. We all know that it's possible to respond unwisely or immaturely when our emotions govern our actions or when we want to impress others. It follows, then, that an adolescent may attack someone else online either because it seems appropriate at that particular moment or just because it feels right or good to do it. For example, a bully may seriously wound his target with his texts or tweets simply because he has "lost" himself in cyberspace; he is conscious of the physical distance and relative immunity from identification and sanction and oblivious to the significance and reality of his harmful actions.

Lack of Supervision

Most everyone agrees that supervision is lacking in cyberspace. There are no regulating authorities or administrative hosts who are watching and policing the posts that people make on social media platforms. Cell phone companies and Internet service providers aren't actively monitoring e-mails or text messages we send and receive (which, for the most part, is a good thing). And while e-mails or other web-based communication may be stored on a server somewhere for a period of time, even after they are deleted from one's device, that is not true of text messages sent through mobile phones.[6]

For the most part, the service providers (e.g., Facebook or AT&T) are off the hook when it comes to inappropriate, hateful, or even criminal communication posted on or through their networks. According to the Communications Decency Act of 1996, "No provider or user of an interactive computer service shall be treated as the publisher or speaker of any information provided by another information content provider" and "[n]o cause of action may be brought and no liability may be imposed under any State or local law that is inconsistent with [Section 230]."[7] This essentially means that social networks are not responsible to proactively police the contents of user-created profiles, pages, or accounts. Despite apparent *legal* absolution, we believe they have a *moral* and *ethical* responsibility to expeditiously investigate any reports filed by users of behavior that violate their Terms of Service (which typically includes cyberbullying, threats, explicit material, etc.). Tech companies that make a profit from their online users should not hide behind an outdated law and use it as a justification not to be proactive. The authors of that law in 1996 had no idea how social media would be employed to harm others, and we would hope that an ethically conscious corporation would find it reasonable and appropriate to help their users instead of turning a blind eye to them.

Virality

Another key feature that makes cyberbullying so problematic is the fact that hurtful or humiliating content can be sent to a large number of people in a short period of time. While spoken rumors sometimes spread around a school like wildfire, this process is greatly expedited when utilizing technology. Text messages can be sent from one electronic device to a limitless number of recipients in a matter of seconds. If a student posts a humiliating photo in the girls' bathroom of another classmate, only those who venture there would be able to view the picture. If the same picture was posted on social media or texted to everyone in the school, many more people would be drawn into the incident, thereby increasing the target's victimization.

This, of course, ties into the element of repetition or repeated harm that is included in most definitions of bullying, which we discussed in Chapter 1. Cyberbullying can be a *viral* phenomenon, as certain content is spread from one person (the source or creator) to another and to another—all at dizzying speed due to the data-processing and sending capabilities of computers and cell phones. Malicious content often gains infamy in this manner and becomes practically impossible to control once a critical mass finds out about it. A student may attempt to cope with one or two classmate's verbal or even physical attacks, but when a large number of people are seemingly in on the harassment, it can be overwhelmingly painful. This is compounded by the fact that online harassment is not confined or constrained to the school day or the school campus, which leads to protracted (and seemingly unending) suffering.

Limitless Victimization Risk

Electronic devices allow individuals to contact and connect with others at all times and almost all places. Many youth who are bullied by others in traditional settings, such as the school lunchroom, the playground, the hallway, at the bus stop, or on the bus, are able to escape the victimization once their school day is over. They can retreat into personal and protected environments, such as the confines of one's home, which provide (at least) temporary relief for targets of bullying and perhaps allows them to recharge and be encouraged by loved ones before venturing out again into a potentially hostile world. However, with so many teens constantly connected to their phones, and almost continuously involved in texting and social media use, would-be bullies can infiltrate the private spaces of potential victims around the clock. There may truly be "no rest for the weary" as cyberbullying penetrates all possible places where victims might seek refuge. Indeed, we have heard one target describe his experience with cyberbullying by saying he was "tethered to his tormenter." Jill, sixteen, from Alabama, explained it this way:

> It's one thing when you get made fun of at school, but to be bullied in your own home via your computer is a disgusting thing for someone to do and I think anyone who gets kicks out of it is disgusting.

As a related point, the coordination of a cyberbullying assault from multiple aggressors can occur with more ease because it is not constrained by the physical location of the bullies or victims. That is, a group of adolescents may decide to orchestrate an attack on a particular individual on social media or a gaming network. These teens could be congregating in their neighborhoods, hanging out in the mall, or in the privacy of their own individual homes, for that matter. And even if the target has been careful to avoid coming into physical contact with the bully, that doesn't prevent an onslaught of mistreatment from afar. Cyberbullying really can greatly expand the reach and augment the intensity of interpersonal harm that occurs.

Finally, everyone must realize how intertwined real space and cyberspace have become when considering the ways in which youth socialize. Many teenagers spend days with their friends in school and nights with those same friends online through social networking, texting, and gaming. That which occurs during the day at school is often discussed online at night, and that which occurs online at night is often discussed and relived during the day at school. That is, face-to-face and device-mediated interactions drift seamlessly between the two realms in contemporary adolescent culture. For many youth, there really is no clear distinction between life as lived in real space and in cyberspace; one social sphere is now a natural and complementing extension of the other. This is difficult to comprehend by an adult population who (1) has not grown up with Internet-based socializing and therefore is not naturally predisposed to it and (2) uses the Internet and their electronic devices to supplement (rather than complement) life as lived in real space. Quite simply, as discussed in Chapter 2, teens use technology differently than most adults and are therefore more tied to, and as a result more affected by, the problems that occur online.

> Cyberbullying really can greatly expand the reach and augment the intensity of interpersonal harm that occurs.

FORMS OF CYBERBULLYING

As mentioned earlier, there are new arrivals to the electronic landscape on a regular basis (e.g., apps, sites, devices), and we do not want you to get overwhelmed with any or all of them. Fundamentally, cyberbullying can and does happen in *any* online environment because of the way in which online interactions can occur—irrespective of what device, website, or app teens are using now or will use in the future. We should not, and cannot, blame the technology at hand in any of these cases. Technology is neutral and can be used for good or for ill, depending on the user. Remember, bullying has been around for generations—long before the invention of the computer, the cell phone, or the Internet. Instead, we need to understand the motives, mechanisms, and outcomes of various forms of high-tech cruelty so that we are informed with how best to prevent and respond to them all.

Following is a brief discussion of some of the many manifestations of cyberbullying. This list is neither exhaustive nor mutually exclusive. Cyberbullying incidents often include examples of behaviors from more than one of these groups, and there are behaviors that don't fit neatly into any of these. That said, this list does comprise the most commonly seen forms of cyberbullying, and it is hoped that our descriptions of them will help to equip you with the knowledge to identify and better understand what is happening and why it is important to respond.

Rumor Spreading

Commonly perpetrated using social media posts and texts, gossip and hearsay about someone can be disseminated very easily online. Rumor spreading tends to be an activity performed more frequently by girls than by boys (see Chapter 4), due in part to the relational aggression and social sabotage that occurs more commonly between girls when rivalries arise.[8] That said, Damian, a seventeen-year-old from California, aptly depicts how boys can also be harmed by rumors that are circulated: "One time someone made me feel so bad that I wanted to kill myself because I believed those things that they said. My friends calmed me down and told me not to do anything dumb. I dislike it when people spread rumors online about you and it has happened to mostly everyone who chats."

The mediums typically used for this form of cyberbullying allow messages to go viral with incredible speed. Within a matter of minutes, the whole school (and beyond) can learn of a rumor and perhaps start treating the target in a cruel way. Furthermore, because these messages can be sent from accounts created solely for the purpose of harassing or impersonating or from disguised identities, it can be difficult at first to determine the origin of the rumors.

I was bullied online anonymously and not anonymously. Called horrible names, had rumors spread, people who used to be my friends making fun of me, calling me fat, a bitch, slut, attention whore, and tons of other things. They'd ignore me in person, make fun of me, my clothes, my voice, my family, the amount of money I had, my life in general. Because of them and the hate I received, it led to anorexia, self-harm, depression, anxiety attacks, and extremely close calls with suicide. This went on for almost 4 months . . . daily.

—Kristen, 14, Colorado

Flaming

Flaming typically involves sending or posting hostile, angry, or annoying messages intended to inflame the emotions and sensibilities of others. These comments or messages do not productively advance or contribute to the discussion at hand but, instead, attempt to wound another person socially or psychologically and to assert authority over others. Most often, flaming occurs on online discussion boards, forums, and the comment sections of articles covering various news (e.g., sports, celebrities, current events). One person who contacted us sent in this example of a flame posted as a comment to another person's creative writing submission on www.fanfiction.net, a site where fledgling authors can share their works:

> You have been chosen to be a recipient of the "Flame Writing Challenge for Flame Rising #2" flame for which I had to write a seething review for pieces of shit like yours using a list of random words given to me by people. What does this mean exactly? It means this story is still a piece of d.o.u.c.h.e.d-up excrement, and I got to use some big, fancy words to tell you so. Feel honored. What is it that's wrong with you that makes you think you have actual talent as a writer, hmm? Is it a calcium deficiency? Or perhaps you ate some rancid tapioca? You see, kiddo, you're being quite mendacious to yourself if you actually think you have what it takes to be a writer.

Receiving such feedback after posting a piece of creative writing in the hopes of being encouraged by others can be quite damaging to the emotional state of an adolescent. If unable to shrug off the comment as a flame, the young person might even have the dream to become a writer extinguished.

The concept of trolling is very similar to flaming, except that the latter is directed at another participant (or other participants) in the discussion, while the former is directed at the subject of discussion. Trolls attempt to cause maximum disruption, annoyance, and arguments in the online thread, and their words and actions have no sincere basis. This is done by posting messages that are often cruel and insulting but are marked by being simply inaccurate, ridiculous, irrelevant, or obtuse. With all of this said, it is our belief that trolls are malicious or act maliciously because they intentionally attempt to provoke unproductive reactions from others. Flaming, on the other hand, often involves being extremely harsh and hurtful when conveying what one thinks is true or right.

Posting of Pictures and Videos

We all have pictures that we don't want others, especially complete strangers, to see, because we find them embarrassing or otherwise negative in their portrayal of us. With everyone carrying their phones wherever they go, there often seems the opportunity to capture someone else in a moment of awkwardness, shame, ugliness, or pain. One of our friends told us about seventh-graders Megan and Bryan, who liked each other and became boyfriend and girlfriend. Everything seemed to be going fine for a while until Megan cheated on Bryan with another classmate. In response, Bryan hacked into Megan's social media account after using her password, posted a sexually suggestive picture of her that she had sent him in confidence, and made it her profile picture. He even changed her password so she wouldn't be able to delete the humiliating photo.

From that day on, Megan became known as a "slut" across her school community. She was so embarrassed, she didn't come back to school for an entire week, and when she finally returned, she had lost a noticeable amount of weight. The entire school gossiped about her for months, and Megan had to deal with people calling her obscene and explicit names and repeatedly requesting sexual favors. In addition, Megan's personality completely changed; a girl who was once outgoing and gregarious now isolated herself and would not talk to anyone—or even bother to defend herself. While Megan was eventually able to remove the picture and delete her account, the damage had already been done as almost everyone had already seen the picture. She ended up having to change her phone number and transfer schools.

It should be noted here that in some places (like bathrooms or locker rooms), people have an expectation of privacy. Taking a picture of someone in those places and publicly posting it without their permission could be grounds for civil or even criminal punishment (we discuss these laws in more detail in Chapter 7). For example, Oregon law considers it a Class A misdemeanor criminal offense and states that "a person commits the crime of invasion of personal privacy if the person knowingly makes or records a photograph, motion picture, videotape or other visual recording of another person in a state of nudity without the consent of the person being recorded."[11] Laws vary depending on the state and jurisdiction, but suffice it to say, some teens unwittingly cross the line when taking and posting curious pictures and videos for fun and entertainment.

Captions, Commenting, and Messaging

Earlier in this chapter, we discussed how disinhibition and deindividuation make it easier for people to be mean online and to say things they

BREAKOUT BOX

Photoshopping

Photoshopping is a neologism referring to the popular image-editing software program, Adobe Photoshop. However, the term applies to image or photo modifications or alterations made using any software program. While sometimes done strictly for clean or even flattering humorous intent, in cyberbullying instances, photoshopping generally involves doctoring images so that the main subject is placed in a compromising or embarrassing context or scene. One of the most widely known examples of photoshopping occurred when a boy named Alex posted online a picture of "Sam," a girl who was moshing (dancing in an aggressive, primal manner) at a punk rock concert in San Diego, California, in January 2005.[9] The picture was then downloaded and altered hundreds of times in funny, humiliating, and even obscene ways, and each new version was redistributed across the Internet. Recalling the incident, Sam later remarked,

> The situation was funny at first, I even laughed, but there was a line crossed, where cruelty came into play and I shouldn't have to be the one saying "please take them down." You can't help but realize that you are being humiliated across the country. In a nutshell, I feel shitty.

Many of these photoshopped images of "Moshzilla" are still available online today.[10]

would likely never say face-to-face. Unfortunately, even some adults are sometimes guilty of mouthing off while behind the touchscreens of their phones or the keyboards of their computers—especially when caught up in an emotional situation or feeling the need to defend themselves. Teens struggle with this and typically have less self-control and instructive life experiences (from which they've learned what not to do!) than adults, and this leads to a lot of hate being posted and sent. Some of it is very overt name-calling, insults, and obscenities. Other times, it is indirect and subtle, involving passive aggressiveness, barbed sarcasm, and twisted wordplay. Sometimes it is done anonymously or by using a pseudonym or fake account to mask the aggressor's identity. Other times, the one who is bullying truly doesn't care that her identity is revealed, and feels free to hurt others blatantly from her own account(s).

A few years ago, a Facebook profile page named "Pompano High's Finest" grew popular within a high school in southeast Florida. It was the source of an incredible amount of extreme gossip. The anonymous user behind this page would copy a photo from a new target's profile page, and then repost it on the "Finest" page with a horrifically nasty caption. For example, when one of the students became pregnant and the news became known to others, her picture was immediately featured on "Pompano High's Finest" with a caption saying, "You shouldn't be pregnant you dumb c***."

The user behind the page also periodically uploaded pictures of people and animals side by side comparing their features. The page became so notorious that everyone was constantly checking it throughout the school day, evenings, and weekends. It was a huge deal; whenever something new was posted, it was the talk of the school and the source of so much new gossip, rumors, and backbiting. Students would think it was hilarious, until one of *their* pictures was featured, which then made them the laughingstock of the entire student body.

Soon enough, teachers and administrators came to learn about the page and tried repeatedly (and unsuccessfully) to take it down and identify the person behind it. An assembly was held, expulsion threats were floated, and students were promised immunity if they came forward. No one ever did, and to this day no one knows who operated the page.

Perhaps you know a teen who has been targeted on a site like this. It might not be as elaborate a production and may simply only involve repeated hateful texts, rude comments to an Instagram photo, or snarky and insulting tweets that go viral. Recently, more cyberbullying incidents have even occurred through the use of hashtags. For example, someone might include mean or hateful hashtags under something they post (in the caption or comments) or that another person posts (in the comments). Popular examples include: #dork, #loser, #fuglyslut, #tryweightwatchers, #crackwhore, #cantbelievesheworethat, or #peoplewhoshouldoffthemselves.

BREAKOUT BOX

Confession Pages

Confessions pages on social media have received some attention in the press recently, and we regularly hear about the experiences of teens on these sites. They allow anyone to share personal secrets, rumors, gossip, and anything else they might want others to know about but are hesitant to post publicly or in a way that is tied to their identity. Anonymous confession posts can vary from sexual fantasies for another student to a crush on someone to revealing one's sexual orientation or another thing that may often be stigmatized or judged. Other posts are cruel and hateful and clearly represent cyberbullying. And, of course, everyone who knows about the page (in a community, school, or other organization) can "like" it and thereby can stay in the loop by receiving any and all updates. At this point, they can then participate as a voyeur, or more actively by liking, commenting on, or sharing specific confessions.[12]

As an example of how it works on, say, Facebook, a user creates a "page" (meaning, one that represents a group or brand or entity, as opposed to a "profile" which is specific to a particular individual).

Once again, we will let your mind come up with a million more that are so much worse. Regardless of how it happens, though, it clearly takes a toll.

Information Spreading

As we have mentioned, one of the major problems with online participation and interaction is that content sent, posted, or shared can be seen in such a short amount of time by such a large number of people. And when teens are acting in a shortsighted manner without considering future implications, some end up spreading things that should have remained private. What sort of information is typically involved in these cases? As a rule, it

Visitors then send private messages to the page with specific confessions, and the administrator of the page posts them publicly to the Wall for all followers to see. Another way to keep posts anonymous is to create an e-mail account specifically to receive confessions from others or to set up a form via free online tools such as Google Docs (or Survey Monkey or even an Ask.fm page). Then, confessors can click on a link, open up the form, share their confession without giving any identifying information, and click send. The person behind it all then receives these anonymous confessions via e-mail and then can post them for all to see.

Students do understand the negatives that arise when these sites are embraced within certain populations. One teen recently stated to the media that "they degrade people and make them feel unnecessarily bad about themselves."[13] But even so, confession pages have garnered tremendous popularity in some circles for the same reasons that other novel environments breed cyberbullying. As we know, people are "more likely to speak their mind" online if their "words can't be traced back to them."[14] Although, as discussed above, very little is ever completely anonymous online since everything posted has a digital footprint.

is personal contact information such as a phone number, e-mail, or home address. It could also be information related to something we don't want broadcasted far and wide like sexual orientation, sexual experiences, physical or medical issues, family problems, or anything else which we are not (yet) comfortable discussing. Sometimes those with malicious intentions find out what a teen doesn't want revealed and has tried to keep secret and figures out a way to use it against them. Other times, youth may be careless with what they've posted to their online friends or followers (or texted to someone they believe they can trust), but somehow it gets into the wrong hands and is disseminated well beyond the intended audience. And we have seen that intimate or private content tends to go viral pretty fast (because of its originally "secret" nature). Even if it's deleted relatively soon after it's posted, it's often too late.

Ginny, from New York, recently shared this story with us, underscoring the effect of information sharing as cyberbullying:

> When I was 15, a freshman in high school, I was bullied over the Internet and at school. I felt like it came out of nowhere. One day the group of girls I called friends turned against me viciously online. They created a fake profile page for me, which contained my cell phone number and instant message name. They photoshopped obscene sexual photographs of me and posted them in this profile. I was getting calls and began being stalked by strange men. These girls would make up sexually explicit rumors about me even though at the time I was a virgin. They would instant message me and tell me I was going to die. They were going to kill me. I was afraid to leave the house, to have friends, to pick up the phone. I lived in fear for so long. I knew they were looking for a fight and I refused to give them one so I deleted all known online presence and changed my number. I became recluse, a prisoner in my own home. Once I graduated high school I applied to college outside of my hometown to run away. Now, I am 22 and still have to live with the effects of these cruel girls. Trauma is hard to recover from but I know it is possible and I am stronger now than I have ever been. I am not that scared 15-year-old girl but I am still haunted by the girl I used to be.

Impersonation

Impersonation occurs when someone assumes another person's identity online. For example, they might create a social media profile and pretend to be you. They might fabricate e-mails that come from your account even though you personally didn't write them. They might pose as you to say or do hurtful things to others while interacting online in a way that ruins your reputation and gets you into serious trouble. We tend to see this as a more calculated form of cyberbullying—it doesn't occur as often as the posting of embarrassing pictures or the barrage of vicious messages or comments, and typically takes more planning and forethought. Here's one story we received from Marija in Croatia that depicts what can happen:

> First, I started to get nasty messages directly, and then my name started to be used to humiliate me, call me names, and assault my looks, my family. My name was used on Facebook statuses in most humiliating way, bullies started to impersonate me and spread personal things, lies and even made notes with the title: The truth about me. I could not fight with it, nor stop it. No matter how much I reported it to Facebook, they were persistent in making fake profiles, stealing pictures where they perceived me as ugly. After some physical threats, I reported them to advisors. However, after that, I started to be bullied anonymously, I got harmful messages, again was impersonated, and even sexual toys were ordered in my name to my home address without me knowing.

Another way impersonation can lead to cyberbullying is through a practice referred to as *catfishing*. Catfishing, at least in the online world, refers to the practice of setting up a fictitious online profile, most often for the purpose of luring another into a fraudulent romantic relationship. This became practiced more widely after a 2010 documentary film highlighted the real-world ramifications of online relationships, and when MTV launched a reality TV show in 2012 to capitalize on interest in this phenomenon.

Misleading another on social media with the intent to cause harm is not new. In 2009, Anthony Stancl, a New Berlin, Wisconsin, eighteen-year-old impersonated two girls ("Kayla" and "Emily") on Facebook. He sent out friend requests to a number of boys in his high school while posing and interacting as these two girls, and soon enough was involved in a number of online romantic relationships. In time, he convinced at least thirty-one of those unsuspecting boys to send him nude pictures or videos of themselves in exchange for pictures of "herself." As if that weren't bad enough, Stancl— still posing as a girl and still communicating through Facebook and AOL Instant Messenger—tried to convince more than half to meet with a male friend and let him perform sexual acts on them. If they refused, "she" told them that the pictures and/or videos would be released for all to see. Seven boys actually submitted to this horrific request and allowed Stancl to perform sex acts on them or they performed sex acts on him. He took numerous pictures of these encounters with his cell phone, and the police eventually found over 300 nude images of male teens on his computer. He was charged with five counts of child enticement, two counts of second-degree sexual assault of a child, two counts of third-degree sexual assault, possession of

BREAKOUT BOX

Self-Cyberbullying

We introduced you to Hannah Smith at the beginning of this chapter. Recall that she committed suicide after being cyberbullied, mainly through messages received on Ask.fm. The tragedy took an even darker turn as evidence emerged that Hannah may have actually sent many of the hurtful messages to herself. Upon investigating the suicide, Ask.fm officials noted that 98 percent of the messages sent to Hannah came from the same IP address as the computer she was using. *Self-cyberbullying* is actually not a new phenomenon. danah boyd, social media researcher and author of the recent book *It's Complicated: The Social Lives of Networked Teens*, wrote about "digital self-harm" a few years ago, focusing on behaviors observed on the now defunct Formspring.me, a social media site that operated a lot like Ask.fm (with the public answering of questions sometimes posed by anonymous people). "There are teens out there who are self-harassing by 'anonymously' writing mean questions to themselves and then publicly answering them," boyd wrote.[16] In 2013, Massachusetts Aggression Reduction Center researcher and psychology professor Elizabeth Englander found that up to 10 percent of college freshmen admitted that they had "falsely posted a cruel remark against themselves, or cyberbullied themselves, during high school."[17]

Those who harm themselves physically (usually by cutting, carving, or burning) are hurting and desperately searching for relief from some perceived insurmountable shortcoming, flaw, or insecurity. It is often a coping mechanism to distract from pain in other areas of their lives. They feel as though they have no other options and resort to a last ditch effort to bring some sense of normalcy or routine to their life. If left to fester, self-harm can eventually result in the ultimate harm to oneself—suicide—though usually the two behaviors are distinct.[18] And even though some might assume that those who choose digital forms of self-harm are at a reduced risk of physical self-harm or suicide (suggesting perhaps that these youth don't actually really want to hurt themselves), Hannah's case certainly casts doubt on that theory. Desperation and despair can lead people to do things that may seem completely irrational to the rest of us. But to them, it appears to be their only option.

To be sure, much more work needs to be done to explore this hidden side of cyberbullying. We don't know how much self-cyberbullying is really going on and whether the causes are comparable to other forms of self-harm. As boyd aptly points out, however, irrespective of who the perpetrator is, targets of cyberbullying need help. "Teens who are the victims of bullying—whether by a stranger, a peer, or themselves—are often in need of support, love, validation, and, most of all, healthy attention."[16]

I had a group of friends who I've been friends with since k-8. At the end of 8th grade year and over the summer just out of the blue the 5 friends just all turned their backs on me. They bullied me through Kik Messenger, Instagram and also Snapchat. The things they said to me were the worst, They called me fat, ugly, space case, cunt, whore, slut. "I hope you kill yourself." "I hope you get raped." "No one even loves you, everyone just pretends." "I hope you become suicidal." "Go cut yourself." And more. All the things they have said to me have never left my mind. I've became a self-harmer. I am suicidal. I have an eating disorder and severe depression & anxiety. I still haven't recovered from being cyberbullied.

—Jess, 14, Florida

child pornography, and repeated sexual assault of the same child and received a fifteen-year sentence in prison in early 2010.[15]

Tagging and Untagging

For those unfamiliar, tagging ties or connects a person (as represented by their online profile or account) to a specific piece of content on social media. Most commonly, individuals are tagged when they appear in a particular image or video. For example, if our friend Amanda posts a picture to her Facebook profile that includes her with both of us, she can link that picture not only to her profile but also to each of ours simply by clicking on the image and adding our names. When she does this, that image will automatically show up on our respective Facebook timelines (unless we have disabled it in our Privacy settings).

When it comes to cyberbullying, what often happens is the target is tagged (or linked) to a statement or picture or video or link that the person really doesn't want to be associated with. For instance, a person can caption a gross, disgusting, or otherwise insulting or demeaning photo with a target's username and perhaps a negative sentiment (for example, uploading a picture of a sumo wrestler and then captioning with something like "this reminds me of @hinduja"). Different from simply adding a username in a caption or a comment, someone can also tag a user in a specific image. On Facebook, you have to be friends with another person to tag him in a photo. However, anyone can be tagged in a photo on Instagram, and if they don't remove the tag or hide it from their profile, then anyone can see it—and it could go viral.

One of our friends, Debbie, had to go through this. When Debbie was twelve, she struggled with obesity. With determination, diet, and exercise, however, she was able to successfully shed over forty pounds before her first year of high school. She was finally healthy and for the first time in her life had increasing levels of confidence. Halfway through her sophomore year, though, a few girls discovered an old picture of Debbie before she had lost the weight. Thinking it would be hilarious, they posted the photo online, tagged her in it, and spread rumors that Debbie had an eating disorder. That was all it took for it to become the talk of the school, which led to unbelievable amounts of harassment, hate, and abuse. For example, after lunch classmates would make snide comments toward her saying, "You gonna go throw up in the bathroom now?" Debbie had worked so hard to be healthy, but the offline and online bullying destroyed her motivation and self-confidence to where she stopped exercising and making healthy diet choices. She is still emotionally scarred by what happened years ago, and can still vividly recollect each and every incident in which she was teased, tormented, and rejected.

Cyberstalking

Cyberstalking can be defined as using technology to induce fear, to threaten, to annoy, or otherwise harass someone else. Cyberstalking is a crime in many states; for example, in North Carolina, it is unlawful for a person to

- Use in electronic mail or electronic communication any words or language threatening to inflict bodily harm to any person or to that person's child, sibling, spouse, or dependent, or physical injury to the property of any person, or for the purpose of extorting money or other things of value from any person.
- Electronically mail or electronically communicate to another repeatedly, whether or not conversation ensues, for the purpose of abusing, annoying, threatening, terrifying, harassing, or embarrassing any person.
- Electronically mail or electronically communicate to another and to knowingly make any false statement concerning death, injury, illness, disfigurement, indecent conduct, or criminal conduct of the person electronically mailed or of any member of the person's family or household with the intent to abuse, annoy, threaten, terrify, harass, or embarrass.[19]

Since we are constantly tethered to our devices and share so much information about ourselves and our whereabouts online, it has become much easier for someone with malicious or perverse motives against you to wield their devices like weapons to wound you emotionally, psychologically, and even physically. Oftentimes, it isn't "strangers" that we should be concerned about—even though the initial uncertainty about who is responsible exacerbates the fear. Instead, research has shown that those most likely to harm you are those you've let into your life somehow: those you've given access to at least some of your personal information.[20]

Social media has made it so simple for stalkers to learn about someone after becoming one of their online friends or followers (or simply by searching for someone and going through their open profiles if they are not locked down and set to private). They can find out what the person likes to do, where she hangs out, who her friends are, what her daily routine tends to be, and so much more. Maybe this

> It has become much easier for someone with malicious or perverse motives against you to wield their devices like weapons to wound you emotionally, psychologically, and even physically.

is OK, if the person is emotionally well-balanced and simply has an appropriate interest in the person. However, some teens do not and take things way too far.

Someone we know, Dani, had to deal with this in high school. She is a sweetheart of a girl whom everyone liked, and she would go out of her way to show care to others. As such, she immediately befriended a new kid at school named Andrew, whose family had recently moved to town. Andrew, of course, didn't have any friends yet, and so Dani started to hang out with him and introduce him to others at school and around town. This soon led to Andrew developing a strong crush on Dani because of all the interest and time he was receiving from her. One day, Dani (naive and sweet as ever) told Andrew that she liked another boy. He briefly hid his devastation but then started to harass her and send her threatening e-mails—even going so far as to talk about killing Dani and himself. Initially, she found the messages creepy and dismissed them while attempting to cut off communication with Andrew. The messages, however, started to get even more vivid and unsettling. Eventually, she told her parents, who talked to Andrew's parents, who then sought psychological help for their son. While Dani had a happy ending to her story, some victims of cyberstalking are simply not as fortunate.

Physical Threats

We sometimes have seen instances of cyberbullying that involve threats to a person's physical safety and well-being. Of course, this type of cyberbullying warrants immediate attention and response by law enforcement to determine whether it is actually a threat with merit, as people often say things to one another that should not be construed as threats. For example, sometimes even youth who are the best of friends will text each other saying, "I am going to kill you if you go out with him!" It is essential to determine the extent to which the language actually implies a threat or if it is simply adolescents being adolescent.

> When I was 13, I started dating a boy from the next town over and apparently a girl from that town had a huge crush on him and was very upset with me when she found out that I was dating him. She started yelling at me and threatening me over msn instant messenger. She scared me so much and when I would try to block her address, she would just create a new profile and continue where she left off. It got to the point where I was scared to go to see my boyfriend in his town because I was scared of running into her and what she would do to me. I am from Ohio.
>
> —Anonymous

You may not know that in the months leading up to the Columbine school shooting in Littleton, Colorado, in April 1999, a parent found a web diary of Eric Harris (one of the shooters) where he threatened to "kill and injure as many of you pricks as I can."[21] The concerned parent reported this to law enforcement, but they were unable to find the website and argued that even if they could, there wasn't enough evidence that a specific crime had been committed. Because of the tragic outcome, the Columbine incident has (hopefully) encouraged school officials and law enforcement to take seriously any threat articulated online.

Some may dismiss electronic bullying as normal behavior that does not actually harm anyone, unlike a punch to the face, for example. Others acknowledge the severity of the psychological and emotional wounds that are caused by insults or intentional embarrassment. In one of our studies, 17 percent of students reported that threats made online are carried out at school, highlighting how cyberbullying can have significant real world ramifications (as illustrated in the Amanda Todd story at the beginning of Chapter 1, and in many others we are sure you can think of). The concept of *harm* stemming from harassing online communications warrants even greater attention so that we can accurately consider its gravity and severity. Fully comprehending how youth are negatively impacted by cyberbullying in very tangible ways is essential to foster a strong and lasting motivation to combat it.

> Words can be just as powerful as fists.
>
> —Alexis, 16, Michigan

SUMMARY

Cyberbullying can take as many different forms as there are popular devices and online environments. Would-be bullies can post hurtful messages on public online platforms or send direct anonymous messages over and over to individual targets. They can use photos, audio recordings, or video to exacerbate the humiliation. While the vast majority of interactions between youth are appropriate and respectful, the ubiquity of technology, its inherent characteristics, and the numerous forms through which cyberbullying can occur create a seemingly endless pool of candidates susceptible to being victimized, or to being an aggressor. And even though the devices, applications, and websites are continuously changing, a constant in society is that some teens will use whatever tools they have at their disposal to harm others.

There is no question that technology makes it *easier* to bully; but little is known about whether cyberbullying is a more troublesome experience for youth. Some have told us that it is. But research really hasn't been able to provide a meaningful response to that question. In the next chapter, we summarize *what is known* based on the research we and others have done over the years. We and many others have made great strides in just the few years since the first edition of this book came out in 2008.

QUESTIONS FOR REFLECTION

1. Do you think anonymity online is always a bad thing? Can you think of any benefits to being anonymous online?

2. What was the most hurtful type of cyberbullying you have heard of or seen? How would it have made you feel if you were the target of that cyberbullying when you were their age? What would you have done in that situation?

3. What would drive a teen to cyberbully themselves? What can schools do to prevent this unique form of cyberbullying?

4. If you found out that a rumor was circulating around school about a student in your class, what would you do?

5. Which do you think is worse from the perspective of the victim: being bullied at school or being bullied online? How about from the perspective of the school?

NOTES

1. Caroline Davies. "Hannah Smith Wrote 'Vile' Posts to Herself Before Suicide, Say Police." *The Guardian*. http://www.theguardian.com/uk-news/2014/may/06/hannah-smith-suicide-teenager-cyber-bullying-inquests.

2. Caroline Davies. "Hannah Smith Wrote 'Vile' Posts to Herself Before Suicide, Say Police." *The Guardian*. http://www.theguardian.com/uk-news/2014/may/06/hannah-smith-suicide-teenager-cyber-bullying-inquests; Martin Fricker. "Hannah Smith: Dad Says Internet Trolls Drove Bullied Schoolgirl, 14, to Hang Herself. *The Daily Mirror*. http://www.mirror.co.uk/news/uk-news/hannah-smith-dad-says-internet-2129280#ixzz37wGf3D1x.

3. Leon Festinger, Albert Pepitone, and Theodore Newcomb. "Some Consequences of Deindividuation in a Group." *Journal of Abnormal and Social Psycholog* 47 (1952): 382–389.

4. Jerome E. Singer, Claudia A. Brush, and Shirley C. Lublin. "Some Aspects of Deindividuation: Identification and Conformity." *Journal of Experimental Social Psychology* 1, no. 4 (1965): 356–378.

5. Edward F. Diener. "Deindividuation: The Absence of Self-Awareness and Self-Regulation in Group Members." In *The Psychology of Group Influence*, edited by Paul B. Paulus, 209–242. Hillsdale, NJ: Lawrence Erlbaum, 1980; Tom Postmes and Russell Spears. "Deindividuation and Antinormative Behavior: A Meta-Analysis." *Psychological Bulletin* 123, no. 3 (1998): 238–259.

6. Patrick Wade. "Cellphone Companies Say They Don't Save Text Messages." Accessed August 26, 2013, http://www.news-gazette.com/news/local/2013-08-26/cellphone-companies-say-they-dont-save-text-messages.html.

7. Communications Decency Act. Pub. L. No. 104-104 (Tit. V), 110 Stat. 133 (1996), codified at 47 U.S.C. §§223, 230.

8. Rachel Simmons, R. *Odd Girl Out*. New York: Harcourt, 2003.

9. Leslie Katz. 2005. "When 'Digital Bullying' Goes Too Far." CNET News. Accessed June 22, 2005, http://news.cnet.com/When-digital-bullying-goes-too-far/2100-1025_3-5756297.html.

10. Moshzilla.com. Accessed June 5, 2011 (Site has been removed).

11. OregonLaws.com. "Invasion of Personal Privacy." Vol. 4, Ch. 163, §163.700 (2011). http://www.oregonlaws.org/ors/163.700.

12. Stephanie Simon. "Students Bare Souls, and More, on Facebook 'Confession' Pages." *Reuters*. http://www.reuters.com/article/2013/03/18/us-usa-facebook-confess-idUSBRE92H0X720130318.

13. Zarah Peer Mohammed. "Bullying at School Gets Dangerous With Facebook 'Confessions' Pages. *The Express Tribune*. Accessed April 14, 2013, http://tribune.com.pk/story/535191/social-stigma-bullying-at-school-gets-dangerous-with-facebook-confessions-pages/.

14. Harry McCracken. "'Secret' iPhone App Is Silicon Valley's Newest Obsession." *Time*. Accessed February 8, 2014, http://time.com/6015/secret-app/.

15. Dinesh Ramde. "Anthony Stancl, 19, Gets 15 Years For Facebook Sex Scam." *Huffington Post*. Accessed February 24, 2010, http://www.huffingtonpost.com/2010/02/25/anthony-stancl-19-gets-15_n_476214.html.

16. danah boyd. "Digital Self-Harm and Other Acts of Self-Harassment." Accessed December 7, 2010, http://www.zephoria.org/thoughts/archives/2010/12/07/digital-self-harm-and-other-acts-of-self-harassment.html.

17. Elizabeth Englander. "Digital Self-Harm: Frequency, Type, Motivations, and Outcomes." http://webhost.bridgew.edu/marc/DIGITAL%20SELF%20HARM%20report.pdf.

18. Raychelle C. Lohmann. "Understanding Suicide and Self-Harm: Discovering the Similarities and Differences Between Self-Harm and Suicide." *Psychology Today*. http://www.psychologytoday.com/blog/teen-angst/201210/understanding-suicide-and-self-harm; Keith Hawton, Daniel Zahl, and Rosamund Weatherall. "Suicide Following Deliberate Self-Harm: Long-Term Follow-Up of Patients Who Presented to a General Hospital." *British Journal of Psychiatry* 182 (2003): 537–542.

19. North Carolina. "Cyberstalking." General Statute § 14-196.3 (2008). http://www.ncga.state.nc.us/EnactedLegislation/Statutes/HTML/BySection/Chapter_14/GS_14-196.3.html.

20. Justin W. Patchin and Sameer Hinduja. "Trends in Online Social Networking: Adolescent Use of MySpace Over Time." *New Media & Society* 12, no. 2 (2010): 197–216.

21. Brooks Brown and Rob Merritt. *No Easy Answers: The Truth Behind Death at Columbine*. Brooklyn, NY: Lantern Books, 2002.

CHAPTER FOUR

What Do We Know About Cyberbullying?

Ryan Halligan was a thirteen-year-old boy from Essex Junction, Vermont, who didn't quite seem to fit in with his peer group. As such, he was teased, taunted, and called "gay" by some of his classmates, both at school and online. In the summer between his seventh- and eighth-grade years, however, things finally seemed to be getting better. During this time, he began a casual Internet friendship with Ashley, a popular girl from his school. Over the course of several weeks of communicating online, he developed a crush on her. Unfortunately, the feelings weren't mutual.

But instead of leveling with him and letting him down easy, Ashley started to pretend she liked Ryan, primarily for the purposes of gaining more personal information about him. When school started back up again in the fall, he was filled with hope for his social life and his future. He approached Ashley in person with romantic gestures—but was rejected as a "loser" and mocked in front of others. Completely devastated, Ryan told Ashley, "It's girls like you who make me want to kill myself."

After enduring months of further humiliation and harassment at the hands of his classmates, he couldn't take it anymore and chose to end his life on October 7, 2003. Ryan's father, John, is clear about the causes of his son's untimely death: "We have no doubt that bullying and cyberbullying were significant environmental factors that triggered Ryan's depression."[1] Based on what we can learn from reports on the story, the main problem wasn't that Ryan was bullied or spurned by his crush. To be sure, these things happen all the time in adolescence. Ryan's father suspects that because these behaviors carried over to the Internet, they were amplified due to the perception that "everyone" in the school knew of the incident. Apparently, Ashley had forwarded or sent very personal excerpts from her instant message exchanges with Ryan to a number of other classmates. It was hard enough to be embarrassed in front of one or two peers—especially by a girl you really thought liked you back. Instead, to Ryan it seemed like the entire school was in on the joke.

Was Ryan's experience typical? Does cyberbullying affect teens in different ways compared to traditional, schoolyard bullying? At the time of the publication of the first edition of this book, very little formal scientific inquiry had taken place. Since then, dozens of studies involving tens of thousands of teens have been conducted and the findings help to inform our understanding of the problem and its possible solutions. This chapter will review that body of research with a particular emphasis on our own empirical work. We begin with a brief discussion of the studies that we have undertaken over the last decade.

OUR CYBERBULLYING RESEARCH

We first began to systematically explore cyberbullying through an online pilot survey in 2003 so that we could learn as much as possible about the nature, extent, forms, and consequences of these emerging behaviors. The primary benefit of using an online survey is the ability to reach a wide number of online teenagers at an economical cost, and therefore worked with our goals for a preliminary inquiry into this phenomenon. Our survey instrument asked youth whether they had experienced online aggression in any way, shape, or form, or knew of others who had such experiences. Very little data had been collected at this time, and so not much was known.

From a very small sample, representing only those youth who volunteered to complete our survey after seeing it linked to a teen-oriented website, we learned that cyberbullying was more of a problem than anyone at the time realized. We modified and replicated that survey in the spring of 2004 among a slightly larger sample (and again in 2005) and confirmed our earlier beliefs that a significant proportion of Internet-using youth had experienced cyberbullying either as a target or an aggressor or both.[2] We also learned that many teens lacked effective skills for dealing with cyberbullies, and that for the most part, teens weren't talking to adults about these experiences.[3]

Despite all of these important initial insights, the utilization of online surveys has certain limitations that leave it susceptible to criticism. While a complete discussion of these is outside the scope of this book, interested readers are encouraged to consult our previous papers cited above. To be sure, there are drawbacks in *any* research endeavor, and ideally several approaches should be utilized to analyze a problem from different vantage points. With that in mind, since 2007, all of our studies have involved random samples of known populations in schools which aimed to be representative of a typical student's attitudes, behaviors, and experiences, so we can be fairly confident in the reliability and validity of the information obtained. In total, we've conducted ten formal surveys involving close to

15,000 middle and high school students. We will restrict our discussion in this chapter to the most recent eight surveys conducted since 2007 that utilized the more rigorous methodologies (see Resource C at the end of the book for our survey instrument and psychometric properties, in case you need them).

In addition to all of the quantitative data that we collect in objectively worded (multiple-choice-type) questions, we also give respondents opportunities in all of our surveys to tell us what they are experiencing, *in their own words*. For example, in each of the surveys, we include the following question:

> Please describe—in as much detail as possible—your most recent experience with **being bullied online**. Please tell us about the online activity in which you were participating, what you know about the others who were involved, how it made you feel, and what you did specifically in response.

We expected short, one- or two-sentence summaries of respondents' recent bullying experiences. What we received instead were rich, detailed stories about how online harassment has made their lives frustrating, miserable, and, in some cases (and in their own words), "not worth living." Some youth wrote so much about their experiences that their responses overwhelmed our database, and we had to modify our data fields to accommodate the lengthy responses. Apart from the surveys, we've also collected stories through focus groups and detailed one-on-one conversations with hundreds of teens. Many of the anecdotes included throughout this book come from these accounts. We feel that it is vitally important to make sure that the "hard data" we present is representative of the actual lived experiences of youth.

Once, I took a silly photo with this girl's camera and she posted it on Facebook. The comments were horrendous. They were about me looking like a possessed demon, and how weird I looked. People were saying how bad they felt that she had to deal with me. Then the rumors came. They started to say I was crazy, talking to bookshelves and I should be put away. People even started to raid my regular photos with remarks. I had to deactivate my Facebook account, but they didn't stop. Text messages came by the dozen.

—Tabitha, 16, New York

PREVALENCE OF CYBERBULLYING

If you pay attention to the news reports of cyberbullying incidents (like we do), you would probably believe that cyberbullying is happening at *epidemic* levels and is impacting legions of young people. When we first started studying cyberbullying, we would literally print out and archive any news article we saw that talked about a cyberbullying incident—because they happened (or at least were reported) so infrequently. Now, it seems, cyberbullying occurs (and is reported or discussed) at an almost constant rate. However, some scholars in certain fields have argued that cyberbullying is not really occurring at levels that merit our significant attention, and the entire phenomenon may be overblown. Well, which is it? How much is going on and to what extent is it affecting our youth? Is it an epidemic or a rarity? We'll examine this question by looking at both our own research and that of others. As you might guess, the answer is somewhere in between.

Our Studies

Overall, approximately 25 percent of the students we have surveyed since 2007 have told us that they have been cyberbullied at some point in their lifetimes (see Chart 4.1). Almost one out of ten (9 percent) said they were cyberbullied in the thirty days preceding the survey. Similarly, about 16 percent of those who we surveyed admitted that they had cyberbullied others at some point in their lifetimes (see Chart 4.2), with about 6 percent saying they had done so in the most recent thirty days.

In our most recent survey, conducted in the spring of 2014, we asked 661 middle school students whether they had experienced cyberbullying. At the beginning of the survey, we informed them that "cyberbullying is when someone repeatedly makes fun of another person online or repeatedly picks on another person through e-mail or text message or when someone posts something online about another person that they don't like." Note that this definition is slightly different from the one used in Chapter 1. We wanted to present it to the students in a way that they would easily understand and ensure that we were all on the same page in terms of what experiences we wanted them to share with us.

The major findings were pretty much in line with what we've regularly found over the years. When asked "Have you been cyberbullied in the last 30 days?" 11.9 percent of students responded yes. When asked "Have you been cyberbullied in your lifetime?" just over one-third of respondents (34.6 percent) said yes. When asked "Have you cyberbullied others in the last 30 days?" 4.2 percent responded yes. When asked "Have you cyberbullied others in your lifetime?" 17 percent of the students said yes. Finally, slightly

Chart 4.1 Lifetime Cyberbullying Experiences Among Middle Schoolers (Victimization): Eight Different Studies, 2007–2014

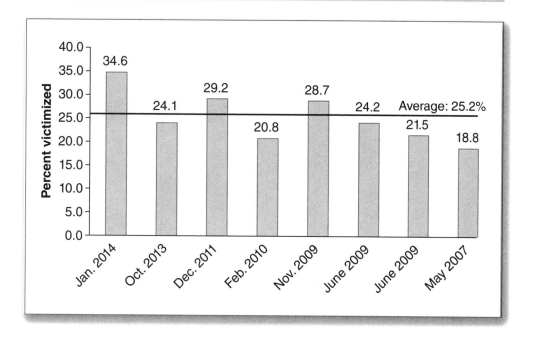

Chart 4.2 Lifetime Cyberbullying Experiences Among Middle Schoolers (Offending): Eight Different Studies, 2007–2014

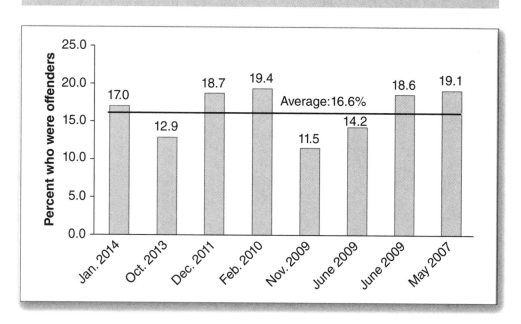

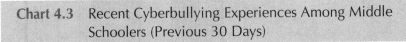

Chart 4.3 Recent Cyberbullying Experiences Among Middle Schoolers (Previous 30 Days)

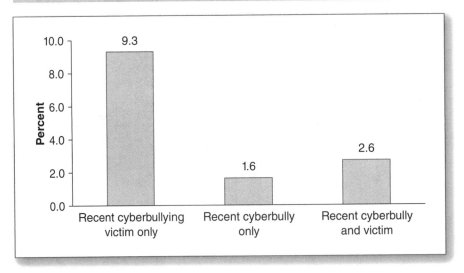

less than 11 percent of students in our most recent sample were both cyberbullying victims and offenders at some point in their lifetime (2.6 percent in previous 30 days). Chart 4.3 summarizes the results of this survey.

When asked about specific types of online harassment and aggression, about 18 percent of the students in our most recent sample had experienced at least one of the following, two or more times in the previous thirty days:

- Been cyberbullied
- Someone posted mean or hurtful comments about me online
- Someone posted a mean or hurtful picture of me online
- Someone posted a mean or hurtful video of me online
- Someone created a mean or hurtful web page about me
- Someone spread rumors about me online
- Someone threatened to hurt me through a cell phone text message
- Someone threatened to hurt me online
- Someone pretended to be me online and acted in a way that was mean or hurtful to me

Even though only about 12 percent of students reported that they had "been cyberbullied" when asked directly, more than 18 percent have experienced behaviors online that many would classify as cyberbullying. As such, it's important to point out that if you ask students if they have "been cyberbullied" and they say no, you may need to inquire further about the specific *types* of behaviors they have experienced while online to make sure you fully understand the nature of what is occurring to them and how often it happens.

Other Published Research

In the fall of 2013, we reviewed all of the published research we could find that included prevalence rates for cyberbullying. This work built on our earlier effort to quantitatively summarize published cyberbullying articles, which we wrote about in our book *Cyberbullying Prevention and Response: Expert Perspectives* (see especially Chapter 2).[4] In total, we have now systematically reviewed seventy-four articles published in peer-reviewed academic journals; fifty-two of those included cyberbullying victimization rates and forty-three included cyberbullying offending rates. Interestingly, rates across all of the studies ranged widely, from 2.3 to 72 percent for victimization and from 1.2 to 44.1 percent for offending. However, the average across all of these studies was remarkably similar to the rates that we found in our work (about 21 percent of teens have been cyberbullied and about 15 percent admitted to cyberbullying others at some point in their lifetimes). Taken as a whole, it seems safe to conclude that at least one out of every five teens has experienced cyberbullying, and about one out of every six teens has done it to others (see Charts 4.4 and 4.5).

> At least one out of every five teens has experienced cyberbullying, and about one out of every six teens has done it to others.

As mentioned earlier, estimates across these studies range widely as to how many youth have experienced online aggression. There are several explanations for the different statistics reported here. First, many of these studies target respondents of varying ages. As expected, the studies that focus on younger populations (middle school samples or younger) tend to report lower prevalence rates than those that target high school students. Second, these studies employ different survey methodologies. That is, respondents could be asked questions through a phone interview, in-class survey, or web-based survey. Those studies that used Internet-based samples tend to report higher numbers of aggressors and victims because they are surveying those who are more regularly participating and interacting online, and therefore most likely to experience cyberbullying. Those that utilized phone interviews reported lower rates, perhaps because in some cases the respondent's parents or siblings were within earshot of the conversation and the teen was therefore reluctant to disclose too much.

Third, some of the youth included in these studies were selected at random, while others were selected deliberately because they were members of some larger group. In some cases, students opted into the study on their own accord. In those cases, students who had experienced cyberbullying are likely overrepresented in the sample since they would possibly be more enthusiastic about sharing their story. Ideally, participants would be

Chart 4.4 Select Published Cyberbullying Research: Cyberbullying Victimization Rates Across Peer-Reviewed Journal Articles (*n* = 52)

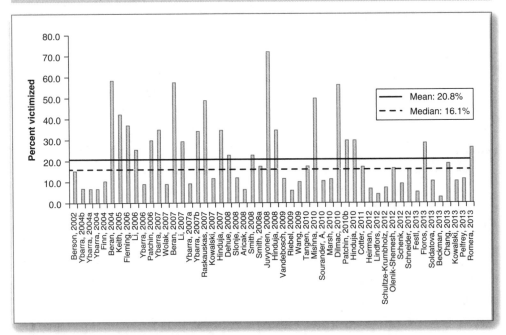

Chart 4.5 Select Published Cyberbullying Research: Cyberbullying Offending Rates Across Peer-Reviewed Journal Articles (*n* = 43)

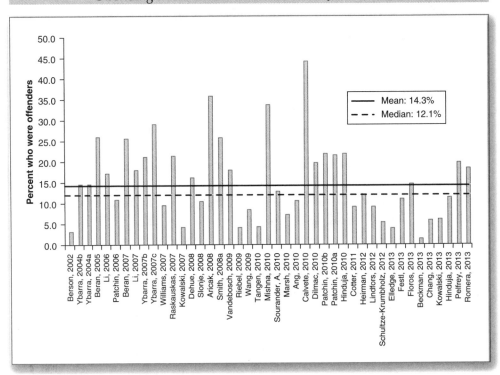

selected randomly from a known population so that the responses of the sample could be used to approximate how the population as a whole might respond. It's problematic, for example, to recruit participants for an online survey about cyberbullying by posting a link on a website that offers resources for teens who are being cyberbullied. This strategy will undoubtedly overestimate the problem because most people who see the link and volunteer to participate likely found it because of their experience with cyberbullying.

Fourth, different studies utilize different reporting periods. When asking adolescents if they have experienced cyberbullying, some surveys asked about experiences over one's lifetime, while others focused on the previous year or just the last month. We settled on asking both about lifetime and recent experiences, reasoning that teens are likely to remember if they had *ever* been cyberbullied and if it happened relatively recently. Finally, one of the biggest differences among these research endeavors is the way that *cyberbullying* is defined. People can't even agree on what to call it (see Box 1.2 in Chapter 1), let alone what behaviors it constitutes. As noted above, we use a very specific definition of cyberbullying but also ask youth about their experiences with various behaviors that can be characterized as online harassment. We think this is the best approach to comprehensively learn about the actual types of behaviors that youth are experiencing.

> Even one child being cyberbullied or cyberbullying others is too many.

It is important to point out, however, that the one number you don't see listed in any of the charts presented is *zero*. We believe that even one child being cyberbullied or cyberbullying others is too many, and imagine you agree.

Trends

Many people understandably assume that cyberbullying rates have been steadily increasing over the last several years. In fact, the media often contact us to confirm that the problem is steadily "growing" and "getting worse." The data, however, really don't demonstrate a clear, significant upward trend. There are only two studies that we are aware of that have explored cyberbullying experiences over a period of time. The first analysis was conducted by our colleagues at the Crimes Against Children Research Center at the University of New Hampshire. Examining the three waves of the Youth Internet Safety Survey (2000, 2005, 2010), they found a slight increase in cyberbullying behaviors over that time period (from 6 percent to 9 percent to 11 percent).[5] The second data source is the School Crime Supplement of the National Crime Victimization Survey (NCVS). In 2011,[6] 9 percent of students said they were cyberbullied compared to 6.2 percent in 2009.[7] Since the

NCVS data are weighted to represent the entire population of twelve- to eighteen-year-olds enrolled in Grades 6 through 12, we can estimate that about 2.2 million students experienced cyberbullying in 2011, up from about 1.5 million in 2009. Overall, even though we don't have a lot of good research to go on, it seems reasonable to presume a slight increase in cyberbullying behaviors over time.

GENDER DIFFERENCES IN CYBERBULLYING

> My most recent experience was with four girls, only one I knew in person (she goes to my school) . . . they kept dogging me and threatening me, laughing at me, and just constantly putting me down. Eventually I blocked them because I was getting so frustrated and felt so vulnerable. It took me months to get over feeling like that (even though it was online) and to finally getting to the point where I could just say F*** you guys and get over the whole thing.
>
> —Jane, 18, Canada

A significant body of traditional bullying research indicates that boys are involved in physical bullying more often than girls.[8] However, research has also consistently noted that adolescent girls tend to participate in more indirect, less visible forms of bullying, including psychological and emotional harassment (e.g., gossip, rumor spreading and other forms of relational aggression).[9] Given the fact that the vast majority of cyberbullying behaviors involve these indirect forms of harassment via texts, posts, and messages, it makes sense that most studies show that girls are just as likely, if not more likely, to be involved in cyberbullying, both as a target and as a perpetrator. The third wave of the Youth Internet Safety Survey found that 69 percent of youth who were harassed were female.[5] In a 2012 survey of over 20,000 high school students from Massachusetts, Shari Kessel Schneider and her colleagues found that 7.2 percent of girls had been cyberbullied, compared to 5.6 percent of boys.[10] Moreover, 11.1 percent of girls had been bullied both online and at school, compared to 7.6 percent of boys (boys were more likely to have experienced bullying at school only).

In the twenty-four peer-reviewed studies we analyzed that included prevalence rates for both boys and girls, eighteen found higher rates for girls, while six found higher rates for boys, though not all of these differences were statistically significant. On average across these studies, 18 percent of boys had been cyberbullied compared to 22 percent of girls. Eighteen studies included cyberbullying offending rates disaggregated by gender and fifteen of those found that more boys admitted to cyberbullying others compared to girls. Again, across all of those studies, 16 percent of the boys cyberbullied others compared to 12 percent of the girls.

The nature of the cyberbullying behaviors, however, seems to vary. In our 2014 study, for example, girls were more likely to be bullied via cell phone text messages or on websites like Instagram and Ask.fm, while boys were more likely to be harassed while playing online games. Girls were more likely to spread rumors online, while boys were more likely to create a mean or hurtful website about another. To note, we have previously found that the two online victimization behaviors reported most frequently by girls were being ignored (45.8 percent) and disrespected (42.9 percent), both of which are relatively mild in nature.[11] It is important, however, to point out that some girls did report more serious forms such as being threatened (11.2 percent) or being scared for their safety (6.2 percent).

So why do girls seem to be experiencing and participating in cyberbullying more frequently than traditional bullying (see Chart 4.6)? There are a number of potential explanations. While some research has shown that boys and girls perpetrate similar amounts of verbal bullying,[12] other research has indicated that girls may experience more verbal and less physical bullying.[13] As such, perhaps the hateful sentiments and harm inflicted via status updates, tweets, captions, comments, and replies are internalized more so by girls than by boys—to the point where they characterize and clearly report it as cyberbullying victimization. To be clear, we are simply making an informed speculation here; much more research must be done on gender differences and bullying experiences to provide more clarity. Secondly (and relatedly), girls may partake in a different *type* of bullying—one that is more emotional and psychological. Girls generally engage in variations of "social sabotage" much more frequently than boys, an activity well facilitated by the mediums of interaction in cyberspace.[14]

Third, girls are arguably less confrontational and more committed to maintaining balance and agreeability in their relationships—at least when face-to-face with another.[15] Communicating online frees them to act out flagrantly from a safe setting behind their phone, tablet, or computer. Vicious statements can be made with a sense of security and power since they have a visible and even authoritative platform from which to widely share candid opinions, feelings, and emotions about others. Fourth, girls have been culturally and socially constrained when it comes to manifesting

Chart 4.6   Cyberbullying by Gender: Victimization

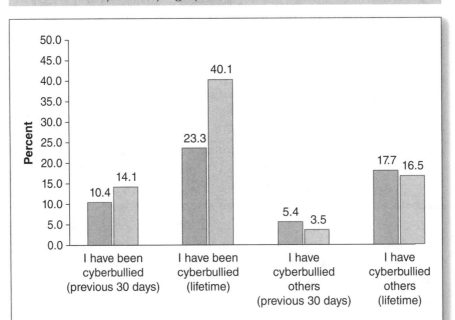

violent or aggressive tendencies but are not bound by those same constraints in cyberspace.[16] Even though vastly more males than females commit violent crime, which might lead one to believe that males are more
violent than females, it is possible that females share the same tendencies
toward hostility as males.[17] However, they have been historically entrenched
in a social structure that forbids them to demonstrate aggression in the
same ways that men do because they are told it is not culturally or socially
appropriate to do so.[18] Simply put, the majority of society believes that it
is not "feminine" and thereby inappropriate to act out in a physically
aggressive manner.

Finally, girls arguably often need peer support to gang up on another girl,
and this can be accomplished with ease through the marshaling of technology. Consider Amanda Todd's experience from Chapter 1; so many other
students were able to band together and collectively torment her both offline
and especially online because of ubiquitous technology access and use. In
this case, incredibly cruel statements, threats, and even blackmail occurred
through video chat, Facebook, YouTube, and texting over the course of
months and years. And the malice followed Amanda, as select girls (and others) continued their torment through social media even when she moved
away to different schools.

RACIAL DIFFERENCES IN CYBERBULLYING

Studies that have examined traditional bullying across different racial groups have been largely inconclusive.[19] The same has been true when focusing on cyberbullying. While our sample size from our 2014 survey wasn't large enough to accurately distinguish experiences by race, we surveyed a diverse sample of over 4,400 middle and high school students back in 2010. In that study, we found that white students were slightly more likely to experience cyberbullying as a victim—especially when they reported on their lifetime experiences (see Chart 4.7). In another recent study, Jing Wang and her colleagues at the National Institutes of Health found that African American students were more likely to be involved in cyberbullying perpetration, while Hispanic youth were more likely to be cyber victims.[20] Finally, Shari Kessel Schneider and her colleagues found that nonwhites were more likely than whites to be victims of cyberbullying but found no difference when comparing whites' to nonwhites' experiences with traditional bullying.[10]

In studies that have revealed differences based on race, some have cited a so-called digital divide—where certain racial and economic groups have less access to technology.[21] In their study, Brandesha Tynes and Kimberly Mitchell found that African American youth were more likely than nonblack youth to access the Internet from a cell phone as opposed to a home computer.[22] In our

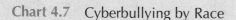

Chart 4.7   Cyberbullying by Race

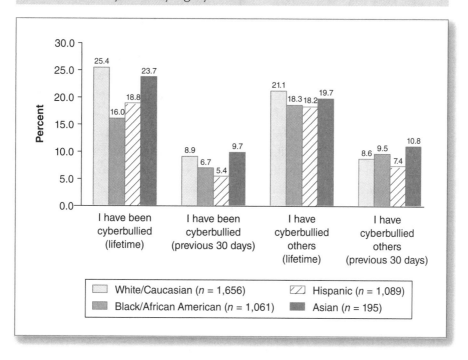

studies, however, different races report relatively similar rates of participation in other online activities (online games, e-mail, chat rooms, etc.), and no clear finding signaled differential levels of access to technology. Of course, that may be related to our particular samples. Or it might mean that the digital divide—at least in the United States—is closing over time.

It also may simply be that certain demographic characteristics, such as race and gender, are rendered less important in an environment where interpersonal communication occurs frequently through textual post, comments, and messages (although, of course, pictures and video are so much more a part of Internet communication than a decade ago). An alternative explanation is that historically less powerful groups may be more powerful (or at least not disadvantaged) when online. Minority groups (irrespective of race or ethnicity)—while potentially unpopular at school—may not be exposed as marginal on the Internet. Moreover, youth who may not (or cannot) stand up for themselves at school may be more likely to do so in cyberspace if the perceived likelihood of retaliation is minimized. Whatever the reason, much more research needs to be done to disentangle the effect that race has on experiences with cyberbullying.[23]

AGE DIFFERENCES IN CYBERBULLYING

Research has consistently indicated that traditional bullying tends to peak in the middle school years and generally decrease as the student progresses through high school.[24] With respect to cyberbullying, the research is less clear. Some studies have noted that cyberbullying tends to peak in the later middle school years (8th Grade)[25] or even into high school.[26] Across the three waves of the Youth Internet Safety Survey (YISS) spanning from 2000 to 2010, Lisa Jones and her colleagues routinely found higher experience with online harassment among thirteen- to fifteen-year-olds when compared to younger (10–12) and older (16–17) students.[5]

In our own study from 2005, older youth tended to be involved in cyberbullying more often, most likely due to their expanded experiences using technology back then. Returning to our 2010 data where we surveyed both middle and high school students, we saw a general trend of increased participation in cyberbullying as teens got older, though it did vary by type of cyberbullying (see Chart 4.8). We would expect to see a greater variety of mediums being used as kids move into their teenage years and become more proficient with different devices and online environments.[27] Indeed, we have also found that youth who spent more time online or who were more computer proficient were more likely to experience cyberbullying, both as victims and as bullies.[3] This mirrors other research into online harassment, which has found that offenders (both those who have only offended as well

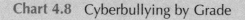

Chart 4.8 Cyberbullying by Grade

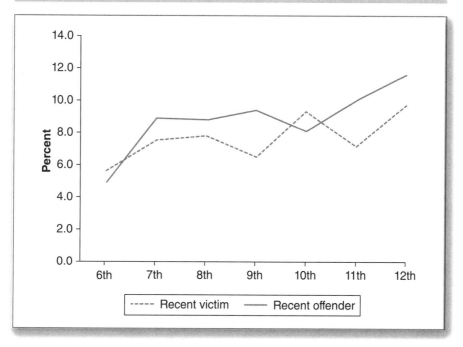

as those who have been both an offender and a victim) tend to use the Internet more frequently and with more proficiency than individuals who have only been victimized.[28] So it may not be that older teens tend to bully online (or be bullied online) more than younger kids because of their age, but rather the fact that they typically have more varied online experiences. That may be changing now as younger and younger children are being introduced to technology, and as a result, we may start to see these children experience online bullying earlier in their lives.

VICTIM/OFFENDER RELATIONSHIP IN CYBERBULLYING

In 8th grade I was constantly bullied by an ex-boyfriend of mine. He made me feel like I was worthless and that I deserved to die. With the help of friends after months of not saying anything I finally told someone. He recently showed up again and I am feeling like I don't deserve to live again. He says rude things and I wonder about not living anymore but I don't want to hurt those I love.

—Chloe, 14, Washington

The relationship between those who are victimized online and their aggressors merits attention, as traditional bullying largely involves adolescents who know each other—whether at school, in the neighborhood, or through some other social connection. This begs the question: Is cyberspace just another setting in which traditional bullying can take place, albeit without face-to-face interaction and the immediate threat of physical harm? Or do online environments somehow embolden individuals (for one reason or another) to harass and mistreat others with whom they have no previous relationship or contact?

In part to answer this question, in 2007, Janis Wolak and her colleagues analyzed data from 1,500 youth between the ages of ten and seventeen from the second wave of the Youth Internet Safety Survey (YISS) and found that 43 percent of Internet harassment victims knew their aggressor.[29] In that same year, Robin Kowalski and Susan Limber found that over half of cyberbullying victims knew the identity of their aggressor.[27] Also based on the YISS data, Michele Ybarra, Kimberly Mitchell, David Finkelhor, and Janis Wolak found that 12.6 percent of all harassed youth report that the same aggressor harms them offline and online, while 10.4 percent of victims report that different individuals mistreat them offline and online.[30] Finally, in the most recent wave of the YISS (2010) 58 percent of youth reported that the aggressor was a school friend or acquaintance.[5] Our own research also found that victims of cyberbullying generally know (or at least think they know) who is harassing them (see Chart 4.9). Like the YISS data, over 60 percent of the students from our 2014 sample who reported that they were cyberbullied said it was by someone from within their social circle (usually a former friend). Even though online bullying provides aggressors with a veil of perceived anonymity, it appears that sooner or later, the target often figures out who is harassing them.

My daughter is not one for starting drama, but will come to the aid of a friend in need and that draws a lot of fire from others sometime. This brings me to her new cyberbully . . . "Gossip Girl." This person is downright toxic. This person has posted long bullying tirades on Instagram. My daughter has shown me these posts. My daughter used to like school, now she is begging me to have her homeschooled. It is pretty obvious that this "Gossip Girl" goes to [school removed] because she knows too much about what goes on in that school.

—Cam, parent, Maryland

THE LINK BETWEEN TRADITIONAL BULLYING AND CYBERBULLYING

Interestingly, a good amount of research suggests a strong connection between cyberbullying and traditional schoolyard bullying.[31] While it is difficult to determine whether traditional bullying occurs before cyberbullying or vice versa, there is a clear correlation between online and offline victimization and offending. In one of our earlier studies, we found that youth who reported bullying others in real life in the previous six months were more than 2.5 times as likely to report bullying others online. Similarly, youth who were victims of traditional bullying in the previous six months were more than 2.5 times as likely to be victims of cyberbullying.[3]

> I feel bad for the people being bullied, it's so rude to pick on someone and they are doing it online where they have proof of what they said and can print it out and pass it around school.
>
> —Faye, 15, Wisconsin

Table 4.1 helps to further illustrate this relationship. It shows, for example, that most students have neither been bullied at school nor online. Most of those who have been cyberbullied have also been bullied at school.

It seems likely that the causes of meanness and cruelty among teens are similar, irrespective of the environment in which it takes place. That is, whatever causes a student to bully online will undoubtedly also cause them to bully somewhere else. As much as technology has made it easier to connect with others at any time and from just about any place, Table 4.1 also shows that the primary location for bullying opportunities still appears to be the school. It will be interesting to see if this might change over time, but it has not as of now. To note, most people we speak to often assume that cyberbullying is occurring with more frequency than traditional bullying. Perhaps this is because most of what we hear about in the news are cases of cyberbullying or because technology is so much more widespread among teens than ever before. The reality, however, is that most bullying is still happening primarily where it has always occurred—at school.

> Most of those who have been cyberbullied have also been bullied at school.

To support this point further, about 12 percent of students had been cyberbullied compared to over 43 percent who had been bullied at school in our most

Table 4.1		Relationship Between Cyberbullying and Bullying at School	

		Been Bullied at School	
		No	Yes
Been Cyberbullied	No	53.9%	33.7%
	Yes	2.6%	9.8%
		Bullied Others at School	
		No	Yes
Cyberbullied Others	No	90.9%	4.7%
	Yes	2.3%	2.0%

Note: Represents recent experiences—within the previous 30 days.

recent sample (in the previous thirty days). And we are not the only researchers to have observed this. The School Crime Supplement of the National Crime Victimization Survey added a handful of cyberbullying questions to their survey in 2009, and in that year and in 2011 (the most recent available), significantly more students reported that they had been bullied at school than online.[32] Specifically, in 2011, 26 percent of students reported being bullied at school, while 8 percent reported being bullied "by electronic means anywhere."[6] As much as societal sentiment would suggest that cyberbullying is occurring with greater frequency than schoolyard bullying, it just isn't.[33]

These findings do raise some intriguing follow-up questions for additional study: Are there certain characteristics that are unique to the group of students who specialize in only one form of bullying? Are interventions that focus on reducing bullying in general also effective at reducing cyberbullying (or vice versa)? Are there certain features of schools (or web environments) that make them more or less inviting of different types of bullying? As has been our mantra throughout this chapter, we once again reiterate that additional research is necessary to flesh out the answers.

I got a Tumblr blog about a year and a half or so ago and someone kept writing me anonymous questions about how I should kill myself and the world would be better off if I was dead and how I'm such a whore etc. Now they're egging my driveway once or twice a week and my parents are just so upset and I feel so bad because I honest to God don't know what I ever did to someone to do this to my family. They usually don't tell me or warn me that they'll egg my house but last week when they did they sent me a message anonymously on Tumblr. I just really want to know if I could go to the police and ask them if they can find out where the anonymous message came from and if they'll be able to do it without my parents present. I don't want to involve my parents with the cops and this situation because my dad is kind of sick and I don't want to stress him even more.

—Sarah, 17, Michigan

RESPONSES OF CYBERBULLYING VICTIMS

One of the first things we learned in our earliest cyberbullying studies was that victims were not telling adults about their experiences. Specifically, fewer than 10 percent of victims told a parent, and fewer than 5 percent told a teacher about their experiences with cyberbullying.[2] As illustrated in Chart 4.9, these numbers have improved, but only slightly in recent years. This may suggest that teens are becoming more willing to confide in adults or that messages about Internet safety are getting through to youth.

Chart 4.9 Who Victims Tell (%)

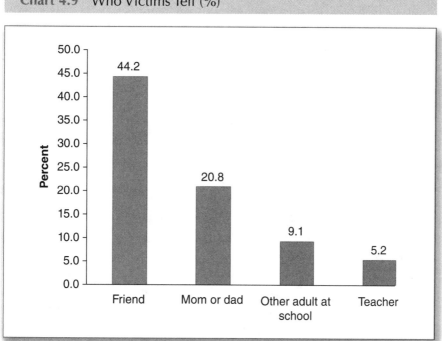

We also have learned that both boys and girls are unlikely to confide in others about their cyberbullying experiences, although girls are generally more likely to report their experiences to others. Even so, approximately 80 percent of recent victims of cyberbullying *do not tell an adult* about their experiences and over one-quarter didn't tell *anyone*—which may be cause for concern. Here also it is clear that more research is required to better understand the extent to which victims are disclosing cyberbullying experiences to adults and perhaps to identify what can be done to encourage it.

There are several commonly stated reasons for the disconnect here. First, victims don't want to be blamed for somehow being partly responsible for what happened and are often afraid that parents will simply remove the source of the problem—the computer or phone. As Sarah, thirteen, from Virginia, told us, "I wanted to tell my parents but I was afraid that they would never let me chat again and I know that's how a lot of other kids feel." The other concern that victims have is that adults are ill-equipped or unwilling to intervene on their behalf (and in a calm, rational manner) to resolve the situation. To be sure, many parents simply don't know what to do when confronted with a cyberbullying problem. It also seems that some teachers are gun-shy in responding to behaviors that happen away from school (this will be clarified in Chapter 5). Finally, law enforcement is unlikely to get involved unless a clear violation of the law can be articulated (which is uncommon in cyberbullying cases). So, to whom can victims turn? For starters, we hope that after reading this book you (yes, you!) will make yourself available and informed so that they will feel comfortable talking to you.

> 80 percent of recent victims of cyberbullying *do not tell an adult* about their experiences and over one-quarter didn't tell *anyone*.

When it comes to responding to minor cyberbullying behaviors, many victims take matters into their own hands. As illustrated in Chart 4.10, almost half of recent victims simply blocked the bully from communicating with them. This is an effective response to social media, e-mail, and even text message bullying. Blocking can be a short-term solution, however, because the bully can always create new accounts, screen names, or alternate identities and thereby continue the assault.

Furthermore, over one-quarter of victims logged off their device for a period of time as a response strategy to being victimized. This can be an effective way to counter many types of cyberbullying because it temporarily removes the target of attack and source of amusement. Nearly 12 percent of youth were forced to change their own screen names or e-mail addresses, which can make communicating with friends or family difficult and, at the very least, causes an inconvenience to let everyone know about the new

Chart 4.10 How Victims Responded

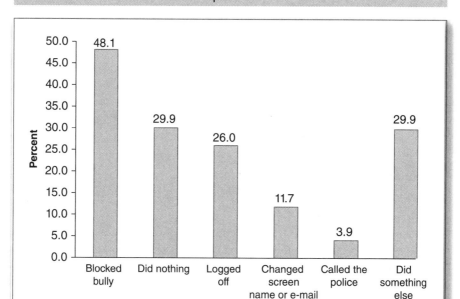

name or account. Also noteworthy is the fact that about 4 percent of victims thought their cyberbullying incident was so severe that they called the police. Incidents that involve a clear threat to the safety of an individual certainly warrant this response. Finally, about 30 percent did nothing. Perhaps they didn't feel like it would help if they sought assistance from an adult and chose to suffer in silence instead. Maybe they thought it would backfire and lead to more harm and retaliation. They might have wanted to avoid being labeled a tattletale or convinced themselves they need to "shrug it off" and "not let it get to them," and that being bullied is just an inevitable part of growing up. And it's also possible they simply did not know what to do out of all of the options available to them. We are saddened to think that almost one-third of students were in this predicament, and one of our primary messages to youth-serving adults is the crucial need to help kids figure it out.

EMOTIONAL AND BEHAVIORAL CONSEQUENCES AND CORRELATES OF CYBERBULLYING

Emotional Consequences

Research has reported a variety of emotional consequences of traditional bullying, pointing to victims often feeling sad, anxious, and depressed when compared to those who are not victimized, and Chapter 1 referred to some of these studies. Recent research of Internet-using adolescents specifically focusing on online harassment and emotional reactions suggests that victims of cyberbullying respond very similarly to traditional bullying victims in terms of the aforementioned negative emotions.[34]

In our own recent study, we found that many cyberbullying victims felt angry, frustrated, sad, embarrassed, or scared (see Chart 4.11). This is particularly noteworthy given that researchers have suggested that delinquency and interpersonal violence can result when these negative emotions aren't dealt with properly.[35] For example, if a victim feels scared about going to school because of cyberbullying, he may be tempted to bring a weapon to school for protection. Similarly, victims may feel so sad or depressed about the incident that they may hurt themselves, or act out irresponsibly or even violently to cope. Future research must clarify how these negative emotions (anger, frustration, sadness, embarrassment, fear) are related to problem behaviors in which youth might participate as coping mechanisms (such as self-harm, eating disorders, and acting out by participating in delinquency or violence). Such research could help explain how aggression in cyberspace can have significant real-world implications.

Traditional bullying research has also shown that those who are bullied (and those who bully) have lower self-esteem than those not involved in bullying.[36] We examined the extent to which this relationship held for cyberbullying behaviors back in 2007. Within our survey of approximately 2,000

Chart 4.11   How Victims Felt

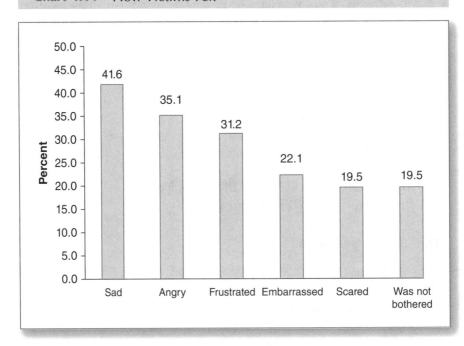

middle school students, we included Morris Rosenberg's well-validated self-esteem scale, which included the following statements:[37]

1. On the whole, I am satisfied with myself.

2. At times I think I am no good at all.

3. I feel that I have a number of good qualities.

4. I am able to do things as well as most other people.

5. I feel I do not have much to be proud of.

6. I certainly feel useless at times.

7. I feel that I'm a person of worth, at least on an equal plane with others.

8. I wish I could have more respect for myself.

9. All in all, I am inclined to feel that I am a failure.

10. I take a positive attitude toward myself.

Response choices ranged from 1 to 4 (from strongly disagree to strongly agree) and were combined in a way that higher scores represented higher self-esteem. As noted in Chart 4.12, youth who have experienced cyberbullying (whether as a target or as an aggressor, and especially those who were both targets and aggressors) had lower levels of self-esteem than those not involved in cyberbullying. And while the differences in the numbers don't look all that dramatic, they are statistically significant. While not surprising, this finding is important because lower self-esteem has been tied to a number of problem behaviors among adolescents.[38] What we can't say, however, is whether experience with cyberbullying *causes* victims to have lower self-esteem or whether youth with low self-esteem are targeted for cyberbullying more often (or whether having low self-esteem results in an impulse to cyberbully). Additional inquiry over an extended period of time is required to clarify how self-esteem is directly and indirectly influenced by online harassment among youth.

> I sometimes didn't want to go to school, my quiz scores went down, and I thought it was my fault.
>
> —Mallory, 13, Maryland

Behavioral Consequences

Chapter 1 also summarized some of the behavioral consequences associated with traditional bullying. Similar behavioral outcomes seem to be linked to cyberbullying—especially for those who are doing the offending. For

Chart 4.12 Cyberbullying and Self-Esteem

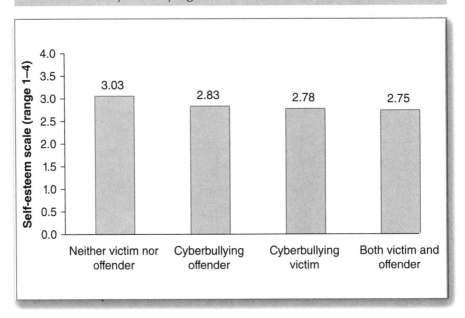

instance, Michele Ybarra and Kimberly Mitchell found that cyberbullies were significantly more likely than youth who didn't cyberbully to be the target of offline bullying (defined as "being hit or picked on by another child during the previous year") and to engage in other problematic behavior (i.e., purposefully damaging property, police contact, physically assaulting a nonfamily member, and taking something that did not belong to the respondent within the previous year).[39] Online aggressors were also found to have low school commitment and to be more likely to consume alcohol and use cigarettes. Ybarra and Mitchell also found that with increasing perpetration of online harassment comes increased aggressive and rule-breaking behavior among those youth.[40] Those who have been cyberbullied have also demonstrated higher levels of offline problematic behaviors, including substance use and violent and sexual behavior.[41] Relatedly, Ybarra, Marie Diener-West, and Philip J. Leaf identified that online victims were eight times as likely as nonvictims to report carrying a weapon at school in the last thirty days.[42]

> This one time this girl that was a lot bigger than me made me cry when I talked to her online because she told me if she saw me in school she was going to stuff me in a locker and that no one was going to find me for a very long time. I faked sick for a week and a half until I found the courage deep inside me to go to school. Nothing bad even happened. I was really relieved.
>
> —Bennie, 18, New York

Our own research has discovered a link between cyberbullying victimization and adolescent problem behaviors, such as recent school difficulties, assaultive conduct, substance use, and traditional bullying.[3] Increased absenteeism also followed, as some students were even hesitant to go to school and did what they could to avoid attending and being victimized there. We also discovered that a significant proportion of victims removed themselves from the online venue in which the cyberbullying occurred, while one in five (20 percent) felt forced to stay offline completely for a period of time.[2]

CYBERBULLICIDE

> People told me I was retarded, that I didn't fit in. This girl said that I was bitch and that she wished I was dead. I never did anything to her but I got really upset and depressed and started cutting myself and started seriously considering suicide. I just ignored them but it still really hurt.
>
> —Lena, 13, Australia

Regrettably, teen suicide is all too common. In 2010, suicide was the second-leading cause of deaths among those between the ages of ten and eighteen (1,449 total deaths).[43] As you are probably aware, there have been many high profile and tragic incidents described in the media linking adolescent suicides to experiences with bullying and cyberbullying. The interest in the connection between suicide and interpersonal aggression is nothing new, as a number of studies have documented the association between bullying and suicide.[44] The term *bullicide* is often used to refer to incidents where teens appear to have been "bullied to death."[45] We introduced the term *cyberbullicide* in the first edition of this book and, while we kept it in this revised version, we recognize that there are problems with each term. Neither is accurate in the sense that usually terms that end in *-icide* refer to the killing of someone else, as in *parricide*, which is the act of killing one's parents (patricide is to kill one's father). And in our case, we do not mean that the victim of bullying killed the one who had bullied them. Nevertheless, both terms are commonly used in educational vernacular, therefore we felt it was important to include them here.

We briefly introduced Ryan Halligan at the beginning of this chapter. He was one of the first in a long line of teens (and tweens) who committed suicide after experiencing bullying and cyberbullying. Like Ryan, thirteen-year-old Megan Meier from Dardenne Prairie, Missouri, also began an online friendship—but one with a boy she didn't actually know in real life. For almost a month, Megan corresponded with him exclusively online because he said he didn't have a phone and was home-schooled. The friendship deepened quickly, as tends to happen in online relationships, as Megan felt a connection to him and found a lot of value in their interactions. One day in October of 2006, however, Megan received a message through her MySpace profile saying, "I don't know if I want to be friends with you any longer because I hear you're not nice to your friends."[46] This was followed by bulletins being posted across the MySpace profiles of her school peers calling Megan "fat" and a "slut." Soon after, Tina Meier found her daughter hanging in her bedroom closet. Though she rushed her daughter to the hospital, Megan died the next day.

Six weeks after their daughter's death, the Meier family learned that the boy with whom Megan had been corresponding never existed. He (and his online profile) was created by Lori Drew, a neighbor and the mother of one of Megan's friends, as a way to spy on what Megan was saying about her own daughter. While a number of details are still unclear even all these years later, some have suggested that the mother and some of her adult friends sent the cruel messages. Interestingly, the district attorney in the case refused to file charges and claimed that no criminal law had been broken. Despite that outcome, a federal prosecutor from Los Angeles indicted Drew, the parent presumed responsible for the creation of the profile. In late 2008, a jury found Drew guilty of three misdemeanor charges of illegally accessing a protected computer (in essence, she was found guilty of violating MySpace.com's Terms of Service). On appeal, however, US District Judge George Wu acquitted Drew of all federal criminal charges. While most agree those responsible for Megan's death need to be held accountable, the federal indictment was really a last-ditch, Hail Mary attempt to prosecute Drew criminally.

Sadly, there have been many other examples since Ryan and Megan. In September of 2013, twelve-year-old Rebecca Sedwick jumped to her death after enduring months of bullying, online and off, from as many as fifteen classmates at Crystal Lake Middle School in Lakeland, Florida. Among the messages were repeated calls for Rebecca to end her life, including "Drink bleach and die" and "Can you Die Please?" As a response, she changed her Kik Messenger profile name to "That Dead Girl" and then did just as they had asked and committed suicide. According to an AP report, one of the tormenters allegedly boasted about her behavior toward Rebecca on Face-book even after the suicide: "'Yes, I bullied Rebecca and she killed herself but I don't give a . . . ' and you can add the last word yourself," Polk County Sheriff Grady Judd noted, referring to a Facebook post.[47] Two students faced felony criminal charges for their involvement, but charges were later dropped as a part of an agreement with prosecutors. Subsequent investigation into this incident has revealed conflicting information about where some of the hurtful messages originated from and some evidence suggests that there wasn't a lot of bullying going on in the weeks or even months right before the suicide.[48] These questions further illustrate the challenges in understanding the link between bullying and suicide, especially when considered within the broader context of a tumultuous adolescent time.

The experiences of Ryan, Megan, and Rebecca, along with others scattered throughout this book, are just a few of numerous examples of incidents where experience with bullying and cyberbullying was followed by suicide. These stories individually and collectively point to the tragic consequences of ignoring cyberbullying. And it's not random. Our research has confirmed a link between suicidal thoughts and online victimization.[49] Based on data analyses we conducted among nearly 2000 middle school students, those who experienced cyberbullying were nearly twice as likely to have attempted suicide as those who had not been cyberbullied. We also examined the relationship between suicidal ideation and cyberbullying experiences, by asking students to respond to the following questions:

1. Did you feel so sad or hopeless almost every day for two weeks or more in a row that you stopped doing some usual activities?

2. Have you ever seriously thought about attempting suicide?

3. Did you make a specific plan about how you would attempt suicide?

4. Did you actually attempt suicide?

Youth who responded yes to more of these questions scored higher on the scale. Youth who experienced cyberbullying scored higher on a suicidal ideation scale than those who did not experience cyberbullying (see Chart 4.13). This finding indicates that youth who are bullied in cyberspace are at an increased risk for suicide, and we therefore should not dismiss it as simply text that can be ignored.

A final cautionary note: It bears mentioning that in addition to the cyberbullying, many of the adolescents who took their own life had other issues going on that may have contributed to their decision. For instance, Ryan Halligan attended special education classes in elementary school and struggled socially and academically. Megan Meier suffered from low self-esteem and depression and was on psychotropic medication when she took her life. Rebecca Sedwick had a history of cutting herself, had major family problems with her stepdad, mom, and dad, and had recently broken up with her Internet boyfriend. Amanda Todd (from Chapter 1) was clinically depressed and

Chart 4.13   Cyberbullying and Suicidal Ideation

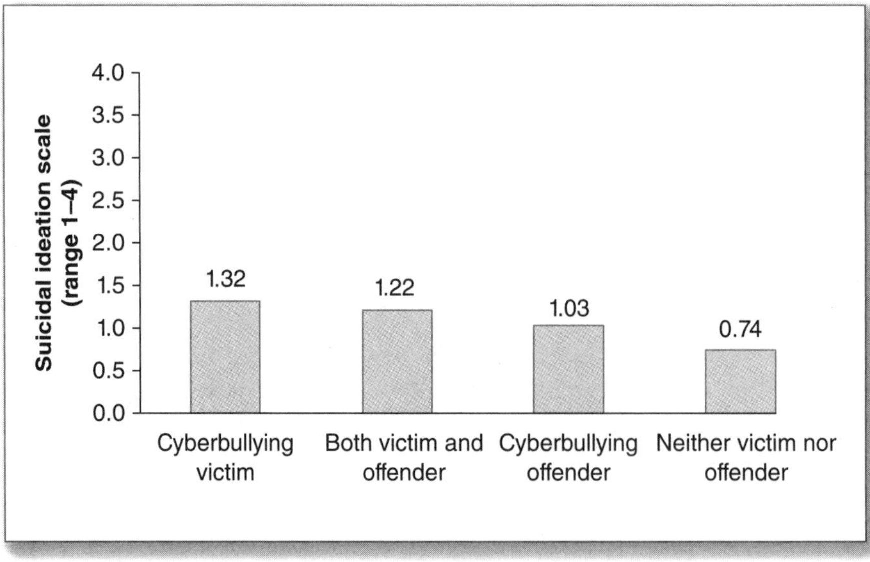

Note: Higher values represent more suicidal thoughts and attempts.

receiving significant formal counseling. From what we've learned, cyberbullying by itself doesn't usually directly lead to youth committing suicide. Rather, it appears that the toll that daily struggles, stresses, and relative hopelessness take on some adolescents is exacerbated when Internet-based harassment is added to the equation.

On Ask.fm you can put it on anonymous. I think one of my best friends is cyber bullying me on there. She posted a very personal question on there. I've only told her and it's my deepest secret. Every time I got a question her phone would light up with an answer. I'm so tired of it. I'm so tired of it. People are starting to ask me about my secret and I've started cutting again . . .

—Denise, 13, Oklahoma

You should now have a pretty good handle on what has been learned in a decade's worth of cyberbullying research. In the next section, we briefly summarize our recent findings on the motivations and incentives for cyberbullying others. This is a question we are asked quite frequently and one that does not have a singular and clear answer. Multiple theories from a variety

BREAKOUT BOX

Does Bullying *Cause* Suicide?

We cringe every time we read the alarmist headlines across popular media outlets which proclaims that "bullying causes suicide." But what does the research actually say about the nature of this relationship? As discussed above, there have been a handful of studies that have identified some truth to the assertion that bullying plays a role in some suicides. But it is also true that the vast majority of teens involved in bullying do not die by suicide. Most people who have spent some time exploring the connection understand that, as with any association in the social sciences, it is often much more complicated than simply *X* causes *Y*. There are a number of known factors related to suicide (such as depression, a mental disorder, family history of suicide) that, combined with other situational or enduring life stressors (such as bullying), can increase risk.[50] Even so, most people who have these elements in their background or current experiences do not decide to take their life.

All of this said, it is just as important to remember, as inappropriate as it may be to assert that "bullying causes suicide," it is equally incorrect to say that "bullying does not cause suicide." The frank truth is that *we really don't know*. We are not aware of any research that has tested the bullying-causes-suicide hypothesis and has found that it does not. Most research that we are aware of, including the few samples of students among which we have included questions about suicidal ideology and attempts, shows a significant but admittedly modest relationship (that experience with bullying is a factor in suicide). Not the opposite. Of course, there are other variables like the risk factors noted above, which play a contributing role. As we concluded in one of our academic papers about the relationship, "it is unlikely that experience with cyberbullying by itself leads to youth suicide. Rather, it tends to exacerbate instability and hopelessness in the minds of adolescents already struggling with stressful life circumstances."[51]

of disciplines could be used to understand the phenomenon better, so we suggest some that seem most relevant based on our discussions with adults and youth. As individuals increasingly recognize the seriousness of cyber-bullying, more scientific studies will surface that explore the important cognitive and behavioral elements involved.

WHY DO YOUTH ENGAGE IN CYBERBULLYING?

Obviously, the answer to this question is critical to understanding the behaviors themselves. As depicted in Chart 4.14, the most frequent explanation given to us from youth who admit to cyberbullying others is that the target deserved it. In addition, almost one in four (23 percent) reported that they did it to get revenge. Victims of traditional bullying may engage in online bullying as retribution against someone else for hurting them, thereby turning the tables on their aggressors through the equalizing characteristics of the Internet and its ability to remove the relevance of physical intimidation.[27] Comments from seventeen-year-old Bella, from Pennsylvania illustrate this:

> I had recently picked on an old friend of mine [because] she had done something to me that was equally as wrong, if not worse. I was disappointed in her, and for that I decided not to be a friend any longer and spread her deepest secrets to everyone, which made her look like a complete fool. I felt somewhat guilty because I had known her for years, at the same time it was pay back and I think she learned from it when it comes to attempting to mess around with me.

Also, about one in ten (8.7 percent) said they did it simply because it was fun. It seems that among some adolescents, cyberbullying behaviors are easily justified and dismissed as comparatively harmless, even though by now you would think they fully understand the serious real-world ramifications. Perhaps some cyberbullies simply just don't see the harm in their behavior and don't classify their actions as *bullying*. "It was just text." "I didn't mean to hurt them." "I was just messing around." These are common replies when youth are asked about their cyberbullying activities. It is therefore important for adolescents to deeply comprehend the harmful consequences that befall victims. They need to hear and empathize with the stories described above of Ryan, Megan, and Rebecca. One major reason cyberbullying is so pernicious is that aggressors don't immediately see (and consequently internalize) the very real consequences of their actions—as we've discussed in Chapter 3.

Chart 4.14   Reasons for Cyberbullying

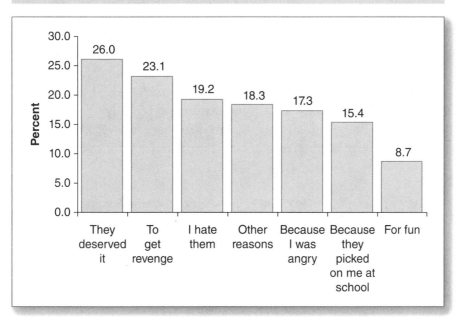

Several developmental factors also make adolescents more susceptible to engaging in cyberbullying. A hallmark of adolescence is the rapid cognitive, social, and emotional changes that youth experience. Psychiatrists Staci Gruber and Deborah Yurgelun-Todd note that "the developmental factors which influence decision making in adolescents may result in choices which are suggestive of cortical immaturity, poor judgment, and impulsivity."[52] That is to say, the brains of many adolescents may not have matured to the point where they can make the most prudent decisions or exercise self-control and restraint.[53]

When presented with the opportunity to harass someone online, some adolescents simply may be unable to hold back. Indeed, they often reflexively respond to the situation or circumstance at hand—and their emotions and attitudes at that moment—instead of carefully considering the acceptability or consequences of their actions. Furthermore, since most of their activities and conversations online are outside of the regular supervision of responsible adult authorities, impulsive youth are free to engage in a variety of inappropriate behaviors without much concern for the potential outcome.

Along these same lines, it is important to remember that adolescents are generally very "now" oriented. They are often most concerned with what is right in front of them at that very moment and sometimes fail to consider the long-term implications. Even though they may fundamentally know that cyberbullying is wrong, they engage in the behavior anyway because they do not have to deal with any immediate consequences and do not witness its immediate, tangible emotional or psychological harm. In other words, usually no automatic or instantaneous cue gives them quick feedback as to the wrongfulness of their actions. If cyberbullying is not detected and disciplined (in some informal or formal way) by parents or educators, then the behavior may be reinforced and continue.

Determining why some youth are more prone to engage in cyberbullying than others is an important direction for future research. To that end, it may be wise to utilize existing criminological, psychological, sociological, or developmental theories to help contextualize cyberbullying. Since traditional and online aggression are deviant behaviors that society wishes to control, it may be instructive to explore the behaviors from a social-science perspective.

For instance, cyberbullying behaviors may be learned from and reinforced by others,[54] or they could be passed down through culture and tradition and therefore viewed as acceptable behaviors.[55] They also may be a manifestation of some underlying personality trait, such as low self-control or impulsivity.[56] An adolescent may turn to cyberbullying others to cope with stressful life experiences,[57] or cyberbullying could result when the adolescent doesn't feel a sense of responsibility for her actions.[58] Because of space limitations, we cannot elaborate on these or speculate on the many other possible theoretical explanations for cyberbullying in this book. We simply wanted to mention a few that—based on our study of this phenomenon—appear relevant and deserve additional inquiry and analysis.

SUMMARY

In this chapter, we reviewed a great deal of research in the hopes of thoroughly equipping you with the latest findings on the nature and extent of cyberbullying among youth today. While it is possible to get overwhelmed by so much data, we encourage you to remember that this book is a resource that you can continually consult when you are curious about some aspect of online aggression. Outside of research findings, we have addressed some of the reasons why youth might engage in this behavior. Deeper analysis of the motives and rationalizations used are necessary so we can better understand the mind-set of bullies at the moment in which they send or post harmful electronic content. Now that you understand the phenomenon in depth, we turn to its impact on schools since educators are often on the front lines in dealing with this problem. In fact, that may very well be your own situation, and a primary goal of this book is to specifically inform your knowledge base and action plans. Before covering ideal prevention and response strategies, though, we must first clarify the legal issues facing schools when it comes to their role in dealing with cyberbullying incidents.

QUESTIONS FOR REFLECTION

1. Why are so many different statistics reported about how many youth experience cyberbullying?

2. Does the research reviewed in this chapter align with what you are seeing in your school or community?

3. Based on your experience, do the youth you've seen cyberbullied generally know who is bullying them? Or do they tend to not know at all who might be behind the harassment?

4. What are some of the emotional, psychological, and behavioral consequences of being cyberbullied?

5. Based on your experience working with or caring for youth, and considering our thoughts on the motivations behind cyberbullying, why do you believe teens engage in the behavior?

NOTES

1. John Halligan. "Ryan's Story: In Memory of Ryan Patrick Halligan 1989–2003. (2006). http://www.ryanpatrickhalligan.org.

2. Justin W. Patchin and Sameer Hinduja. "Bullies Move Beyond the Schoolyard: A Preliminary Look at Cyberbullying." *Youth Violence and Juvenile Justice* 4, no. 2 (2006): 148–169. doi: 10.1177/1541204006286288.

3. Sameer Hinduja and Justin W. Patchin. "Cyberbullying: An Exploratory Analysis of Factors Related to Offending and Victimization." *Deviant Behavior* 29, no. 2 (2008): 1–29. doi: 10.1080/01639620701457816; Sameer Hinduja and Justin W. Patchin. "Offline Consequences of Online Victimization: School Violence and Delinquency." *Journal of School Violence* 6, no. 3 (2007): 89–112. doi: 10.1300/J202v06n03_06.

4. Justin W. Patchin and Sameer Hinduja. "Cyberbullying: An Update and Synthesis of the Research." In *Cyberbullying Prevention and Response: Expert Perspectives*, edited by Justin W. Patchin and Sameer Hinduja, 13–35. New York: Routledge, 2012.

5. Lisa M. Jones, Kimberly J. Mitchell, and David Finkelhor. "Online Harassment in Context: Trends From Three Youth Internet Safety Surveys (2000, 2005, 2010)." *Psychology of Violence* 3, no. 1 (2013): 53–69.

6. National Center for Educational Statistics. "Student Reports of Bullying and Cyber-Bullying: Results From the 2011 School Crime Supplement to the National Crime Victimization Survey" (2013). http://nces.ed.gov/pubs2013/2013329.pdf.

7. National Center for Educational Statistics. "Student Reports of Bullying and Cyber-Bullying: Results From the 2009 School Crime Supplement to the National Crime Victimization Survey (2011). http://nces.ed.gov/pubs2011/2011336.pdf.

8. Mark G. Borg. "The Extent and Nature of Bullying Among Primary and Secondary Schoolchildren." *Educational Research* 41 (1999): 137–153; Dorothy Seals and Jerry Young. "Bullying and Victimization: Prevalence and Relationship to Gender, Grade Level, Ethnicity, Self-Esteem and Depression." *Adolescence* 38 (2003): 735–747; Dorothy L. Espelage, Kris Bosworth, and Thomas R. Simon. "Examining the Social Context of Bullying Behaviors in Early Adolescence." *Journal of Counseling and Development* 78 (2000): 326–333; Kirsti Kumpalainen, Eila Rasanen, and Irmeli Henttonen. "Children Involved in Bullying: Psychological Disturbance and the Persistence of the Involvement." *Child Abuse and Neglect* 23 (1999): 1253–1262.

9. Laurence Owens, Rosalyn Shute, and Phillip T. Slee. "'I'm In and You're Out': Explanations for Teenage Girls Indirect Aggression." *Psychology, Evolution and Gender* 2, no. 1 (2000): 19–46; Nicki R. Crick and Jennifer K. Grotpeter. "Relational Aggression, Gender, and Social-Psychological Adjustment." *Child Development* 66 (1995): 610–722; Kaj Björkqvist, Kirsti M. J. Lagerspetz, and Ari Kaukianin. "Do Girls Manipulate and Boys Fight? Developmental Trends in Regard to Direct and Indirect Aggression." *Aggressive Behavior* 18 (1992): 117–127; Rachel Simmons. *Odd Girl Out*. New York: Harcourt, 2003; Rosalind Wiseman. *Queen Bees and Wannabes: Helping Your Daughter to Survive Cliques, Gossip, Boyfriends and Other Realities of Adolescence*. New York: Crown, 2002.

10. Shari Kessel Schneider, Lydia O'Donnell, Ann Stueve, and Robert W. Coulter. "Cyberbullying, School Bullying, and Psychological Distress: A Regional Census of High School Students." *American Journal of Public Health* 102, no. 1 (2012): 171–177.

11. Amanda Burgess-Proctor, Justin W. Patchin, and Sameer Hinduja. "Cyberbullying and Online Harassment: Reconceptualizing the Victimization of Adolescent Girls." In *Female Crime Victims: Reality Reconsidered*, edited by Vanessa Garcia and Janice Clifford. Upper Saddle River, NJ: Prentice Hall, 2009.

12. Herbert Scheithauer, Tobias Hayer, Franz Petermann, and Gert Jugert. "Physical, Verbal, and Relational Forms of Bullying Among German Students: Age Trends, Gender Differences, and Correlates." *Aggressive Behavior* 32, no. 3 (2006): 261–275; Sarah Woods and Eleanor White. "The Association Between Bullying Behaviour, Arousal Levels and Behaviour Problems." *Journal of Adolescence* 28, no. 1 (2005): 381–395.

13. Erika D. Felix and Susan D. McMahon. "Gender and Multiple Forms of Peer Victimization: How Do They Influence Adolescent Psychosocial Adjustment?" *Violence and Victims* 21, no. 6 (2006): 707–724; Valerie E. Besag. *Understanding Girls' Friendships, Fights and Feuds: A Practical Approach to Girls' Bullying*. Maidenhead, Berkshire, UK: Open University Press, 2006.

14. Rosalind Wiseman. *Queen Bees and Wannabes: Helping Your Daughter to Survive Cliques, Gossip, Boyfriends and Other Realities of Adolescence*. New York: Crown, 2002; Marion K. Underwood, Britt R. Galen, and Julie A. Paquette. "Top Ten Challenges for Understanding Gender and Aggression in Children: Why Can't We All Just Get Along?" *Social Development* 10, no. 2

(2001): 248–266; Laurence Owens, Rosalyn Shute, and Phillip T. Slee. "'Guess What I Just Heard!': Indirect Aggression Among Teenage Girls in Australia." *Aggressive Behavior* 26 (2000): 67–83.

15. Eleni Andreou. "Bully/Victim Problems and Their Association With Coping Behavior in Conflictual Peer Interactions Among School-Age Children." *Educational Psychology* 21 (2001): 59–66; Patrice Marie Miller, Dorothy L. Danaher, and David Forbes. "Sex-Related Strategies for Coping With Interpersonal Conflict in Children Aged Five to Seven." *Developmental Psychology* 22 (1986): 543–548.

16. Carolyn Zahn-Waxler. "The Development of Empathy, Guilt, and Internalization of Distress: Implications for Gender Differences and Externalizing Problems." In *Anxiety, Depression, and Emotion: Wisconsin Symposium on Emotion*, edited by Richard J. Davidson, 222–265. New York: Oxford University Press, 2000; Marion K. Underwood. "The Comity of Modest Manipulation: The Importance of Distinguishing Among Bad Behaviors." *Merrill-Palmer Quarterly* 49, no. 3 (2003): 373–389; Lyn Mikel Brown. *Girlfighting*. New York: New York University Press, 2003.

17. Nicki R. Crick and Jennifer K. Grotpeter. "Relational Aggression, Gender, and Social-Psychological Adjustment." *Child Development* 66 (1995): 610–722; Kaj Björkqvist and Pirkko Niemelä. "New Trends in the Study of Female Aggression." In *Of Mice and Women: Aspects of Female Aggression*, edited by Kaj Björkqvist and Pirkko Niemelä, 3–16. San Diego, CA: Academic Press, 1992.

18. Lyn Mikel Brown. *Girlfighting*. New York: New York University Press, 2003.

19. Dorothy Seals and Jerry Young. "Bullying and Victimization: Prevalence and Relationship to Gender, Grade Level, Ethnicity, Self-Esteem and Depression." *Adolescence* 38 (2003): 735–747; Tonja R. Nansel, Mary Overpeck, Ramani S. Pilla, W. June Ruan, Bruce Simons-Morton, and Peter Scheidt. "Bullying Behaviors Among U.S. Youth: Prevalence and Association With Psychosocial Adjustment." *Journal of the American Medical Association* 285, no. 16 (2001): 2094–2100; Sandra Graham and Jaana Juvonen. "Ethnicity, Peer Harassment, and Adjustment in Middle School: An Exploratory Study." *Journal of Early Adolescence* 22 (2002): 173–199; Asha Goldweber, Tracy E. Waasdorp, and Catherine P. Bradshaw. "Examining Associations Between Race, Urbanicity, and Patterns of Bullying Involvement." *Journal of Youth and Adolescence* 42, no. 2 (2013): 206–219.

20. Jing Wang, Ronald J. Iannotti, and Tonja R. Nansel. "School Bullying Among US Adolescents: Physical, Verbal, Relational and Cyber." *Journal of Adolescent Health* 45, no 4 (2009): 368–375.

21. Pippa Norris. *Digital Divide: Civic Engagement, Information Poverty, and the Internet Worldwide*. New York: Cambridge University Press, 2001.

22. Brendesha M. Tynes and Kimberly J. Mitchell. "Black Youth Beyond the Digital Divide: Age and Gender Differences in Internet Use, Communication Patterns, and Victimization Experiences." *Journal of Black Psychology* 40, no. 3 (2014): 291–307.

23. Sabina Low and Dorothy Espelage. "Differentiating Cyber Bullying Perpetration From Non-Physical Bullying: Commonalities Across Race, Individual, and Family Predictors." *Psychology of Violence* 3, no. 1 (2013): 39–52.

24. Dorothy Seals and Jerry Young. "Bullying and Victimization: Prevalence and Relationship to Gender, Grade Level, Ethnicity, Self-Esteem and Depression." *Adolescence* 38 (2003): 735–747; Tonja R. Nansel, Mary Overpeck, Ramani S. Pilla, W. June Ruan, Bruce Simons-Morton, and Peter Scheidt. "Aggression Behaviors Among US Youth: Prevalence and Association With Psychosocial Adjustment." *Journal of the American Medical Association* 285 (2001): 2094–2100; Dan Olweus. "Bullying at School: Basic Facts and Effects of a School Based Intervention Program." *Journal of Child Psychology and Psychiatry* 35 (1994): 1171–1190.

25. Kirk R. Williams and Nancy G. Guerra. "Prevalence and Predictors of Internet Bullying." *Journal of Adolescent Health* 41 (2007): S14–S21. doi: 10.1016/j.jadohealth.2007.08.018; Janis Wolak, Kimberly J. Mitchell, and David Finkelhor. "Does Online Harassment Constitute Bullying? An Exploration of Online Harassment by Known Peers and Online-Only Contacts." *Journal of Adolescent Health* 41 (2007): S51–S58. doi: 10.1016/j.jadohealth.2007.08.019; Wanda Cassidy, Margaret Jackson, and Karen N. Brown. "Sticks and Stones Can Break My Bones, But How Can Pixels Hurt Me?" *School Psychology International* 30 (2009): 383–402.

26. Michele L. Ybarra and Kimberly J. Mitchell. "Online Aggressor/Targets, Aggressors and Targets: A Comparison of Associated Youth Characteristics." *Journal of Child Psychology and Psychiatry* 45 (2004): 1308–1316. doi: 10.1111/j.1469–7610.2004.00328.x; Michele L. Ybarra and Kimberly J. Mitchell. "Prevalence and Frequency of Internet Harassment Instigation: Implications for Adolescent Health." *Journal of Adolescent Health* 41 (2007): 189–195. doi: 10.1016/j.jadohealth.2007.03.005.

27. Robin M. Kowalski and Susan P. Limber. "Electronic Bullying Among Middle School Students." *Journal of Adolescent Health* 41 (2007): S22–S30.

28. Michele L. Ybarra and Kimberly J. Mitchell. "Online Aggressor/Targets, Aggressors and Targets: A Comparison of Associated Youth Characteristics." *Journal of Child Psychology and Psychiatry* 45 (2004): 1308–1316. doi: 10.1111/j.1469–7610.2004.00328.x; Ilene R. Berson, Michael J. Berson, and John M. Ferron. "Emerging Risks of Violence in the Digital Age: Lessons for Educators From an Online Study of Adolescent Girls in the United States." *Journal of School Violence* 1, no. 2 (2002): 51–71.

29. Janis Wolak, Kimberly J. Mitchell, and David Finkelhor. "Does Online Harassment Constitute Bullying? An Exploration of Online Harassment by Known Peers and Online-Only Contacts." *Journal of Adolescent Health* 41 (2007): S51–S58. doi: 10.1016/j.jadohealth.2007.08.019; Kirk R. Williams and Nancy G. Guerra. "Prevalence and Predictors of Internet Bullying." *Journal of Adolescent Health* 41 (2007): S14 -S21. doi: 10.1016/j.jadohealth .2007.08.018.

30. Michele L. Ybarra, Kimberly J. Mitchell, David Finkelhor, and Janis Wolak. "Examining Characteristics and Associated Distress Related to Internet

Harassment: Findings From the Second Youth Internet Safety Survey." *Pediatrics* 118, no. 4 (2007): 1169–1177.

31. Robin M. Kowalski and Susan P. Limber. "Psychological, Physical, and Academic Correlates of Cyberbullying and Traditional Bullying." *Journal of Adolescent Health* 53, no. 1 (2013): S13–S20. doi:10.1016/j.jadohealth.2012.09.018; Juliana Raskauskas and Ann D. Stoltz. "Involvement in Traditional and Electronic Bullying Among Adolescents." *Developmental Psychology* 43, no. 3 (2007): 465–475. doi: 10.1037/0012–1649.43.3.564.

32. National Center for Educational Statistics. "Student Reports of Bullying and Cyber-Bullying: Results From the 2011 School Crime Supplement to the National Crime Victimization Survey" (2013). http://nces.ed.gov/pubs2013/2013329.pdf; National Center for Educational Statistics. "Student Reports of Bullying and Cyber-Bullying: Results From the 2009 School Crime Supplement to the National Crime Victimization Survey (2011). http://nces.ed.gov/pubs2011/2011336.pdf.

33. Nathaniel Levy, Sandra Cortesi, Urs Gasser, Edward Crowley, Meredith Beaton, June Casey, and Caroline Nolan. "Bullying in a Networked Era: A Literature Review" (Research Publication No. 2012–17). Cambridge, MA: Berkman Center for Internet & Society, 2012. Available at http://dmlcentral.net/sites/dmlcentral/files/resource_files/ssrn-id2146877.pdf.

34. Ybarra and Kimberly J. Mitchell. "Prevalence and Frequency of Internet Harassment Instigation: Implications for Adolescent Health." *Journal of Adolescent Health* 41 (2007): 189–195. doi: 10.1016/j.jadohealth.2007.03.005; Ilene R. Berson, Michael J. Berson, and John M. Ferron. "Emerging Risks of Violence in the Digital Age: Lessons for Educators From an Online Study of Adolescent Girls in the United States." *Journal of School Violence* 1, no. 2 (2002): 51–71; Robin M. Kowalski and Susan P. Limber. "Psychological, Physical, and Academic Correlates of Cyberbullying and Traditional Bullying." *Journal of Adolescent Health* 53, no. 1 (2013): S13–S20. doi:10.1016/j.jadohealth.2012.09.018; Helen Cowie and Lucia Berdondini. "The Expression of Emotion in Response to Bullying." *Emotional and Behavioural Difficulties* 7, no. 4 (2002): 207–214; Jing Wang, Tonja R. Nansel, and Ronald J. Iannotti. "Cyber and Traditional Bullying: Differential Association With Depression." *Journal of Adolescent Health* 48, no. 4 (2010): 415–417; Linda Beckman, Curt Hagquist, and Lisa Hellström. "Does the Association With Psychosomatic Health Problems Differ Between Cyberbullying and Traditional Bullying?" *Emotional and Behavioural Difficulties* 17, no. 3/4 (2012): 421–434.

35. Robert H. Aseltine, Susan Gore, and Jennifer Gordon. "Life Stress, Anger and Anxiety, and Delinquency: An Empirical Test of General Strain Theory." *Journal of Health and Social Behavior* 41, no. 3 (2000): 256–275. doi: 10.2307/2676320; Paul Mazerolle, Velmer Burton, Francis T. Cullen, David Evans, and Gary L. Payne. "Strain, Anger, and Delinquent Adaptations: Specifying General Strain Theory." *Journal of Criminal Justice* 28 (2000): 89–101. doi: 10.1016/S0047–2352(99)00041–0; Lisa M. Broidy and Robert Agnew. "Gender and Crime: A General Strain Theory Perspective." *Journal of Research in Crime and Delinquency* 34, no. 3 (1997): 275–306. doi: 10.1177/0022427897034003001; Paul

Mazerolle and Alex Piquero. "Linking Exposure to Strain With Anger: An Investigation of Deviant Adaptations." *Journal of Criminal Justice* 26, no. 3 (1998): 195–211. doi: 10.1016/S0047–2352(97)00085–8; Justin W. Patchin and Sameer Hinduja. "Traditional and Nontraditional Bullying Among Youth: A Test of General Strain Theory." *Youth and Society* 43, no. 2 (2011): 727–751. doi: 10.1177/0044118X10366951; Carter R. Hay, Ryan C. Meldrum, and Karen Mann. "Traditional Bullying, Cyber Bullying, and Deviance: A General Strain Theory Approach." *Journal of Contemporary Criminal Justice* 26, no. 2 (2010): 130–147.

36. Tonja R. Nansel, Mary Overpeck, Ramani S. Pilla, W. June Ruan, Bruce Simons-Morton, and Peter Scheidt. "Aggression Behaviors Among US Youth: Prevalence and Association With Psychosocial Adjustment." *Journal of the American Medical Association* 285 (2001): 2094–2100; Denise L. Haynie, Tonja R. Nansel, Patricia Eitel, Aria Davis Crump, Keith Saylor, and Kai Yu. "Bullies, Victims and Bully/Victims: Distinct Groups of At-Risk Youth." *Journal of Early Adolescence* 21, no. 1 (2001): 29–49. doi: 10.1177/0272431 601021001002; Dorothy Espelage and Susan M. Swearer. "Research on School Bullying and Victimization: What Have We Learned and Where Do We Go From Here." *School Psychology Review* 32, no. 3 (2003): 265–383; Jaana Juvonen, Sandra Graham, and Mark A. Schuster. "Bullying Among Young Adolescents: The Strong, the Weak, and the Troubled." *Pediatrics* 112, no. 6 (2003): 1231–1237.

37. Justin W. Patchin and Sameer Hinduja. "Cyberbullying and Self-Esteem." *Journal of School Health* 80, no. 12 (2010): 616–623; Morris Rosenberg. *Society and the Adolescent Self-Image*. Princeton, NJ: Princeton University Press, 1965.

38. Mark R. Leary, Lisa S. Schreindorfer, and Alison L. Haupt. "The Role of Self-Esteem in Emotional and Behavioral Problems: Why Is Low Self-Esteem Dysfunctional?" *Journal of Social and Clinical Psychology* 14 (1995): 297–314.

39. Michele L. Ybarra and Kimberly J. Mitchell. "Online Aggressor/Targets, Aggressors and Targets: A Comparison of Associated Youth Characteristics." *Journal of Child Psychology and Psychiatry* 45 (2004): 1308–1316. doi: 10.1111/j.1469–7610.2004.00328.x.

40. Michele L. Ybarra and Kimberly J. Mitchell. "Prevalence and Frequency of Internet Harassment Instigation: Implications for Adolescent Health." *Journal of Adolescent Health* 41 (2007): 189–195. doi: 10.1016/j.jadohealth.2007.03.005.

41. Brett J. Litwiller and Amy M. Brausch. 2013. "Cyber Bullying and Physical Bullying in Adolescent Suicide: The Role of Violent Behavior and Substance Use." *Journal of Youth and Adolescence* 42, no. 5 (2013): 675–684.

42. Michele L. Ybarra, Marie Diener-West, and Philip J. Leaf. "Examining the Overlap in Internet Harassment and School Bullying: Implications for School Intervention." *Journal of Adolescent Health* 41 (2007): S42–S50. doi: 10.1016/j.jadohealth.2007.09.004.

43. Centers for Disease Control and Prevention. "Web-Based Injury Statistics Query and Reporting System" (WISQARS, 2010). http://www.cdc.gov/injury/wisqars/index.html.

44. Anna C. Baldry and Frans Willem Winkel. "Direct and Vicarious Victimization at School and at Home as Risk Factors for Suicidal Cognition Among Italian Adolescents." *Journal of Adolescence* 26, no. 6 (2003): 703–716; Ken Rigby and Phillip T. Slee. "Suicidal Ideation Among Adolescent School Children, Involvement in Bully-Victim Problems, and Perceived Social Support." *Suicide and Life Threatening Behavior* 29, no. 2 (1999): 119–130; Carla Mills, Suzanne Guerin, Fionnuala Lynch, Irenee Daly, and Carol Fitzpatrick. "The Relationship Between Bullying, Depression and Suicidal Thoughts/Behavior in Irish Adolescents." *Irish Journal of Psychological Medicine* 21, no. 4 (2004): 112–116.

45. Brenda High. *Bullycide in America – Moms Speak Out About the Bullying/ Suicide Connection*. Darlington, MD: JBS-Publishing, 2007.

46. Steve Pokin. "'My Space' Hoax Ends With Suicide of Dardenne Prairie Teen." *St. Charles Journal.* A http://www.stltoday.com/suburban-journals/stcharles/news/stevepokin/my-space-hoax-ends-with-suicide-of-dardenne-prairie-teen/article_0304c09a-ab32–5931–9bb3–210a5d5dbd58.html.

47. Mike Schneider and Jennifer Kay. 2013. "Rebecca Ann Sedwick Suicide: Two Girls Arrested For 'Terrorizing' Bullied Victim." *Huffington Post Miami.* http://www.huffingtonpost.com/2013/10/15/rebecca-ann-sedwick_n_4100350.html.

48. Emily Bazelon. "The Sheriff Overstepped: Grady Judd Got the Spotlight, But No Justice, in Charging Two Teenage Girls in the Rebecca Sedwick Suicide Case." http://www.slate.com/articles/news_and_politics/doublex/2014/04/rebecca_sedwick_suicide_sheriff_grady_judd_never_should_have_arrested_katelyn.html.

49. Sameer Hinduja and Justin W. Patchin. "Bullying, Cyberbullying, and Suicide." *Archives of Suicide Research* 14, no. 3 (2010): 206–221. doi: 10.1080/13811118.2010.494133; Erick Messias, Kristi Kindrick, and Juan Castro. "School Bullying, Cyberbullying, or Both: Correlates of Teen Suicidality in the 2011 CDC Youth Risk Behavior Survey." *Comprehensive Psychiatry* 55, no. 5 (2014): 1063–1068.

50. Centers for Disease Control and Prevention. "Suicide: Risk and Protective Factors." http://www.cdc.gov/ViolencePrevention/suicide/riskprotectivefactors.html.

51. Sameer Hinduja and Justin W. Patchin. "Bullying, Cyberbullying, and Suicide." *Archives of Suicide Research* 14, no. 3 (2010): 206–221. doi: 10.1080/13811118.2010.494133.

52. Staci A. Gruber and Deborah A. Yurgelun-Todd. "Neurobiology and the Law: A Role in Juvenile Justice?" *Ohio State Journal of Criminal Law* 3 (2006): 321.

53. Daniel Romer. "Adolescent Risk Taking, Impulsivity, and Brain Development: Implications for Prevention." *Developmental Psychobiology* 52, no. 3 (2010): 263–276; Dustin Albert and Laurence Steinberg. "Judgment and Decision Making in Adolescence." *Journal of Research on Adolescence* 21, no. 1 (2011): 211–224.

54. Sabina Low and Dorothy Espelage. "Differentiating Cyber Bullying Perpetration From Non-Physical Bullying: Commonalities Across Race, Individual, and Family Predictors. "*Psychology of Violence* 3, no. 1 (2013): 39–52; Charern Lee. "Deviant Peers, Opportunity, and Cyberbullying: A Theoretical Examination of

a New Deviance." Thesis, Southern Illinois University, 2013; http://opensiuc.lib. siu.edu/cgi/viewcontent.cgi?article=2132&context=theses; Sameer Hinduja and Justin W. Patchin. "Social Influences on Cyberbullying Behaviors Among Middle and High School Students." *Journal of Youth and Adolescence* 42, no. 5 (2013): 711–722; B. F. Skinner. *Science and Human Behavior*. New York: MacMillan, 1953; B. F. Skinner. *Verbal Learning*. New York: Appleton-Century-Crofts, 1957; Albert Bandura. *Social Learning Theory*. Englewood Cliffs, NJ: Prentice-Hall, 1977.

55. Stephen Eugene Brown, Finn-Aage Esbensen, and Gilbert Geis. *Criminology: Explaining Crime and Its Context*. Cincinnati, OH: Anderson, 2001.

56. Alexander T. Vazsonyi, Hana Machackova, Anna Sevcikova, David Smahel, and Alena Cerna. "Cyberbullying in Context: Direct and Indirect Effects by Low Self-Control Across 25 European Countries." *European Journal of Developmental Psychology* 9, no. 2 (2012): 210–227; Michael R. Gottfredson and Travis Hirschi. *A General Theory of Crime*. Stanford, CA: Stanford University Press, 1990.

57. Sameer Hinduja and Justin W. Patchin. "Offline Consequences of Online Victimization: School Violence and Delinquency." *Journal of School Violence* 6, no. 3 (2007): 89–112. doi: 10.1300/J202v06n03_06.

58. Edward Diener and Mark Wallbom. "Effects of Self-Awareness on Antinormative Behavior." *Journal of Research in Personality* 10, no. 1 (1976): 107–111; Edward Diener. "Deindividuation: The Absence of Self-Awareness and Self-Regulation in Group Members." In *The Psychology of Group Influence*, edited by Paul B. Paulus, 209–242. Hillsdale, NJ: Lawrence Erlbaum, 1980; Leon Festinger, Albert Pepitone, and Theodore Newcomb. 1952. "Some Consequences of Deindividuation in a Group." *Journal of Abnormal and Social Psychology,* 47 (1952): 382–389.

CHAPTER FIVE

Legal Issues

Protecting Your Students, Your School, and Yourself

In December of 2005, seventeen-year old Justin Layshock used his grandmother's computer to create a parody MySpace profile about his high school principal Eric Trosch. Layshock copied a photo of Trosch from the school's website and included it in the profile, along with bogus answers to a variety of survey questions, such as, "In the past month have you smoked: big blunt. In the past month have you gone Skinny Dipping: big lake, not big dick. Ever been Beaten up: big fag."[1] Most agreed that the profile was crude, but nonthreatening and not all that obscene, yet the school responded by suspending Layshock for ten days.

Just over a year later, eighth-grade honor roll student J.S. and two friends also created a parody MySpace profile about their principal James McGonigle. The profile did not include the principal's or school's name but did use his photo (copied from the school district website). In addition, it was created on a weekend using J.S.'s home computer. According to reports, "The profile contained crude content and vulgar language, ranging from nonsense and juvenile humor to profanity and shameful personal attacks aimed at the principal and his family."[2] The "About Me" section stated, in part, "it's your oh so wonderful, hairy, expressionless, sex addict, fagass, put on this world with a small dick PRINCIPAL"[2] As a result, his school suspended J.S. for ten days.

These are just two of the many incidents that have occurred where students have created parody online profiles of their school administrator(s). Some are more egregious than others, but the aforementioned examples aren't altogether that uncommon. These two almost identical incidents occurred at schools within the same state (Pennsylvania), and both schools responded the same: a ten-day suspension for each student. But was this an appropriate response? Did the school even have the authority to discipline the students for what they posted when not at school? If so, is it even their responsibility? Moreover, at what point do insults and disparagement of another person posted online cross a threshold where the behavior can be punished at school? And what can we take away from this (and similar cases) when students are cyberbullied?

Before attempting to answer some of these questions through the discussion of relevant case law and our experience working with numerous schools across the United States, it is important to note at the outset of this chapter that **we are not lawyers**. Even those who are, and who specialize in student speech cases, struggle with the complexities involved in applying antiquated case law to new forms of electronic communications. Because the law is continuously evolving and little crystal clear consensus has been reached regarding key constitutional and civil rights questions, schools are tasked with figuring out how to appropriately address problematic online behaviors committed by students while simultaneously avoiding any civil liability.

Many school personnel are reluctant to get involved in cyberbullying cases because they fear they will overstep their legal authority. Unfortunately, some administrators seem too focused on protecting the status quo at their institutions rather than proactively protecting the youth they supervise, educate, and mentor. In the same vein, law enforcement officials are hesitant to get involved in cyberbullying cases unless there are obvious violations of criminal law (e.g., harassment, stalking, felonious assault). It is important to remember, however, that inaction *is* action. Not doing something is actually demonstrating passive acceptance or ambivalence toward the issue at hand. Please remember that school administrators have a moral (and often legal) obligation to take action when harassment is brought to their attention.[3]

This chapter describes some of the critical legal questions faced by school administrators and seeks to illuminate the procedural and disciplinary issues related to electronic communication generally and cyberbullying specifically. We begin with a discussion of several foundational court rulings and legislative actions that have shaped the way schools intervene and discipline the behavior of students. These are important insofar as they have served as precedent in more recent cases involving online harassment. We then summarize a number of these court findings. This should equip you with an appreciation of the central factors upon which courts focus when deciding the outcome of such cases.

> School administrators have a moral (and often legal) obligation to take action when harassment is brought to their attention.

Finally, many states have proposed or passed legislation related to cyber-bullying and the school's role in addressing and preventing its relevance among students. We have reviewed numerous legislative actions and policies with the intent of parsing out the most essential components. We have then worked to present them as a guiding framework for school professionals who need a helping hand in creating or modifying policies and procedures. This framework encompasses what we believe is an ideal way to (1) define *cyber-bullying;* (2) include language that shows that violations can result in formal discipline, even in some circumstances when they occur off campus; and, (3) examine how incidents should be investigated, reported, and prevented on a general, prescriptive level.

> It's pretty difficult to figure out what to do. The law seems so complex. I just know that we have got to do something, because it [cyberbullying] is leading to other problems on my campus and under my watch.
>
> —Middle school administrator, Florida

IMPORTANT JUDICIAL RULINGS AND LEGISLATION APPLICABLE TO SCHOOLS

Harassment, Discrimination, and Civil Rights

Harassment has always occurred among individuals, but it has been explicitly outlawed for only about the last half century in the United States. The monumental matter of harassment (in the form of discrimination) and public education first arose in the Civil Rights Act of 1964.[4] Among its other aspects, this law specifically outlawed segregation based on race in the school system, but more generally led to the prohibition of harassment based on race, ethnicity, or religion in public places.

The Civil Rights Act was followed by the equally important Educational Amendments of 1972 (especially Title IX), which involved the intersection of sexual harassment and public education in the United States. Specifically, Title IX states the following:

No person in the United States shall, on the basis of sex, be excluded from participation in, be denied the benefits of, or be subjected to discrimination under any education program or activity receiving Federal financial assistance.[5]

Together, these pieces of legislation (along with others, such as the Americans with Disabilities Act) compel school administrators to take action when they observe or are made aware of behavior that is discriminatory in nature or that violates the civil rights of students. This position has been reiterated by a recent "Dear Colleague letter" written by the US Department of Education's Office of Civil Rights:

> Once a school knows or reasonably should know of possible student-on-student harassment, it must take immediate and appropriate action to investigate or otherwise determine what occurred. If harassment has occurred, a school must take prompt and effective steps reasonably calculated to end the harassment, eliminate any hostile environment, and prevent its recurrence. These duties are a school's responsibility even if the misconduct also is covered by an anti-bullying policy and regardless of whether the student makes a complaint, asks the school to take action, or identifies the harassment as a form of discrimination.[6]

The Office of Civil Rights has also clarified that Title IX doesn't just apply to harassment directed at females. More broadly, it also applies when *any* student is harassed "either for exhibiting what is perceived as a stereotypical characteristic for their sex, or for failing to conform to stereotypical notions of masculinity and femininity."[7] For example, a boy teasing another boy for being gay by calling out his effeminate behaviors or for criticizing him for his interest in clothing, crafts, and other stereotypically "girly" activities, could fall under Title IX.

Two US Supreme Court rulings have further clarified that Title IX protects students from having to endure sexual harassment at school. In *Gebser v. Lago Vista Independent School District* (1998), a student who had been in a sexual relationship with a teacher sued the school district for sexual harassment because the district failed to provide her with an avenue for reporting the abuse. The Court acknowledged that school districts can be held liable for damages under Title IX if an employee "with supervisory power over the offending employee actually knew of the abuse, had the power to end the abuse, and failed to do so."[8] In the end, the Court ruled there was no evidence a district official with the authority to take corrective action knew about the misconduct and failed to respond. With the decision, though, the Court confirmed that if deliberately indifferent to harassment or discrimination by a teacher against a student, a school district could be held responsible.

The Court reaffirmed this ruling and expanded it to student-on-student harassment just one year later in *Davis v. Monroe County Board of Education* (1999). In this case, evidence demonstrated that school officials did in fact know of the sexual harassment of a student by another student yet failed to adequately respond. Noteworthy here was the Court's reminder that "the common law, too, has put schools on notice that they may be held responsible under state law for their failure to protect students from the tortious acts of third parties."[9]

A relatively recent case heard by the US Court of Appeals for the Second Circuit in New York in 2011 applied these broad principles to instances of bullying based on race.[10] Anthony Zeno moved to Stissing Mountain High School midway through his freshmen year (in 2005). Very early on, he was inundated with threats and subject to racial slurs from students at the predominantly white school (Anthony is half white and half Latino). When his mother reported the first incident to the school, Principal John Francis Howe reportedly told her that "this is a small town and you don't want to start burning your bridges."[10] So the harassment continued. Anthony repeatedly reported incidents to the school and his mother contacted the district superintendent and school board. Unfortunately, nobody at the district level even responded. In some cases individual students were warned and even suspended at his school, but the behaviors continued.

The incidents escalated in his sophomore year with students threatening him in the cafeteria and on the football field. "Zeno is dead" and "Zeno will die" was scrawled on the school bathroom walls. On multiple occasions, he was threatened with specific references to a lynching. Again, the school responded by suspending students for individual cases and moving one of the aggressors to another school; Principal Howe instructed staff to keep an eye on Anthony. Still, the incidents continued into his senior year. Though less frequent, they reportedly became more serious. According to the lawsuit, in one incident, "a student called Anthony's sister a 'slut' and threatened to kick Anthony's 'black ass.'"[10] Eventually, a violent fight erupted and one of Anthony's friends was choked to the point of losing consciousness.

Despite the racially motivated nature of the threats, the school's Title IX compliance officer did not investigate the allegations (she was also responsible for enforcing Title VI of the Civil Rights Act of 1964). During Anthony's sophomore year, the school contracted with an individual to provide information to students, staff, and parents on bullying and harassment, but the program did not include any substantive discussion of racial discrimination. In his junior year, the school hired someone to train faculty and staff on racial diversity and stereotypes and to conduct student focus groups and surveys. However (and oddly), no actual training was conducted that year.

In July of 2007, Anthony sued the school, alleging discrimination based on his race. He argued that he was denied educational benefits as a result of the racial harassment. The trial began in March of 2010 and a jury found that the school district had violated Anthony's civil rights under Title VI and awarded him $1.25 million. A subsequent district court ruling reduced that award to $1 million plus attorney's fees. The US Court of Appeals for the Second Circuit concurred with the earlier ruling, agreeing that the school was deliberately indifferent to the harassment that was taking place, even though punishment was meted out after most incidents. The court pointed out that victims "do not have a right to specific remedial measures,"[10] but noted that "the sufficiency of a response, however, must be considered."[10] Even though the school district "suspended every student who was identified as harassing Anthony," the behaviors became increasingly severe.[10] As such, the court agreed that the school *should have done more*.

These rulings seemingly have opened the door for federal and state courts to extend this standard broadly to issues involving other forms of harassment and bullying and, in principle, to cases involving cyberbullying that have implications at school. In short, school districts may be found liable and responsible for monetary damages if they become aware of discrimination or violations of civil rights and fail to take appropriate action (that is, if they are *deliberately indifferent*).

Restricting and Disciplining *On-Campus* Student Behavior and Speech

A number of court rulings over the last forty-five years have provided some direction to schools in terms of when they can discipline students for their behavior or speech. A few landmark Supreme Court cases warrant discussion here. First, in *Tinker v. Des Moines Independent Community School District* (1969), the Court ruled that the suspensions of three public school students for wearing black armbands to protest the Vietnam War violated the free speech clause of the First Amendment. Specifically, Justice Fortas, writing for the majority, stated that

> a prohibition against expression of opinion, without any evidence that the rule is necessary to avoid substantial interference with school discipline or the rights of others, is not permissible under the First and Fourteenth Amendments.[11]

The key phrase in this opinion is *substantial interference*. Because the school district could not articulate that such a disruption occurred, the students' behavior could not be restricted. According to the rule of law, then, for school district personnel to intervene in similar situations, they must demonstrate that such behaviors "materially and substantially interfere with the requirements of appropriate discipline in the operation of the school."[11]

While the quiet, passive expression of a political viewpoint in the *Tinker* case was upheld by the Court, in *Bethel School District v. Fraser* (1986), the

Court ruled that not all expressions are protected by the First Amendment. The Court considered the case of Matthew Fraser, a student who used "an elaborate, graphic, and explicit sexual metaphor" in a nominating speech at a school assembly for a friend who was running for student body vice president.[12] The school responded by suspending Fraser for three days.

After Fraser sued and the case made its way through the system, both the US District Court for the Western District of Washington and US Court of Appeals for the Ninth Circuit sided with Fraser, citing the *Tinker* ruling. The Supreme Court, however, reversed the decision, arguing that there is a substantive difference between a nondisruptive expression and "speech or action that intrudes upon the work of the schools or the rights of other students."[12] Moreover, the Court maintained that schools have an interest in "teaching students the boundaries of socially appropriate behavior" and therefore must play a role in restricting behavior and speech that is considered "highly offensive or highly threatening to others."[12] Highly offensive or threatening material communicated electronically *from school grounds,* then, may fall under the *Fraser* ruling and, therefore, may be restricted.

Another classic Supreme Court case foundational for understanding whether schools can respond in contemporary incidents is *Hazelwood School District et al. v. Kuhlmeier* (1988). Here, the Court reviewed the extent to which school personnel may censor the contents of school newspaper articles authored by students. First, the Court reiterated its earlier ruling in *Tinker:*

> Students in the public schools do not "shed their constitutional rights to freedom of speech or expression at the schoolhouse gate." They cannot be punished merely for expressing their personal views on the school premises—whether "in the cafeteria, or on the playing field, or on the campus during the authorized hours,"—unless school authorities have reason to believe that such expression will "substantially interfere with the work of the school or impinge upon the rights of other students."[13]

Next, the Court restated its earlier ruling in *Fraser*—that the school environment is fundamentally unique and that school officials can in fact censor speech or behaviors on campus that the government could not necessarily interfere with outside of school. As such, the Court stated that

> educators do not offend the First Amendment by exercising editorial control over the style and content of student speech in school-sponsored expressive activities so long as their actions are reasonably related to legitimate pedagogical concerns.[13]

This case may be particularly appropriate when considering electronic material created or disseminated using school-owned computers or other technological devices or within or through content that is seemingly or actually endorsed by the school. School districts have the authority to discipline students who misuse school-owned property, resources, or materials to cause harm to other individuals, as long as their policies clearly proscribe such behavior.

Another case involving student expressions on or near the school campus, *Morse v. Frederick* (2007), received a great deal of public attention—perhaps because of the setting and surrounding circumstances.[14] In 2002, high schoolers in Juneau, Alaska, were released from class during the school day to line both sides of the street outside and watch the Winter Olympics' torch pass through the city. At the opportune moment when the most attention could be garnered, a senior named Joseph Frederick (with the help of several other students), unfurled a large banner that read "BONG HiTS 4 JESUS." Upon seeing the act take place across the street from the school (and therefore not on school property), the school principal grabbed the banner and suspended Frederick for ten days for the inappropriate behavior. Frederick promptly sued the district for violating his right to free expression, and the case was argued before the US Supreme Court in 2007.

The majority opinion concluded that Frederick's First Amendment rights were not violated and upheld the suspension. This decision was based on the arguments that (1) the banner was displayed during a school event, which made the expression "school speech" rather than "free speech"; (2) the banner undeniably referenced illegal drugs and could be reasonably interpreted as advocating the use of illegal drugs; and (3) that the government (and, by extension, schools) has an important and compelling interest in deterring drug use by students.[14] The Court therefore reaffirmed the school's ability to discipline students for inappropriate speech. Even though the students were off campus, the Court ruled that the activity was a school event (basically like a field trip), and therefore, they could be disciplined.

Educators' Ability to Restrict and Discipline Off-Campus Student Behavior and Speech

In our district, we are seeing students using the Internet to defame teachers . . . writing ludicrous, hideous things about them and posting their pictures as well. And we are seeing students bullying other students, resulting in the victims taking their own life. It seems we do not have any recourse for these online student behaviors that occur off-campus.

—Principal, Florida

It is important to point out right at the beginning of this section that courts have traditionally compartmentalized expressions by students on campus as appropriate for restrictions, while disallowing constraints on off-campus speech. As summarized in *Thomas v. Board of Education Granville Central School District* (1979),

> [W]hen school officials are authorized only to punish speech on school property, the student is free to speak his mind when the school day ends. In this manner, the community is not deprived of the salutary effects of expression, and educational authorities are free to establish an academic environment in which the teaching and learning process can proceed free of disruption. Indeed, our willingness to grant school officials substantial autonomy within their academic domain rests in part on the confinement of that power within the metes and bounds of the school itself.[15]

This principle was clearly illustrated in the case of *Klein v. Smith* (1986),[16] which involved student-on-staff harassment. In a restaurant parking lot after school hours in April of 1986, a high school student showed one of his teachers his middle finger. Upon hearing of the incident, the school administration suspended the student for ten days for "vulgar or extremely inappropriate language or conduct directed to a staff member."[16] This promptly led to civil action by the student, who claimed that his First Amendment free speech rights had been violated.

In an interestingly worded opinion, the US District Court for the District of Maine ruled that "the First Amendment protection of freedom of expression may not be made a casualty of the effort to force-feed good manners to the ruffians among us."[16] The court concluded that school officials failed to demonstrate that the vulgar gesture had negatively impacted the school environment or its orderly operation, and therefore sided with the student. This point is pivotal and depicts the importance of identifying a "nexus" between off-campus behavior and the school itself (its goals, purpose, mission, and value system).

Several key issues surface when considering the ability of school districts to restrict off-campus student speech. In general, students have a right of free expression, both at school and away from school, but those rights are more easily restricted on campus. Although none of the previously discussed cases specifically involved electronic communication or content, you should be able to extrapolate how the principles raised can be applied to new technology situations that schools are currently facing. We now focus on a few recent examples that do involve schools responding to the online behaviors of their students. The important distinction for these cases is that they all involve conduct away from school using a personal device and Internet connection.

ELECTRONIC HARASSMENT AND SCHOOLS

School Authority Is Not Universal

Accompanying the widespread adoption and use of electronic devices and the Internet over the last decade has come a rise in harassment cases involving teens and these technologies. For instance, in 1998, a Westlake High School (Ohio) junior created a website from home that disparaged his band teacher as "an overweight middle-aged man who doesn't like to get haircuts" and who "likes to involve himself in everything you do."[17] When made aware, the school proclaimed that the website disrupted the school environment, undermined the teacher's authority, and violated a rule in the student conduct handbook, which stated that "students shall not physically assault, vandalize, damage, or attempt to damage the property of a school employee or his/her family or demonstrate physical, written, or verbal disrespect/threat."[18]

The student was consequently suspended for ten days. The student's family argued that the suspension violated their child's constitutional right to free speech and sued the district for $550,000. The district court agreed with the constitutional violation, stating that "the involvement by the school in punishing plaintiff for posting an Internet Web site critical of defendant . . . raises the ugly specter of Big Brother."[18] School officials were required to expunge the suspension from the student's records and pay him $30,000 to drop the lawsuit. The superintendent of the school district also wrote a letter of apology, stating, "I wish to offer my sincere apology for the misunderstanding which resulted in the imposition of this disciplinary action. Please know that it is neither the Board's policy nor the administration's practice to abridge students' legitimate exercise of their constitutional rights."[18] It was also publicly acknowledged that "the Board recognized that this right [to freedom of speech] extends to students who, on their own time and with their own resources, engage in speech on the Internet."[18]

In another case, the US District Court for the Western District of Washington reviewed an incident where a senior (who had a 3.95 GPA and was captain of the basketball team) created a web page from home titled the "unofficial Kentlake High Home Page," which included mock obituaries of students and a mechanism for visitors to vote on "who should die next."[19] Interestingly, it included a disclaimer that the page was not sponsored by the school and was for entertainment purposes only. Nonetheless, after an evening news story referenced the page as containing a "hit list," the student was placed on emergency expulsion (although this disciplinary action was later reduced to a five-day suspension) for intimidation, harassment, disruption to the educational process, and violation of school copyright.

Similar to the aforementioned cases, the court here again ruled that the school had overstepped its bounds because the website was not produced at school or using school-owned equipment. Even though the court recognized that the intended audience included members of the high school, "the speech was entirely outside the school's supervision or control."[19] Furthermore, the court ruled that the school district failed to demonstrate that the website was "intended to threaten anyone, did actually threaten anyone, or manifested any violent tendencies whatsoever."[19] That is, the school district was unable to show that anyone listed on the site was actually intimidated or threatened by the site or that the site resulted in a significant disturbance at school. With these rulings, the court has issued clear reminders that school districts should tread lightly when intervening in the off-campus behaviors of students when there doesn't appear to be any impact at school.

School Discipline Is Allowed Under Certain Circumstances

Despite these examples where schools overstepped their authority, various courts have consistently held that school districts are allowed to intervene in situations where off-campus speech is *clearly harassing and threatening to students or staff and/or disruptive to the learning environment*. For example, in *J.S. v. Bethlehem Area School District* (2000), the Commonwealth Court of Pennsylvania reviewed a case in which J.S. was expelled from school for creating a web page that included threatening and derogatory comments about Kathleen Fulmer, an algebra teacher.[20] The web page included lists for "Why Fulmer Should Be Fired" and "Why Should She Die." Reasons listed included "She shows off her fat F—ing legs," "The fat f—smokes," and "She's a bitch." The writer of the web page also added, "give me $20.00 to help pay for the hitman."[20]

Fulmer indicated she had been traumatized by the incident, which had led to physical problems (headaches and loss of appetite, sleep, and weight) and psychological problems (anxiety and depression) and to an inability to teach for the rest of the year. The school district also argued that the web page "had a demoralizing impact on the school community" and "caused an effect on the staff . . . comparable to the effect on the school community of the death of a student or staff member because there was a feeling of helplessness and a plummeting morale."[20] Furthermore, law enforcement got involved, with the local police and the Federal Bureau of Investigation conducting investigations to ascertain the validity of J.S.'s threat (which was eventually determined to not be credible). Based on these factors, the court upheld the expulsion of the student. An interesting side note: Fulmer also sued the family of J.S. in civil court and was awarded $500,000.[21]

In a similar case, eight-grader Aaron Wisniewski created a graphic icon of his English teacher's head being shot with a bullet from a gun along with the text "Kill Mr. Vandermolen."[22] He then sent the icon via instant message to fifteen of his friends, among whom it circulated for three weeks before the teacher was informed. After hearing from the distressed teacher, the principal of the school decided to suspend Wisniewski—an action that prompted a lawsuit from his parents. The district court found in favor of the school district, but the case was appealed by Wisniewski's parents to a higher court. In July of 2007, the US Court of Appeals for the Second Circuit upheld the lower court's decision, arguing that the icon represented a threat that the student should have known would cause a *disruption to the school environment*.[22]

> Schools do have the authority to reasonably discipline students for off-campus behaviors that result in significant on-campus disruptions.

The courts in the *J.S.* and the *Wisniewski* cases ruled that schools do have the authority to discipline students when speech articulated or behavior committed off-campus results in (or has a high probability of resulting in) a clear disruption of the classroom environment. The appellate courts in these cases referenced the *Tinker, Fraser,* and *Kuhlmeier* cases to argue that student expressions can be suppressed if and when they substantially and materially disrupt the mission and discipline of the school or infringe upon the rights of others. This was again exemplified in another somewhat recent case in western Washington.

In June 2006, a senior at Kentridge High School in Washington posted a link from his MySpace page to a video on YouTube that made fun of a teacher's hygiene, organizational habits, body weight, and classroom conduct. The footage, covertly recorded in class, also involves close-up shots of the teacher's buttocks and a student making faces, giving her "bunny ears," and giving pelvic thrusts in her direction from behind. The students responsible were suspended for forty days, with twenty days "held in abeyance" if a research paper was completed during the suspension. After one student sued for violation of his First Amendment rights, the court in *Requa v. Kent School District No. 415* (2007) upheld the suspension, alluding to opinions from *Tinker* and *Fraser*:

> The school district is not required to establish that an actual educational discourse was disrupted by the student's activity. The "work and discipline of the school" includes the maintenance of a civil and respectful atmosphere toward teachers and students alike—demeaning, derogatory, sexually suggestive behavior toward a non-suspecting teacher in a classroom poses a disruption of that mission whenever it occurs.[23]

The crux of the argument in favor of the school district involved (1) that covert video recording in the classroom violated school policy, and (2) that the video substantially and materially disrupted the work and discipline of the school. It is also important to point out that the sexually suggestive pelvic thrusts could be construed as sexual harassment and, therefore, should be disciplined based on the relevant district policy.[23] A school resource officer from Minnesota told us that his own district successfully prosecuted a student for disorderly conduct in 2013 when a video surfaced of the student walking behind a teacher in a classroom making pelvic thrusts. Again, it is imperative that schools intervene and discipline students for behaviors that may constitute harassment based on sex or race. Failure to do so may open the district up to liability, as discussed above.

The Difficulty in Determining What You Should Do

At the beginning of the chapter we introduced you to Justin Layshock and J.S., two students who had been suspended by their respective schools for creating parody MySpace profiles about their principals. The facts of the cases were nearly identical, and so too was the response by the schools: ten day suspensions. In both cases, the students sued, arguing that the school overstepped their authority in disciplining them for their off-campus speech. The lower court judge in Layshock's case initially sided with the school, ruling that the "actions appear to have substantially disrupted school operations and interfered with the right of others, which, along with his apparent violations of school rules, would provide a sufficient legal basis for Defendants' actions."[24]

But that wasn't the end of the story. The judge actually reversed himself in July 2007. The court found that multiple MySpace profile pages had been created of the school principal and that the school district could not specify exactly which profile led to the disruption on campus. Also, upon more carefully examining the facts of the case, the court found that the disruption was not substantial nor did it undermine the school's basic educational mission. Finally, the school was not able to demonstrate that the profile created by Layshock—rather than the investigative response of administrators—led to the disruption at school. Essentially the school was unable to provide adequate evidence of the disruption and its cause. The school was ordered to pay $10,000 to the Layshocks, contingent on appeal. The US Court of Appeals for the Third Circuit upheld the lower court ruling.

The lower court refused to grant the student a temporary restraining order or preliminary injunction in the *J.S.* case, ruling that schools can in fact discipline students for lewd off-campus behavior, even if such behavior didn't necessarily cause a substantial disruption. Interestingly, a separate panel from *the same court of appeals that ruled against the school in* Layshock *ruled in favor of the school in* J.S.

To resolve these disparate views, the court of appeals agreed to review the cases collectively (en banc) to offer a perspective. In short, the court reasserted the known standard that schools cannot punish students for off-campus behavior or speech without evidence of a substantial disruption at school (or a high likelihood that such a disruption will occur). In the Layshock case, the school district conceded that the creation of the MySpace parody profile did not cause a disruption at school, making it clearly outside the boundaries of formal school discipline.[25] The court also listed several cases where schools were allowed to discipline students for the off-campus behavior (e.g., *J.S. v. Bethlehem Area School District* [2002], *Wisniewski v. Bd. of Educ. of Weedsport Cent. School District* [2007], and *Doninger v. Niehoff* [2008]), noting that "each of those cases involved off-campus expressive conduct that resulted in a substantial disruption of the school, and the courts allowed the schools to respond to the substantial disruption that the student's out of school conduct caused."[25]

In *J.S. v. Bethlehem Area School District*, the district did initially attempt to argue that the student's activities resulted in a significant disruption at school, but neither the district court nor the court of appeals accepted that argument and so they backed off. In the original hearing, the district court supported the disciplinary actions of the school, not because there was evidence of a substantial disruption, but because the content of the off-campus speech was "vulgar, lewd, and potentially illegal."[20] This was consistent with Supreme Court decisions in *Fraser* (1986) and *Morse* (2007) discussed earlier. In its review, however, the court of appeals noted that in both of these cases, the speech was delivered at school (*Fraser*) or a school-sponsored activity (*Morse*). As such, the vulgarity of the speech was irrelevant and therefore the singular issue to consider is whether the off-campus speech results in a substantial disruption.

In a divided opinion (8–6) the court of appeals overturned the district court, concluding that "the school district violated J.S.'s First Amendment free speech rights when it suspended her for speech that caused no substantial disruption in school and that could not reasonably have led school officials to forecast substantial disruption in school."[20] The presiding judge noted in a concurring opinion, however, that "the issue is whether the Supreme Court's decision in *Tinker* can be applicable to off-campus speech. I believe it can, and no ruling coming out today is to the contrary."[20]

So where does this leave us? Well, the key issue to keep in mind is whether a student's off-campus speech or behavior results in, or has a high likelihood of resulting in, a substantial disruption at school. There is little additional clarity regarding what that actually looks like, but school administrators know a bit more about what it isn't. Staff accessing a student-created profile that harasses a teacher or administrator at school does not constitute a substantial disruption. A student bringing a printed copy of a web page to school at the request of staff does not necessarily cause a substantial disruption. A few students talking in class about a cyberbullying situation does not always mean that there will be a substantial disruption.

It also appears that vulgarities and cruel sentiments directed toward school officials *from an off-campus location* are not automatically subject to school discipline. Now, if that speech substantially or materially disrupts learning at school, it may be fair game for sanction. Some free speech advocates have referred to these rulings as a victory for students, suggesting these opinions are evidence that there are no conditions under which schools can discipline students for their off-campus speech. This is simply not true and an incorrect interpretation of the facts. It has long been known that students have free speech rights. It is also true that those rights are constrained a bit while at school and where they substantially disrupt the school environment. That hasn't changed.

> The key issue to keep in mind is whether a student's off-campus speech or behavior results in, or has a high likelihood of resulting in, a substantial disruption at school.

It is important to also point out that both of these cases involved students who were targeting staff. In *Kowalski v. Berkeley County Schools* (2011), a student created an online profile disparaging another student—which seemingly precipitated another instance when a substantial disruption took place. We first introduced you to Kara Kowalski in Chapter 2. Recall that she was the high school senior who created the "S.A.S.H." MySpace group page which she claimed in her deposition was an acronym for "Students Against Sluts Herpes." However, other classmates later admitted that it was an acronym for "Students Against Shay's Herpes," referring to another Musselman student, Shay N. (the main subject of discussion on the web page). Kowalski sued the school for violating her free speech rights and due process. Upon deliberation, the lower court upheld the suspension and the case was appealed to the US Court of Appeals for the Fourth Circuit, which affirmed the lower court opinion, stating, "Kowalski used the Internet to orchestrate a targeted attack on a classmate, and did so in a manner that was sufficiently connected to the school environment as to implicate the School District's recognized authority to discipline speech which 'materially and substantially interfere[es] with the requirements of appropriate discipline in the operation of the school and collid[es] with the rights of others.'"[26]

My friend has been arguing with her boyfriend, who hangs around with a group of girls and a couple of boys and they call themselves "the gang" and the girls who he hangs around with have made a fake Facebook account pretending to be my friend. They have been writing horrible things like calling her a "slag" and a "slut" and "fat pig." Also they have been messaging her friends saying she wants a fight with them and this is causing people to argue and fight. Our school is saying they can't do anything about it because it happened outside of school. These girls have been also prank calling us all weekend early hours in the morning. My friend is so upset and scared to tell people she is also worried to eat since they have been calling her "fat."

—Lucy, 14, unknown location

You Don't Need to Wait Until the Horse Has Left the Barn Before Closing the Door

It's important that you know that you don't need to wait until a significant disruption occurs at your school before intervening in a way that prevents such a disruption. In fact, early intervention may preempt a number of problems and hassles which might be completely avoidable. This standard was tested at the Supreme Court in 2008 with the case *Barr v. Lafon* (2008). Here, the US Court of Appeals for the Sixth Circuit upheld the discipline of a student for refusing to remove or cover up the image of a confederate flag on a T-shirt.[27] The student argued that the image represented passive, free speech like that allowed in *Tinker*. The school argued that a history of racial tensions demand that certain expressions be prohibited.

The student claimed that no one had complained about the shirt and therefore no disruption was present. Nevertheless, according to *Lowery v. Euverard* (2007), and cited in *Barr v. Lafon*, "*Tinker* does not require disruption to have actually occurred."[28] Instead, the court "must evaluate the circumstances to determine if [the school's] forecast of substantial disruption was reasonable."[28] The court of appeals agreed with the school, ruling that "appellate court decisions considering school bans on expression have focused on whether the banned conduct *would likely trigger disturbances* such as those experienced in the past"[28] [emphasis added] and pointed to the fact that the high school in this case had even positioned law enforcement officials on campus in previous years to maintain order in an environment of racial hostility and violence.[28] The Supreme Court refused to hear the case, signaling tacit agreement with the finding of the lower court.

SO . . . WHEN CAN EDUCATORS INTERVENE?

Knowing when a school can intervene in cases involving off-campus or electronic speech or behaviors is critically important because the potential implications can be significant. As we've mentioned, you must tread lightly. Some districts have even been required to pay significant sums to students who have sued them for overstepping the bounds of their authority in punishing off-campus, online speech. For instance, we referenced the Westlake High School case earlier in this chapter where the school was required to pay $30,000 to the student who was wrongly punished. In *Beidler v. North Thurston School District* (2000), a high school student in Washington was suspended in 1999 for creating a parody web page that ridiculed the assistant principal. Similar to the findings in *J. S. v. Bethlehem* and *Layshock v. Hermitage*, the court ruled that the school district failed to prove that a substantial disruption had occurred, and the student's First Amendment rights had been violated. This led to the district agreeing to pay the student $52,000 in attorney's fees and $10,000 in damages.[29] In yet another case (*Killion v. Franklin Regional School Board* [2001]), a district was required to pay $65,000 for violating the online speech of a student after suspending him for making fun of his school's athletic director in a mass e-mail.[30]

Such outcomes tend to undermine disciplinary action by schools because the threat of civil litigation and bad publicity seems too great. This is unfortunate, because as noted above, there are a number of situations when it is completely appropriate (and necessary) for school officials to get involved. Table 5.1 succinctly summarizes each of the cases we've covered (and some we haven't) and includes a statement of potential precedent stemming from the respective court ruling. We hope this serves as a quick and easy reference when you must consider the legal implications of certain school actions. In general, however, US courts are oriented toward supporting First Amendment rights of free expression. Still, certain expressions are *not protected* and allow intervention and discipline, including those that

- substantially or materially disrupt learning;
- interfere with the educational process or school discipline;
- utilize school-owned technology to harass; or
- threaten other students or infringes on their civil rights.

Even though many school personnel are understandably hesitant to get involved in cases of cyberbullying that occur off campus (especially given the uncertainty of the current legal footing), as long as administrators can point to the aforementioned exceptions, their restrictive response is probably within the boundaries of the law.[3] As we have stressed, the current standard

Table 5.1 Notable Court Cases Relevant to Student Speech, Electronic Behaviors, and Cyberbullying

Court Case	Implications
Tinker v. Des Moines Independent Community School District (1969)	For school district personnel to restrict student expression of controversial or inflammatory opinions, they must demonstrate that such behaviors substantially interfere with school discipline or the rights of others.
Fenton v. Stear (1976)	Lewd, obscene, profane, and libelous language (including fighting words) are not protected speech and school administrators can reasonably sanction students for their use, even when used while students are away from school.
Bethel School District No. 403 v. Fraser (1986)	Highly offensive speech on a school campus can be restricted if it infringes upon the rights of others or is inconsistent with the values being promoted at school.
Klein v. Smith (1986)	Schools cannot discipline students for off-campus behavior that does not negatively affect the school environment.
Hazelwood School District v. Kuhlmeier (1988)	Schools can exercise editorial control over speech or content that appears to be (or is) part of a school-sponsored expressive activity, if the activity is related to legitimate pedagogical goals.
Beussink v. Woodland R-IV School District (1998)	Schools cannot restrict a student's inflammatory online speech that occurs off campus simply because it expresses an unpleasant, unpopular, or upsetting viewpoint.
Gebser v. Lago Vista Independent School District (1998)	A school district can be liable for damages in a staff-on-student sexual harassment case only if it is determined that an employee with supervisory power over the accused is deliberately indifferent to the misconduct.
Davis v. Monroe County Board of Education (1999)	A school district can be liable for damages in a student-on-student sexual harassment case only if it is determined that school officials were deliberately indifferent to the misconduct. Harassment must be "so severe, pervasive, and objectively offensive that it can be said to deprive the victims of access to the educational opportunities or benefits provided by the school."[9]
Emmett v. Kent School District No. 415 (2000)	Schools must provide evidence that seemingly threatening online speech is, in fact, threatening to others or disturbs school operations.
J.S. v. Bethlehem Area School District (2000)	Schools can restrict off-campus online speech that threatens the safety of another person when they can demonstrate harm to the victim.

Court Case	Implications
Wisniewski v. Board of Education of Weedsport Central School District (2006)	Students who create online content that could reasonably cause a disruption at school can be sanctioned, particularly when it involves a threat.
Klump v. Nazareth Area School District (2006)	School administrators cannot violate students' Fourth Amendment protection against unreasonable searches of their cell phones for voicemails or text messages, unless they have clear, articulated, documentable, and reasonable suspicion that school policy has been violated.
Drews v. Joint School District No. 393 (2006)	School districts are not responsible in cyberbullying cases between students when the victim cannot show that any educational benefits were denied or that any rights were infringed.
Morse v. Frederick (2007)	Schools can restrict controversial expressions during school-sponsored events, especially if those expressions appear to endorse behavior that is contrary to their educational mission.
A.B. v. State of Indiana (2007)	Some off-campus online speech by a student may be protected, if it can be considered "political speech" that legitimately criticizes a school administrator.
Requa v. Kent School District No. 415 (2007)	Covert digital video recordings of teachers made by students and then posted to YouTube materially and substantially disrupt the work and discipline of the school, particularly when they involve demeaning, derogatory, and sexually suggestive behavior.
Barr v. Lafon (2008)	Schools can ban political speech if it is likely to cause a disruption at school. Schools do not need to wait for a substantial disruption to occur at school before taking action.
Layshock v. Hermitage School District (2011) and *J.S. v. Blue Mountain School District* (2011)	Schools must diligently and comprehensively collect and provide evidence proving that a substantial and material disruption occurred within the school environment to support their position in a court case.
Kowalski v. Berkeley County Schools (2011)	Schools can discipline students for their online, off-campus speech, consistent with *Tinker*. Speech or behavior that is sufficiently connected to the school environment that materially and substantially interferes with the operations of the school or infringes on the rights of others is subject to appropriate educational discipline.
Zeno v. Pine Plains Central School District (2012)	Once educators learn of harassment taking place, they have an obligation to do everything in their power to ensure that it stops.

reached over forty-five years ago in *Tinker* and reflected in many subsequent cases regarding the extent to which schools can discipline students for inappropriate behavior is whether that behavior resulted in a substantial disruption at school. Actual, material disruption to the school environment—irrespective of where the behavior took place (on or off campus)—perennially seems to be the primary issue in these cases.

From a cyberbullying perspective, it is clear that many forms of electronic harassment carried out off campus would impact the learning environment, at least for the individuals who are the target of the harassment, because they wouldn't be able to concentrate or feel safe there (seeing as how the aggressor[s] tend to be peers at school, as pointed out in the previous chapter). However, the question remains: At what point does such behavior "substantially and materially" disrupt the school environment as a whole? Florida law (HB 609), which took effect in May of 2013, states that schools are allowed to discipline students for off-campus harassment when it "substantially interferes with or limits the victim's ability to participate in or benefit from the services, activities, or opportunities offered by a school or substantially disrupts the education process or orderly operation of a school."[31]

Also in 2013, California clarified the ability of schools to intervene in these situations by defining an *electronic act* as something that can be created or transmitted "on or off the schoolsite" if the behavior results in, or "can be reasonably predicted to have the effect of" [32] a substantial disruption (see Box 5.1).

Box 5.1

Criteria for Educator Intervention in Bullying and Cyberbullying

California law specifies that bullying, including bullying via an electronic act created or transmitted on or off the schoolsite, is subject to school discipline if it results or is reasonably likely to result in one or more of the following:

a. Placing a reasonable pupil or pupils in fear of harm to that pupil's or those pupils' person or property.

b. Causing a reasonable pupil to experience a substantially detrimental effect on his or her physical or mental health.

c. Causing a reasonable pupil to experience substantial interference with his or her academic performance.

d. Causing a reasonable pupil to experience substantial interference with his or her ability to participate in or benefit from the services, activities, or privileges provided by a school.[32]

On its face, we believe the approach taken by California is well conceived and detailed and, therefore, should be used as a model to provide clarity to an otherwise vague clause or concept (other states, such as Iowa, include nearly identical language in their laws).

When a particular student is targeted in a way that disrupts his or her ability to learn or feel safe at school, appropriate school intervention is allowed (and perhaps required). But what about circumstances where off-campus behaviors don't necessarily target one person? The Arkansas Legislature (Public Act 115) defined "substantial disruption" more generally to include incidents where bullying results in the following:

(i) Necessary cessation of instruction or educational activities;

(ii) Inability of students or educational staff to focus on learning or function as an educational unit because of a hostile environment;

(iii) Severe or repetitive disciplinary measures are needed in the classroom or during educational activities; or

(iv) Exhibition of other behaviors by students or educational staff that substantially interfere with the learning environment.[33]

For example, perhaps students are constantly chattering about a hate account on Instagram filled with juicy rumors and gossip to the point where their behavior affects a teacher's ability to deliver instruction. Perhaps one or more students are unable to pay attention in class because of the fallout from a distressing website created about them and fear for their own safety. Perhaps repeated verbal correction by teachers or administrative staff fails to quiet the uproar stemming from mean and inflammatory messages circulating on Facebook. Perhaps fights are breaking out between classes in the hallways because of hostile texts being forwarded from one cell phone to another across the entire student body. All of these instances could be classified as a "substantial disruption" within the meaning of *Tinker*, thereby allowing the school to apply appropriate and reasonable discipline to deal with the problem.

In short, there are a number of circumstances that allow for educators to intervene, even if behaviors occur or originate away from school. But more than that, schools also have an obligation to demonstrate clearly that they are exercising reasonable care to address cyberbullying so as to not appear deliberately indifferent to behaviors that disrupt the ability of students to learn. The important word in this sentence is *reasonable*. It isn't expected that you have full knowledge of all of the intricacies of the law. (Again, many lawyers disagree about these issues.) The standard really has become *reasonableness*. In most of the cases described above where the school district lost at court, the discipline applied was unreasonable. Schools will not be sued for having a conference with a student and parents to discuss questionable online behavior. Similarly, it is highly unlikely that giving detention, requiring Saturday school, or assigning a project-based creative sanction (described later in this chapter) will lead to legal action. In the cases described above, the courts got involved when students were given a long-term suspension or expulsion. Be reasonable with your response and you will have nothing to worry about.

It's also important that schools and districts have clear policies regarding bullying and harassment, and that those policies include reference to electronic forms and mediums. Even though this seems obvious, many schools are lagging behind. As a result, most state legislatures have stepped in and passed legislation that requires districts to update their policies accordingly. In the section that follows, we point out the most common elements of such legislation and discuss the essential features that comprise an effective cyberbullying policy.

STATE BULLYING LAWS

Forty-nine states (all but Montana) now have anti-bullying laws, and all of these include provisions for electronic forms of bullying (see www .cyberbullying.us/laws for more details and the most recent updates). While each of the laws varies to some extent, they generally involve one (or more) of the following elements:

- Direct school districts to have anti-bullying policies.
- Direct school districts to add cyberbullying to existing anti-bullying policies.
- Criminalize or provide specific penalties for cyberbullying.
- Include new provisions to allow administrators to take action when off-campus actions have affected on-campus order.
- Require schools to develop new reporting and disciplinary procedures in cyberbullying cases.
- Mandate that school districts create and implement Internet safety, ethics, and etiquette training and curriculum.

The primary problem that legislators face is how to craft a law that protects students but does not overly restrict student speech, thus violating the First Amendment's guarantee of free expression. Also at issue is whether laws have explicitly authorized schools to intervene in electronic misbehaviors that do not involve school resources or that originate from off-campus sources. As discussed at length above, however, there are consistently clear areas where school personnel can, and must, step in. Many states are currently working (in some capacity) to update their existing anti-bullying legislation in an attempt to keep up with the ever-changing nature of these behaviors. We urge legislatures to adopt language that clearly demonstrates that any and all forms of bullying, no matter where it occurs, that (1) disrupts the ability of a student to learn, (2) infringes on the rights of a student (including the right to be "let alone" at school), or (3) creates a hostile learning environment, is subject to reasonable school discipline. Specifically, we advocate for a slightly modified version of New Hampshire's 2010 anti-bullying law (HB 1523). Here is our recommended language:

> Schools have the authority and responsibility to apply reasonable and educationally based discipline, consistent with a pupil's constitutionally granted privileges, to any harassment, intimidation, or bullying that (a) occurs on or is delivered to school property or a school-sponsored activity or event on or off school property; or (b) occurs off of school property or outside of a school-sponsored activity or event, if the conduct interferes with a pupil's educational opportunities, creates a hostile environment for that pupil or others, or substantially disrupts the orderly operations of the school or school-sponsored activity or event.

Similar language has also been adopted in New Jersey and Connecticut law recently. We have modified it minimally to ensure that students' constitutionally protected speech is not infringed upon by threatening to discipline students who are exercising their rights. As *Tinker* clearly stated, students have free speech rights, but they are not free to disrupt the learning environment at school (create a major scene, threaten or infringe on the rights of others, etc.). With all of this in mind, and taking into consideration the unique requirements included in particular state laws, schools have been tasked with constructing anti-bullying policies that are clear, comprehensive, and constitutionally valid.

SCHOOL DISTRICT POLICY

All state anti-bullying laws require schools to have anti-bullying policies. After carefully reviewing the language from many of the laws discussing this issue with policymakers, we have come up with the six primary elements of what would constitute an effective school policy. This approach moves beyond simply adding "electronic bullying" to existing district policies. Box 5.2 lists these six components, and we discuss each of them in more detail below.

Box 5.2

Elements of an Effective School Cyberbullying Policy

1. Specific definitions of *harassment, intimidation,* and *bullying* (including the electronic variants)

2. Graduated consequences and remedial actions

3. Procedures for reporting cyberbullying

4. Procedures for investigating cyberbullying

5. Language specifying that if a student's off-campus speech or behavior results in "substantial disruption of the learning environment" or infringes on the rights of other students, the student can be disciplined

6. Procedures for preventing cyberbullying

1. Definition of Relevant Terms

It is important that the policy clearly defines the behaviors it seeks to proscribe. The more specific the policy is, the more likely it will withstand legal challenges. As William Shepherd, former statewide prosecutor at the Florida Office of the Attorney General, cautions, however, "the law or policy should be specific, but behavior changes over time, so you must have the ability to grow with the times." In Box 5.3, we provide a sample definition of bullying that you should consider including in your policy. This comes from Nancy Willard's analysis of definitions in relevant research, case law, and consent decrees. In Box 5.4, we list several forms of bullying that should be clearly delineated in your policy. Generally speaking, any communication that has been perceived by a student as unwanted, vulgar, obscene, sexually explicit, demeaning, belittling, or defaming in nature or is otherwise disruptive to a student's ability to learn and a school's ability to educate its students in a safe environment or that causes a reasonable person to suffer substantial emotional distress or fear of bodily injury should be subject to discipline. It is also important to remember that many districts already have policies in place that prohibit various forms of harassment, including harassment based on race or sex. Any behavior that constitutes sexual harassment, for example, should be handled under those provisions, whether or not the behavior is also considered bullying or cyberbullying.

Box 5.3

Sample Policy Definition

Bullying is

Pervasive or persistent hurtful acts directed at another student that have taken place at school, while traveling to or from school, during school activities, or while off campus, that have caused, or can reasonably be forecast to cause: A) physical harm or threat of harm to the student or his or her property; or B) distress resulting in a significant interference with the ability of the student to receive an education or participate in school activities.[34]

Box 5.4

Forms of Bullying

Bullying can occur by one individual or a group of individuals, can be direct or indirect, and can take the following forms:

a. **Physical bullying:** Demonstrations of aggression by pushing, kicking, hitting, gesturing, or otherwise invading the physical space of another person in an unwelcome manner or the unwanted tampering with or destruction of another person's property

b. **Verbal bullying:** Demonstrations of aggression through insults, teasing, cursing, threatening, or otherwise expressing unkind words toward another person

c. **Relational bullying:** Demonstrations of aggression through rumor spreading, exclusion, rejection, and isolation to damage a person's position and relationship within a social group

d. **Cyberbullying:** Willful and repeated harm inflicted through the use of computers, cell phones, and other electronic devices

Cyberbullying can result in discipline whether it occurs on or off campus, irrespective of whether it involves an electronic device at school, at home, or at a third-party location; or if it infringes on the rights of other students or results in, or has a reasonable likelihood of resulting in, a substantial disruption of the school learning environment as defined in this policy.

2. Graduated Consequences and Remedial Actions

Any student found to be participating in, contributing to, or encouraging acts of cyberbullying or harassment toward another student or staff member must be disciplined. Your school's policy should identify what specific actions may be taken. To determine the severity of the harassment or discrimination, the following may be considered:

- how the misconduct affected one or more students' education;
- the type, frequency, and duration of the misconduct;
- the number of persons involved;
- the subject(s) of harassment or discrimination;
- the situation in which the incident occurred; and
- other related incidents at the school.

Any cyberbullying that could be a criminal act, such as stalking or a threat to one's physical safety, should be subject to discipline and result in the notification of law enforcement.

Discipline can include a number of different actions (see Box 5.5). As we discuss in detail in Chapter 7, it is important to link specific behaviors with specific disciplinary outcomes so that students know exactly what may happen if they are caught engaging in cyberbullying behaviors. Don't be afraid to think creatively about alternative sanctions instead of relying on traditional options like detention or suspension. For example, cyberbullies could be required (based on the gravity of the grievance) to research and write an essay on the negative effects of cyberbullying or create a campaign to raise awareness of its dangers. They could also be required to write a formal apology to the aggrieved party or parties. Disciplinary outcomes should be considered and carried out on a case-by-case basis.

3. Procedures for Reporting Cyberbullying

Every student should be encouraged and empowered to report instances or evidence of cyberbullying to a teacher or staff member. In order to do so, they must be made aware of the proper channels through which to report inappropriate behaviors of all varieties. In fact, some state bullying laws require school policies to include explicit information about how students or others should go about reporting bullying (see, for example, laws in New York and West Virginia). As we will discuss in Chapter 6, every school should designate one or more staff members to serve as *trustees* who are specifically trained to deal with cyberbullying incidents. Students should feel comfortable confiding in them when they experience or witness cyberbullying.

Box 5.5

Disciplinary Options

- Parental contact
- Behavioral contracts
- Loss of privileges (either in-school or extracurricular: time on sports team, field trip with club, going to homecoming, prom, or graduation, etc.)
- Conferences with students, parents, teachers, or administrative staff
- Interventions by school guidance personnel
- School service work or student work detail
- Removal of student from class
- Loss of bus privileges (parents are thus responsible for transportation)
- In-school alternative assignments or intervention programs
- Detentions (before, during, or after school or on Saturday)
- Restitution
- Assignment to alternative program in lieu of suspension days
- Restorative intervention (mediation, victim-impact panel, conferencing)
- Suspension—removal of student from school for up to ten days
- Assignment to an alternative educational facility
- Expulsion—removal of student from school for remainder of year plus one additional year

Also, an anonymous reporting system should be set up so that youth can inform adults of a problem without fear of repercussions (see Chapter 7 for a detailed discussion of this). Retaliation or reprisal against any student who anonymously or publicly reports an act of bullying or cyberbullying must be expressly forbidden (and addressed strongly if that occurs). Of course, intentionally false accusations by a student against another must also be subject to discipline.

4. Procedures for Investigating Cyberbullying

We believe *all* forms of cyberbullying, no matter how minor, need to be investigated and documented. Even if you don't feel the school has the authority to discipline the student for the behavior, the incident should be investigated and put in the student's file for future reference. It is important to track the behavioral history of youth, even relatively minor incidents, as this history might be instructive in future considerations. A number of minor behaviors can add up to something more serious. Also, cyberbullying behaviors can signal that something more serious is going on with a particular student; therefore, they must be thoroughly investigated—every single time.

Investigations typically involve collecting statements from the victim(s), the alleged target(s), and any witness(es) or bystander(s). This may also involve collecting and documenting electronic evidence from computers, mobile devices, storage drives, optical media, external or flash drives, server and network logs, Internet service providers or cellular service providers, and related locations. It is important to remember that in many cases, you may need a warrant to search personal property where a student has an expectation of privacy. While the Supreme Court has ruled that the probable cause requirement of the Fourth Amendment does not apply to students at school,[35] a student search must nevertheless satisfy the "reasonableness" requirement[36] (more on this in Chapter 7). We have included a comprehensive "Cyberbullying Incident Tracking Form" (Resource D) that you can use to record and document all instances of cyberbullying.

5. Substantial Disruption

It is worth mentioning again that if cyberbullying resulted in a substantial disruption of the school learning environment or infringed upon the rights of other students or staff (whether the behavior occurred at school or online), the school district can restrict student speech or behavior and discipline those responsible. As pointed out earlier, substantial disruption occurs when an incident forces the cessation of instructional activities, prevents students or staff from focusing on learning and accomplishing the educational goals of the institution, leads to severe or repetitive disciplinary measures to keep students on task or preempt further interpersonal conflict, or otherwise leads to conduct that detracts from the educational process and requires intervention to restore orderly operation. All of these factors must be spelled out in your school's policy so that students and parents fully understand the circumstances under which school authority can reach beyond the school walls. They shouldn't be surprised when discipline is applied for off-campus behaviors since your policy clearly delineates when that might occur.

6. Procedures for Preventing Cyberbullying

It is important, and in some cases even required, that each school educates its students and staff on a regular basis regarding the nature and consequences of, and prohibitions and penalties associated with, all forms of bullying including cyberbullying so that constant and updated awareness of the problem is promoted. Education should occur through training workshops and seminars, as well as formalized continuing education initiatives for all members of the school community. Students should be exposed to cyberbullying prevention programming through signage at school, assemblies with compelling and vetted speakers, the dissemination of interactive materials, and with creative strategies to combat hate among peers and promote a healthy and respectful school climate. Training modules also should be implemented in Grades K–12 with the intent of instructing youth on healthy and appropriate interactions online and off and to help safeguard them from victimization (Chapter 6 covers these and other prevention efforts in greater detail).

SUMMARY

Like the technology that is popular today, the legal principles concerning student speech and behavior are constantly changing and becoming more refined. As such, while the information contained in this chapter was current at the time this book went to press (summer of 2014), new developments in case law and statutory law are continually affecting the state of cyberbullying legal issues. For the most up-to-date information, the reader is encouraged to consult with an attorney who has expertise in school and Internet law. Similarly, students' online misuse and abuse will continue to evolve as communications technology (hardware and software) evolves. Vigilance is important in continually modifying and improving the base of school policies that address electronic harm.

After reading this chapter, you can see why so many educators are confused about what they can and cannot do with respect to intervening in incidents involving off-campus speech and behavior. We hope, however, that we have clarified these issues sufficiently to give you a general understanding of how to approach these situations. Simply put, you cannot formally discipline students for speech or behavior, which you merely disagree (or are uncomfortable) with, that occurs away from school. That said, please don't use this principle as justification for staying uninvolved. As we will discuss in Chapter 7, you can utilize a number of strategies to respond to a variety of cyberbullying situations (those that occur on campus and off). Before we explain how you should address responses to cyberbullying, though, Chapter 6 covers many of the best practical solutions you can implement to help keep it from occurring in the first place.

QUESTIONS FOR REFLECTION

1. Should legislatures step up and pass laws that criminalize electronic harassment? If yes, what punishments should be provided?

2. Is the policy at your school effective at addressing cyberbullying? (If your answer is "I don't know," you have a lot of work to do!)

3. How would a student at your school go about reporting cyberbullying? Do the students at your school know this procedure?

4. When can a school district discipline a student for cyberbullying?

5. How would you define *substantial disruption*? What are some examples of behaviors that would meet this standard in your view?

NOTES

1. Layshock v. Hermitage School District. 593 F.3d 249 (3rd Cir. 2010).
2. Snyder v. Blue Mountain School District. 593 F.3d 286 (3d. Cir. 2010), vacated, 2010 BL 80170.
3. Shaheen Shariff and Dianne L. Hoff. "Cyberbullying: Clarifying Legal Boundaries for School Supervision in Cyberspace." *International Journal of Cyber Criminology* 1, no. 1 (2007): 76–118.
4. *The Civil Rights Act of 1964.* Pub. L. 88–352, 78 Stat. 241 (1964).
5. *Title IX of the Educational Amendments of 1972.* http://www.dol.gov/oasam/regs/statutes/titleix.htm.
6. US Department of Education. "Dear Colleague Letter Harassment and Bullying." US Department of Education, Office for Civil Rights (October 26, 2010): 2. http://www2.ed.gov/about/offices/list/ocr/docs/dcl-factsheet-201010.pdf.
7. Russlynn Ali. "Dear Colleague" Letter. US Department of Education, Office for Civil Rights (October 26, 2010): 7–8. http://www2.ed.gov/about/offices/list/ocr/letters/colleague-201010.pdf.
8. Gebser et al. v. Lago Vista Independent School District. 106 F.3d 1223 (5th Cir 1998).
9. Davis v. Monroe County Board of Education. 120 1390 (F.3d 1999).
10. Zeno v. Pine Plains Central School District. 10–3604-cv (C.A. 2, Dec. 3, 2012).
11. Tinker et al. v. Des Moines Independent Community School District. 503. 393 U.S. 503 (1969).
12. Bethel School District v. Fraser. 478 U.S. 675 (1986).
13. Hazelwood School District et al. v. Kuhlmeier. 484 U.S. 260 (1988).
14. Morse v. Frederick. 551 U.S. 393 (2007).
15. Thomas v. Board of Education, Granville Central School District. 607 F.2d 1043, 1052 (2nd Cir. 1979).
16. Klein v. Smith. 635 F.Supp. 1440 (Dist. Me. 1986).

17. Terry McManus. " Home Web Sites Thrust Students Into Censorship Disputes." (1998). *New York Times*. Accessed July 21, 2014, http://partners.nytimes.com/library/tech/98/08/circuits/articles/13cens.html.

18. David Hudson. "Censorship of Student Internet Speech: The Effect of Diminishing Student Rights, Fear of the Internet and Columbine." Paper presented at Telecommunication Policy and Law Symposium, Washington, DC, April 18, 2000.

19. Emmett v. Kent School District No. 415. 92 1088 (W.D. Wash. 2000).

20. J.S. v. Bethlehem Area School District 412. 593 F.3d 249 (2000) (3d Cir. 2011).

21. Kathleen Conn. *Bullying And Harassment: A Legal Guide For Educators*. Alexandria, VA: ASCD, 2004.

22. Wisniewski v. Board of Education of the Weedsport Central School District. 494 F.3d 34 (2d Cir. 2008).

23. Requa v. Kent School District No. 415. 2007 WL 1531670 (W.D. Wash. May 24, 2007).

24. Layshock v. Hermitage School District. 2:06-cv-00116-TFM (2007).

25. Layshock v. Hermitage School District. 2:06-cv-00116-TFM (2007), *aff'd* 3d Cir. 2011.

26. Kowalski v. Berkeley County Schools. 652 F.3d 565 (4th Cir. 2011).

27. Barr v. Lafon. 538 F.3d 554 (6th Cir. 2008).

28. Lowery v. Euverard. 497 F.3d 584, 592 (6th Cir. 2007).

29. Beidler v. North Thurston School District No. 3. No. 99–2–00236–6 (Wash. Super. Ct. 2000).

30. Killion v. Franklin Regional School Board. 136 F.Supp. 2d 446 (2001).

31. Florida House of Representatives. Bullying in the Public School System. CS/CS/HB 609 (2013). http://www.flsenate.gov/Session/Bill/2013/0609/BillText/er/PDF.

32. State of California. Grounds for Suspension and Expulsion: Bullying. Assembly Bill No. 256 (2013). http://leginfo.legislature.ca.gov/faces/billNavClient.xhtml?bill_id=201320140AB256.

33. State of Arkansas. HB1072 86th General Assembly (2007). Accessed July 29, 2014, http://www.arkleg.state.ar.us/assembly/2007/R/Acts/Act115.pdf.

34. Nancy E. Willard. *Positive Relations @ School (& Elsewhere): Legal Parameters & Positive Strategies to Address Bullying & Harassment*. Embrace Civility in the Digital Age: Eugene, OR, 2014.

35. New Jersey v. T.L.O. 469 U.S. 325 (1985).

36. Klump v. Nazareth Area School District. 425 F. Supp. 2d 622 (E.D. Pa. 2006).

CHAPTER SIX

Preventing Cyberbullying

Jeff Johnston was a fifteen-year-old honor student in southwest Florida who loved computers and Japanese comic books. When a popular girl at school became his girlfriend, another boy became jealous and decided to send and post cruel statements and slanderous gossip through e-mail and on the web: "jeff is a fagget [sic]. he needs to die. it seems everythime [sic] i write on the computer i build up rage."[1] One tormenter even hacked into a web page hosting an online game that Jeff and his friends had designed and replaced it with a hate page in a type of "cybervandalism." As other kids joined in on the harassment, it became too much for Jeff to take. Six weeks before he took his life in June of 2005, he wrote a suicide note on his computer: "I'm just writing to tell you I won't be in school anymore. I decided to commit suicide because my life is too hard to live with."[1]

As we have previously discussed, most kids who experience cyberbullying do not commit suicide. But some do. And others consider or attempt it. Most of those victimized struggle emotionally and psychologically as they face day after day of hate and harassment. We trust that the pages you have read so far have gotten you fired up and motivated to do something to prevent cyberbullying. But you may not know where or how to start. In this chapter, we identify and share a number of practical approaches to help decrease the frequency and seriousness of online harassment among youth. While there is no singular solution that will keep all forms of harassment from occurring, implementing some of these informed strategies can cumulatively work to minimize the likelihood and extent of harm associated with cyberbullying.

To begin, though, a word of caution is warranted. Understandably shaken by the tragedies they hear about in the news, and determined to do *something* or *anything* to keep other kids from the same horrific outcomes, some adults reflexively decide to simply forbid (or substantially restrict) youth from going online. However, we believe this is the *least* appropriate course of action. Think about it for a moment. Would you agree that visiting and touring Washington, DC, would be a fantastic learning opportunity for students? Sure it is: The war memorials, presidential monuments, and governmental buildings are all great places for kids to see and come to appreciate.

Maybe you would like to take the students in your class or school to the nation's capital for a tour. Well, how would you go about it? You certainly wouldn't just drop them off in front of the White House and say, "Have fun!" You know that in addition to all of the wonderful educational opportunities in Washington, DC, there are many things you wouldn't necessarily want your students to see: violence, prostitutes, homeless people, drunkards, gang members, and so forth. That urban environment holds a number of dangers; in fact, Washington, DC, has one of the highest crime rates in the United States. Still, that doesn't mean we should prohibit our students from visiting the city and taking advantage of its historical, political, and cultural attractions.

The Internet should be approached in the same manner. It contains in its seedier corners many things we just don't want our kids to see: foul language, racist and sexist speech, pornography, bomb-making instructions— and the list goes on. The Internet also has many potential dangers: sexual predators, kidnappers, and others with malicious or perverse intent who may want to bring harm to children. Just as we wouldn't leave our kids alone to explore Washington, DC, we shouldn't leave them alone to explore the Internet without supervision, guidance, and explicit age-appropriate instruction. It is critical to provide them with a clear road map and framework for staying safe and being responsible online and to check in on them regularly to make sure they are following through.

Eventually, all children will be exposed to content on the web, on social media, or via text that is problematic. What they do at that point depends on the education they have received and the habits they have developed. The time, energy, and effort you put in toward this end will pay great dividends in the lives of those you invest in. While it is not a lost cause to talk to adolescents about appropriate Internet use when they are seventeen or eighteen years old, so much should be done a lot earlier. We encourage introducing this topic as early as possible—and definitely before they start exploring the Internet alone. We find that between third and fifth grade, students begin to use computers and the Internet more often and for more varied purposes, and we have spoken with quite a few very young children who are vastly more proficient than their teachers and parents. You may not have taught them how to use a phone, tablet, or laptop, but they seem to have learned it *somewhere.*

Kids will undoubtedly become well versed with technology at an increasingly younger age as we continue to make progress in the 21st century. What is encouraging is that adults have a great deal of influence and can meaningfully shape behavior at these earlier ages. You may know from experience that this influence lessens as youth approach the teenage years, and so it is vital to step in as soon as possible. This simply means *now,* if it hasn't happened already. We believe that they'll not only hear you speak but actually listen to what you are saying.

In addition, a comprehensive strategy to prevent cyberbullying, or any other form of adolescent aggression, requires the cooperation of a number of important stakeholders. Parents, students, and other community leaders themselves all have an important part to play and none will be able to do it by themselves. We first, though, turn our attention to the critical role of educators. Their responsibilities include formally assessing the current level of cyberbullying, teaching and informing students and other staff, establishing clear rules, utilizing the expertise of students, maintaining a safe and respectful school climate, implementing and evaluating formal anti-cyberbullying programming, and educating parents.

> I've been bullied for 10 years of my life with a school transfer and a homeschooling program. I've lost everyone including myself. I guess some of you are thinking that I should be used to it by now, but the truth is that you never get used to it. I am told to kill myself on an everyday basis online and offline. Plus the pressures of school, and social hubs, and trying to be yourself in this obscure world, it makes life so hard. I am trying to stay strong and fight through this and now that I have friends for the first time, true friends, I don't feel as alone anymore knowing that there are people in my life who actually have my back.
>
> —Chris, 14, Florida

THE EDUCATOR'S ROLE IN PREVENTING CYBERBULLYING

Assessment

The first proactive step you can take is to assess the level of cyberbullying occurring in your school, and the impact it is having on the student body and educational environment. You may not have formal training as a researcher, and you may even cringe when presented with this suggestion, but it is vital to measure the extent of the problem. Determining the current state of online behaviors among your school population can best be accomplished through an anonymous survey of students and staff, and should be done on a regular basis so that trend data can be reviewed to determine whether certain problems are improving or worsening over time. There are a number of general concepts specific to cyberbullying that your assessment instrument should attempt to address (see Box 6.1).

Box 6.1

Sample Assessment Questions

- How big of a problem is cyberbullying among students at this school?
- Have you ever been the victim of cyberbullying?
- How did you cope?
- What aspects of your life did it affect?
- Who did you approach for help?
- Have you ever been afraid to come to school because of something somebody said to you online?
- Have you ever cyberbullied another student?
- If so, why did you do it?
- What should schools do to help prevent cyberbullying?
- What should students do to help prevent cyberbullying?

In your survey instrument, it is important that you clearly define what *cyberbullying* is to students so they understand the kinds of behaviors that you are referring to. For example, in our surveys, we inform respondents that "cyberbullying is when someone repeatedly harasses, mistreats, or makes fun of another person online or while using cell phones or other electronic devices." Just asking them if they have been cyberbullied, without clearly describing what it is, can lead to confusion among students and make interpreting the results difficult.

If the assessment is coordinated districtwide, numbers can be broken down by school, demographic characteristics (e.g., age, gender, race), region, special populations, and any number of other variables and even compared and contrasted with districtwide data on the general makeup and distribution of students. This analysis can be very instructive in identifying exactly which schools or groups require the most support, education, and resources to deal with cyberbullying. In addition, findings from your data collection can help imbue requests for additional assistance with credibility and legitimacy, since it illustrates exactly what is going on in *your* school. Those holding the purse strings often hesitate to open them up unless you can demonstrate a clear negative impact to your students and community; this will go a long way toward articulating a need.

To get you started, we have included a copy of the cyberbullying survey questions we constructed and used when collecting our data from middle schoolers in 2014 (Resource C). This instrument has been refined in ten formal studies over the last decade involving nearly 15,000 middle and high school students. Of course, feel free to modify it to suit your school population. All we ask is that you contact us to let us know that you are using it and for you to provide proper attribution. Additionally, your school may want to consider partnering with a local college or university to help with the collection, analysis, interpretation, and presentation of these data. University faculty generally have experience conducting assessments and can assist in all aspects of the project. You can also reach out to us if need be. If you want to do it on your own, though, know that outstanding and helpful resources are available online that provide clear guidance to administrators about conducting a meaningful and thorough assessment (we also discuss student surveying in more detail in our book *School Climate 2.0: Preventing Cyberbullying and Sexting One Classroom at a Time*).[2]

Educate Students and Staff

It almost goes without saying that schools must educate both students and staff about the harmful nature of online aggression. In fact, schools that receive discounts for their technology through the very popular e-Rate program are *required* to educate students about online safety and cyberbullying. In 2011, the US Congress amended the Children's Internet Protection Act (CIPA), adding the provision that schools must "provide for educating minors about appropriate online behavior, including interacting with other individuals on social networking websites and in chat rooms, and cyberbullying awareness and response."[3] School administrators, therefore, have an obligation to learn about these issues and pass this important information along to teachers and counselors. As just one example, a district could convene a staff meeting related to youth Internet safety and bring a specialist in to speak on the topic, provide actual case studies, summarize the latest research findings, and share proven prevention and response strategies that can be valuable in your respective schools.

After being so equipped, teachers and counselors need to pass this information on to students. Teachers should take time to discuss appropriate social media and electronic device use in their classrooms throughout the school year. While some may balk at this and argue that coverage of this material should be reserved for stand-alone digital literacy or online civility classes, many schools do not have room in their curriculum for such courses. And even if they do, we firmly believe that all teachers—regardless of their subject matter expertise—should broach the topic. You might feel completely unprepared to do so, but you must remember that this is their world nowadays, and therefore worth time, inquiry, and attention. We find that regardless of your level of comfort with technology, you just need to bring up a story, current event, headline, or new app or device and the students will take the topic and run with it. And that will give you the opportunity to learn from them, encouraging the right attitudes and actions while correcting the wrong ones.

Tell Relatable Stories

As you consider how to talk through these issues with youth, we'd like to suggest a particular tack to take. Interesting incidents often surface in the media about students from other schools who have misused their cell phones, laptops, webcams, or other devices and paid a significant price (on a social, reputational, financial, civil, or even criminal level). For example, we remember the story about the high school student who boasted on social media about the age-discrimination lawsuit her father recently won against the school. By mentioning the case publicly, however, the daughter unwittingly violated the confidentiality terms of the settlement, thereby costing her father $80,000.[4] Or the time a seventeen-year-old honor student and captain of the football team was suspended from school for seven weeks for a two-word tweet. Some friends sarcastically asked him if he had made out with a particular teacher and his response, "Yes, actually," got him kicked out of school.[5]

These stories (and others like them) should be shared with students to constantly remind them about the reality of fallout from unwise electronic communications. It is hard sometimes for now-focused adolescents to deeply consider the consequences of their actions, but regular reminders reinforced with concrete examples of cases where their peers got into trouble should help. When giving talks to youth, we share plenty of real-world examples of how teenagers and young adults inadvertently allow personal, private, and sometimes provocative information to be collected and oftentimes used against them through the connecting of their candid posts and messages online. We believe that teachers of every subject can assist in spreading this message by infusing important lessons about online safety and responsibility into a variety of classroom activities in similar ways to which youth can really relate and empathize with. If all teachers touch on the topic of online safety and responsibility, even briefly, then students will learn all adults in the school are serious about this issue. We've also provided some cyberbullying scenarios in Resource A of this book, as well as on our website (www .cyberbullying.us).

All of this said, we also advocate the sharing of inspiring stories of teens who are intentionally spearheading movements of kindness to change the climate at their school. One example is how Kevin Curwick used an anonymous

Twitter account to express compliments about others at his school (google "Nice it Forward" to learn about this). These true stories will hopefully get a student to think to themselves, "I like technology and I'm always on social media . . . and I want to do something to combat bullying and make a difference among my student body. And it's so simple, and I can do it 'behind the scenes' so no one knows it's me or gives me a hard time or even any attention about it. And slowly but surely, maybe the words I express will matter and somehow contribute to people less often being jerks here, and more often being cool to each other!" We are so big on this idea that we covered it extensively in our book for teens (*Words Wound: Delete Cyberbullying and Make Kindness Go Viral*) and have heard from a number of students at schools across the nation that they've been doing this on Twitter, Instagram, and with Facebook pages. As a final point, sharing these stories demonstrates that a lot of kids are doing the right thing with technology—and that the potential for good is so much stronger and larger than the potential for bad. You can find positive stories to share with students on www.WordsWound.org, www.Upworthy.com, or Huffington Post's Good News section, and many other pages.

Encourage Teens to Pause Before They Post

Another key point to convey is the importance of creating and maintaining a clean digital reputation. Adolescents (and adults!) seem to fly through Internet-based actions and interactions—doing so much in such a short amount of time (mere seconds, usually), because it is so easy to type out a message or upload a picture on an electronic device. Many times, we are multitasking with many windows and applications open—and we just don't stop to thoroughly give our attention to the content of our creation. We just post it—often based on emotion or a felt urgency to respond—and assume nothing bad will come from it. Generally speaking, nothing bad *does* come of it. But sometimes, we realize we should have been a little more careful. We recognize that if we could do it all over again, we would have slowed down and thought it through. Because now, the content is out there and it could lead to a misunderstanding or a misinterpretation or simply bad feelings. Or worse. Maybe it could lead to some serious drama or a lot of hate or vicious cyberbullying. And maybe only one person saw what we posted, or maybe it was viewable by many, including those whose friendships and relationships matter on a personal or professional level. And maybe one small mistake makes that teen's life a living hell.

Call Upon Outside Professionals for Help

We also recommend that schools supplement their own efforts to convey this guidance and wisdom with quality age-appropriate presentations to students by vetted and highly recommended external professionals in the field.

Sometimes youth discount the wisdom offered to them by adults they know well (familiarity breeds contempt!). However, hearing the same message from someone on the outside who regularly works with teens may be much more hard hitting and convincing. There are a number of "experts" who have surfaced in recent years to capitalize on the bullying prevention phenomenon, and this makes it hard to determine who to invite. This decision is critical, however, because a mediocre presentation by someone who doesn't know what he is talking about or has not studied exactly what to convey and how best to present it can do a great deal of damage at your school. As an example, an Illinois high school student recently committed suicide after viewing an anti-bullying video assembly presentation at school.[6] He was reportedly harassed frequently by members of the school's football team and became suicidal after viewing the film, which included stories and pictures of youth who had taken their life. His parents are now suing the school and the presenters of the assembly. Talk to some of your colleagues at schools in your area (or beyond) and find out if they have had someone speak to students or staff about these issues in a way that was compelling, relatable, and effective.

> Do your part to help create a generation of future-focused teens.

Overall, educators must do their part to help create a generation of future-focused teens, as it seems this is becoming increasingly unnatural across youth who are so used to immediate gratification of information, diversion, and entertainment with their devices. We need educators, parents, and other adults to take the time to connect with youth, invest in them, model appropriate attitudes and behaviors (walk the walk!), and basically be someone that can be admired and esteemed. Students reared in homes and taught in classrooms that engender responsibility, integrity, and respect will work extra hard to avoid putting anything online that will damage their relationship with the people they care about.[2] Even though parents and teachers can't directly supervise the behaviors of youth 24/7, a strong bond to a parent or teacher will result in adolescents who will consider the response of these caretakers before doing anything online or off that will disappoint them. In criminology, we call this *informal social control*—and it can be incredibly powerful in guiding and constraining human behavior.

Convey and Reinforce Clear Expectations Regarding the Use of Digital Devices

School officials have a responsibility to address the online misbehaviors of their students when they are made aware of them (in the next chapter we will outline several specific strategies and guidelines toward this end). It is important from a prevention perspective, however, to ensure appropriate responses are articulated in school policy and followed through on. Having a policy that states that "any student who posts inappropriate content online will be expelled" is unreasonable. Very rarely, if at all, will this type of response be warranted. When made aware of inappropriate content online that was created by a student, educators should inform the student's parents. Administrators may want to make an electronic or physical copy of the content in question so that if it is deleted or changed, there will be a version that has not been altered. They should also keep any evidence that clearly links the content to a particular student as the student may deny involvement. If the online content results in, or has the real potential to result in, a *substantial disruption of the school environment* (as discussed in Chapter 5), then school officials must take actions to maintain an appropriate school climate. This may be detention, suspension, loss of extracurricular privileges, or other school-based restrictions placed on the student(s) involved. Again, it is highly likely that the problems can be handled informally in the vast majority of cases without resorting to these options.

Schools should also take the time to regularly revisit their policies that govern all school-owned technology, as well as student technology brought to campus (cell phones, laptops, etc.). These policies should clearly state that students can be disciplined for (1) any misuse of school-owned technology, (2) misuse of student-owned technology while on school property or at school functions, and (3) any online behaviors that substantially disrupt the learning environment or infringe on the rights of other students or staff members. Consider convening a team that includes teachers, administrators, parents, and students to review the current policies and make suggestions for improvements. You should know by now that zero-tolerance policies are unlikely to be useful because each incident is different and therefore demands the discretion of informed educators to respond appropriately based on the particular facts of the incident.

In addition to a broad policy, it is also beneficial to post specific principles to guide the behavioral choices of students as they adopt and embrace increasing social media, gaming, and web use. When we were in seventh-grade shop class, we remember spending several weeks at the beginning of the school year studying the safety practices and procedures associated with the power tools before being allowed to use them. Before being permitted to drive a car a couple of years later, we were required to take a comprehensive driver's education course and pass both a written exam and a road test. Society recognizes that power tools and automobiles can be dangerous if used improperly or irresponsibly, so we take the time to educate students about the inherent dangers in their operation. The same approach should be taken before students are allowed to use electronic devices at school. Youth cannot be naturally expected to exercise complete wisdom in new situations. They need to be taught clearly and repeatedly how to use technology

BREAKOUT BOX

Deterring Teen Bullying: Dos and Don'ts

What can be done to prevent teens from engaging in bullying and cyberbullying? Here are some Dos and Don'ts:

DON'T increase formal sanctions. A number of people have been pushing for increased criminal penalties to be leveled against those who participate in bullying. Bills have been passed or proposed in most states even while legislation has been languishing at the federal level for almost five years. New laws that clarify and support the roles of educators in responding to bullying are helpful, but those that seek to further criminalize are not likely to be effective at preventing the behaviors. The problem is that most teens (and many adults for that matter) simply don't stop to consider the possible costs prior to participating in a behavior (especially possible criminal consequences).

DON'T enact zero-tolerance policies. Zero-tolerance policies require school administrators to apply a specific, generally severe sanction (often suspension or even expulsion) to a student who is found to have participated in some proscribed behavior. These policies were most often originally focused on curbing weapon and drug possession at school, but in recent years, they have been expanded to include other forms of violence and bullying. Don't get us wrong, zero tolerance is a fine idea in theory. Educators do want to clearly communicate that they have zero tolerance for weapons or drugs or bullying in their schools and that those who violate this standard are certain to be punished. The problem is that these policies, by definition, do not allow educators to use their discretion to handle situations outside the letter of the policy. Bullying is largely a relationship problem and educators, working with parents, need to use their knowledge of the situation to apply a reasonable sanction that is more uniquely designed to address the particular problem at hand. One-size-fits-all responses frequently fall short in issues involving teens.

DON'T utilize public shaming. Shame is a powerful force that can be used to encourage conformity and compliance. But when misused, it can result in the exact opposite response. Historically, societies have used shame to induce guilt among those who behave in ways that are counter to societal norms. Shaming can also have the unintended side effect of severing the emotional bond between the person(s) doing the shaming and the one being shamed. Even when done with the best intentions in mind, public shaming is too risky when applied to adolescents whose self-esteem is generally underdeveloped and fragile. The importance of the parent-child emotional bond cannot be overstressed, and permanent damage could be done. Praise publicly, punish privately.

DO give students a stake in conformity. The threat of punishment only works if someone has something of value in their life that they would put at risk of losing if punished. For instance, earning a bad grade only hurts if a student cares about good grades or is aiming for college or a scholarship. After-school detention is most powerful when a student has something else they really like to do after school that they would miss out on (such as an extracurricular activity). As Bob Dylan famously sang, "when you ain't got nothing, you got nothing to lose." The best thing we can do for students to deter them from mistreating others is to get them involved in prosocial activities that they really enjoy so that the threat of school sanction or parental punishment holds weight.

DO connect and interact. Another reason many people refrain from misbehavior is because they don't want to disappoint the people in their lives that they care about. Prevention is all about relationships. Even though many teens are not deterred by the threat of formal punishment, they *are* dissuaded from participation in behaviors that they know their friends, parents, or other valued adults would frown upon. When teens are emotionally attached or socially bonded to others, they internalize their norms and values and do not want to disappoint them by behaving in a way that is contradictory to those principles.

DO develop a positive school climate. A positive school climate is one that stimulates and encourages respect, cooperation, trust, and a shared responsibility for the educational goals that exist there. Educators, students, and everyone connected to the school take ownership of the mission of the school and work together toward a shared vision. If a climate like this is established, everything else seems to fall into place. Research consistently demonstrates that the more positive the climate of the school is, the fewer problems there are with bullying (and cyberbullying). A sense of collective concern is cultivated where students just seem to look out for each other more and believe that the adults in the school are genuinely there to help.

in responsible ways. Just as there are rules for using power equipment or cars, there should also be clear rules about what is expected when interacting online. As long as students know the rules, they cannot plead ignorance if they are caught violating them. They should also know the potential consequences for any wrongdoing. (This is discussed in more detail in the Chapter 7).

In Box 6.2, we list several specific rules that educators might consider posting near the workstations in a computer lab or classroom. At the bottom of the list, we also recommend specifying certain websites and software applications that are forbidden at school.

Box 6.2

Rules for School-Owned Technology Use by Students

I understand that utilizing school-owned devices is a privilege that is subject to the following rules:

1. I am allowed to use these devices for approved, educational purposes only.

2. I will only play games authorized by my teacher.

3. I will not alter device settings or damage any hardware.

4. I agree never to write or post anything online that I would not want my teacher or parents to see.

5. I will not use any device to bring harm to anyone else.

6. I will not type profanity or otherwise offensive language.

7. If I receive harassing messages or accidentally view any offensive or inappropriate content, I will report it to my teacher immediately.

8. I will use the Internet to search only areas appropriate to the school curriculum.

9. I agree not to download and install apps, software, shareware, freeware, or other files without obtaining permission from my teacher.

10. I will only save material in my personal folder appropriate for educational use.

11. I will only alter my own files and documents.

12. I will not plagiarize from the Internet (copy someone else's information and pass it off as my own).

13. If I ever feel uncomfortable about an experience online, I will immediately tell my teacher. I understand that my teacher is willing to help me and will not punish me as long as these rules are followed.

14. I will not agree to meet with anyone I have met online without adult approval. If anyone wants to meet with me and makes me uncomfortable, I will bring it to the attention of an adult I trust.

15. I will not share any of my passwords (my school network account, my e-mail account, my social media account, etc.) with anyone else other than an adult I trust.

16. I will not use a proxy to attempt to access websites or other forms of Internet content and communications technology that have been blocked from my school network. I will also report any instances of other kids trying to do so.

17. I am prepared to be held accountable for my actions and for the loss of school-owned device privileges if these policies are violated.

List of prohibited websites, apps, and software:

In addition to classroom computer use, students need to know which (if any) of their personally owned electronic devices are allowed on campus or in class—and when and how they are able to use them. In fact, this is a much larger issue than specifying rules with school-owned technology because they have everything they need on their smartphones. And there is little you can do to truly stop them unless you can get them on board with your policies.

According to data from the Pew Internet and American Life Project, 24 percent of teens in the United States say that they attend schools that are completely prohibitive—and forbid having a cell phone at all times.[7] Nearly two-thirds (62 percent) of teens say they go to schools that allow them to have a phone on campus but not in class. Finally, 12 percent of teens go to schools which are completely permissive—and allow them to have a phone at all times (but of course have rules in place for their misuse). These results are from data collected in 2009 (but the most recent available), so it is very likely that now, over five years later, even more schools have a more liberal policy when it comes to allowing students to use their devices in the classroom. In fact, even back then over half (58 percent) of teens who went to schools that prohibited all phones still said that they had sent texts during class.[7] The point is that we believe you are fighting a losing battle if you continue to try to clamp down on the presence and use of phones. It is going to happen and you might as well get used to it rather than spend hours each day trying to enforce prohibitions, confiscate phones and discipline violators, and deal with angry parents who need to get in touch with their child at times via their devices. A better approach is to have clearly specified guidelines for when and where the devices are allowed and what will happen if a student is caught using a device at a prohibited time or place.

We would also like to emphasize here that when portable electronic devices are confiscated, educators should resist searching their contents, even when there is a clear violation of school policy. This is best left either to parents or to law enforcement, who know when the circumstances call for such an intrusion of privacy. While school officials likely do have the authority to conduct a limited search for the purposes of obtaining known evidence of a violation of school policy, the legal issues are complicated and even well-meaning administrators can find themselves on the wrong side of the often fuzzy line (more on this in Chapter 7).

Utilize the Expertise of Students Through Peer Mentoring

> Growing up I would always talk to my older brother about problems that I didn't feel comfortable talking to my mom about, so I can understand the theory behind peer mentoring. Most kids will feel more comfortable talking to an older teen because they feel that person has been through the same thing or that they won't get in trouble for what might've happened.
>
> —Ryan, unknown US location

Peer mentoring generally involves educators training student leaders to advise and counsel students about issues affecting them, such as bullying and cyberbullying. Mentors can also be utilized to help other students appreciate the responsibilities associated with the misuse of electronic devices, social media, gaming networks, and the Internet in general. Overall, the goal is to encourage teens to take responsibility for the problem and to work together in coming up with a solution. It also seeks to foster respect and acceptance of others—no matter what—and to get kids to see how their actions affect others and how they can purposefully choose behaviors that promote positive peer relations.

> I have started to talk to others who have had a similar experience and try and help them because they are going through the same thing that I went through and it helps to talk to people who understand. I tell them to be brave and not to worry because everything will be OK.
>
> —Sam, England

Peer mentoring has been fruitful in reducing traditional bullying and interpersonal conflict within schools[8] and, as such, should be considered in a comprehensive approach to preventing cyberbullying as well. Accordingly, newer cohorts of students can learn from the wisdom of others who have already had some of these experiences and have figured out effective ways to deal with them. This wisdom may sink in more quickly and deeply since it comes from peers rather than adults, as kids have the tendency to tune out adults when being taught certain life lessons. As a mom from California told us, "Parents and teachers can get up and preach, but if they hear it from another kid, they will remember it." On a larger scale, these efforts can significantly and positively affect the social climate within the school community, benefitting youth and their families, teachers and staff, and the community as a whole.[9] We cannot more strongly emphasize the need to encourage teens themselves to rise up and become powerful catalysts for change.

The power of peer relationships can be exploited in a number of useful ways. For example, high school leaders could talk to other students in the cafeteria during lunch about these issues. A few high school students could also organize a presentation for small classroom–size groups (20–30 students). One-on-one sessions might even be held in which a trained student meets with a cyberbullying victim to offer support and help. Finally, skits can be presented in auditoriums or cafeterias by high school students for assemblies of their peers or of younger students in nearby middle or elementary schools. All of these interactions can consist of one or more activities. Box 6.3 lists several messages that can be communicated to the school community using trained student mentors. Over time, additional formal and informal lessons—as well as continued interaction between the mentors and mentees—can occur. And eventually the mentee can become the mentor and pass valuable information on to the next generation. The more students who become involved in mentoring, the more effective it may be at decreasing problem behaviors and setting the tone for a student body that chooses to engage with technology in respectful and responsible ways.

Mentor Messages

Schools can utilize student leaders to convey a number of important messages of Internet safety to others, including the following:

- Reiterating that they are not alone in experiencing victimization
- Encouraging them to speak up and not remain silent when confronted with cyberbullying
- Sharing one or more highly relatable vignettes or stories about cyberbullying
- Discussing the consequences (legal, social, and professional) of sending or posting hurtful or sexually explicit images online
- Describing positive ways in which conflict between peers can be deescalated or resolved
- Using role-playing examples to get students thinking about the various ways to address a cyberbullying situation
- Providing an opportunity to discuss and answer any questions, clarify any confusion, and reinforce how to deal with online problems and issues

Maintain a Safe and Respectful School Climate

School climate can be defined as the "sum of the values, cultures, safety practices, and organizational structures within a school that cause it to function and react in particular ways."[10] Overall, it is critical for educators to develop and promote a safe and respectful school climate, which will go a long way in reducing the frequency of many problematic behaviors at school, including bullying and harassment. In this setting, educators should demonstrate emotional support, a warm and caring atmosphere, a strong focus on academics and learning, and a fostering of healthy self-esteem.

In our research, we found that students who experienced cyberbullying (both those who were victims and those who admitted to cyberbullying others) perceived a poorer climate or culture at their school than those who had not experienced cyberbullying. Specifically, we asked students how much they agreed with the following statements:

- I feel safe at my school.
- I feel that teachers at my school care about me.
- I feel that teachers at my school really try to help me succeed.
- I feel that students at my school trust and respect the teachers.
- I feel that teachers at my school are fair to all students.
- I feel that teachers at my school take bullying very seriously.

Students responded to each of these questions using a four-point scale ranging from "strongly disagree" (0) to "strongly agree" (3). Scores from the six questions were averaged for each student and each school was given an average score based on responses from a random sample of students in that school. The analysis resulted in school climate scores ranging from 1.41 to 2.16, with higher numbers indicating a better overall climate. Then three groups were created by looking at natural breaks that included roughly one-third of the schools so that average climate scores for each group were low (1.55), medium (1.71), and high (1.90). Those who admitted to cyberbullying others or who were the target of cyberbullying were less likely to agree with those statements. As illustrated in Chart 6.1, schools that were rated by students to have relatively low school climate had more reports of cyberbullying than those rated as medium or high.

It is important to acknowledge the preliminary nature of this research. We were only able to include thirty-three schools from one school district, though we do want to encourage others to replicate this work with larger and more diverse samples. Ideally, scores of schools from around the United States (and abroad!) would be sampled and analyzed to obtain a more comprehensive picture of the nature of the relationship between climate and online behaviors. Moreover, while we don't know whether a poor school climate *caused* cyberbullying behaviors (or was the result of them), we do know that the variables are linked.

There are a number of specific steps that schools can take to help promote a quality climate (for a comprehensive discussion of these issues, see our book *School Climate 2.0: Preventing Cyberbullying and Sexting One Classroom at a Time*).[2] Along these lines, it's crucial that educators promote bonding among students (and between students and adults at the school), as this is related to personal, emotional, behavioral, and scholastic success. Toward this end, we often champion what can be termed a *respect policy* or honor code when working with schools. An example, one with which we are familiar, reads as follows:

Respect is the cornerstone of our relationships with each other. We are committed to respecting the dignity and worth of each individual at North High School and strive never to degrade or diminish any member of our school community by our conduct or attitudes. We benefit from each other. Our diversity makes us strong.[11]

The goal of such a statement is to specify clearly to students and staff alike that all members of the school community are expected to respect each other and that such respect should govern all interpersonal interactions and attitudes among students, faculty, and staff on campus (and hopefully off campus as well). Respect policies serve as reference points against which every questionable thought, word, and deed can be measured and judged. Every instance of harm between individuals lacks a measure of respect for the victim, including those that occur through the use of electronic devices.

Apart from their inclusion in policy manuals, respect policies should be disseminated within school materials to both students and parents and posted

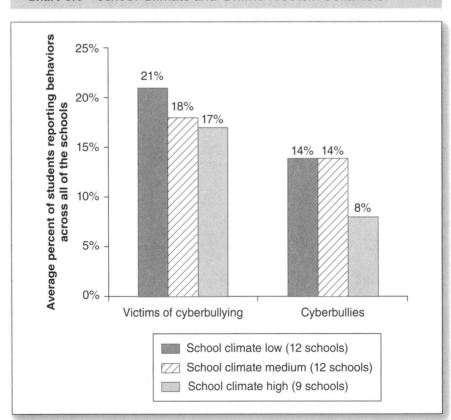

Chart 6.1   School Climate and Online Problem Behaviors

Note: Low, medium, and high school climate scores are only relative to this particular sample. On a scale that ranges from 0–3, the average score for each category was: low (1.55), medium (1.71), and high (1.90).

visibly in hallways and classrooms. While one might wish that students would automatically and naturally treat each other (and the adults in their lives) with respect, we know that in reality this does not always happen. As such, the respect policy reminds them of a standard that has been set and will be enforced.

It is also crucial that the school seeks to create and promote an environment where certain behaviors or language simply is not tolerated—by students and staff. In a school with a positive climate, students know what is appropriate and what is not. In these schools, there are a number of behaviors that the community as a whole would agree are simply "not cool." It isn't cool to bring a weapon to school. It isn't cool to get up in the middle of class and walk out of the classroom. It isn't cool to assault a teacher physically. It isn't cool to use racial slurs. Certain behaviors are simply not acceptable in the eyes of both adults and youth.

We hope that with education and effort, cyberbullying will someday be deemed "not cool." This ideal might be considered by some as wishful thinking, but we believe it is worth pursuing. All forms of bullying, no matter how minor, need to be condemned—with the responsible parties disciplined. If teachers deliberately ignore minor (or even serious) bullying because they just don't want to deal with it, what message does that send to the students? Kids need to see that their teachers, counselors, and administrators take these behaviors seriously.

Install Monitoring and Filtering Software

CIPA, discussed above, requires that public schools (and libraries) install filtering software on computers that have access to the Internet if they want to remain eligible for federal funding assistance. Filtering software blocks Internet content that is deemed inappropriate for children (e.g., violent or pornographic material). This is typically done in two ways: site blocking and content monitoring.

Site-blocking filters typically prohibit computer users from accessing sites designated as inappropriate (those on a "black list"). Alternatively, some site-blocking filters only allow users to access sites that have been preapproved (those on a "white list"). Ideally, this includes certain social media and gaming environments as well, apart from peer-to-peer (P2P) applications that are undesirable (such as those used for the piracy of books, software, music, and movies).

Content monitoring, on the other hand, generally uses a key word-blocking approach. Here, data are analyzed against a library of user-defined words and phrases deemed unsuitable. The software then blocks that data regardless of the software (or medium) through which it comes. In addition, most network-level software at schools allow IT administrators to block specific categories of problematic sites (such as those that revolve around alcohol and tobacco, dating and personals, guns, hatred, etc.). Overall, most schools employ an approach that combines site blocking and content monitoring, which does a fairly good job in protecting most students. Nevertheless, for some students it is still relatively easy to access these sites and programs from school by intentionally circumventing such controls.

Hundreds of constantly updated websites called *proxies* redirect individuals to sites that have been "blacklisted," or prohibited by hardware or software rules at school. Basically, adolescents can access Facebook (for example) on a school device with their web browser—even if it is blocked by the school network administrators—by first accessing another website (such as www.hidemyass.com), inputting "www.facebook.com" into a web page form field, and then being rerouted to that site (thereby circumventing a direct connection to Facebook and bypassing the block or filter). The proxy serves as an intermediary site (that is not prohibited) from which a user can access a prohibited site because the school network has allowed a connection to the proxy site (It is virtually impossible to block all of these types of sites!). Finally, tweaked portable web browsers found on the Internet can be run off of a pocket USB drive (also known as a flash, thumb, or key drive) that a student brings to school and plugs into the school computer. Those programs use a proxy site to reroute the student's connection and gain access to any site, again bypassing the blocks that are in place.

We can all agree that the Internet is an amazing instructional tool but that its content varies in quality and appropriateness. While schools are able to evaluate text books and library books carefully before approving them for school use, this remains a difficult task when dealing with online material. Filtering and blocking software is a necessary, but regrettably a largely insufficient method of preventing students from accessing inappropriate content from school. The discussion of proxies is becoming less and less relevant because of the ubiquity of smartphones among teens, which use a cellular connection to access the Internet instead of the school network (which is restricted) means students pretty much have complete access to whatever they want. A more proactive approach is therefore required, whereby students come to recognize that it is in their best interest to avoid getting involved in inappropriate online activities. In keeping with this philosophy, Nancy Willard, the director of Embrace Civility in the Digital Age, aptly points out, "By developing a comprehensive approach to address such concerns, schools can help young people develop effective filtering and blocking systems that will reside in the hardware that sits upon their shoulders."[12]

> Students come to recognize that it is in their best interest to avoid getting involved in inappropriate online activities.

Implement and Evaluate Formal Anti-Bullying Programming

School officials should also actively work to develop and implement an anti-bullying curriculum that includes training modules on online aggression. Before implementation, it may once again be helpful to partner with researchers from a nearby university so that a scientific evaluation of the programming can occur to determine its worth. Otherwise, the rest of us never find out what works and what doesn't, and educators keep having to reinvent the wheel and trying new things. To be sure, very little evaluation research has been done in this area in order to inform the masses. A study published in 2014 involving a national sample of 3,391 youth ages five to seventeen from 2011 did identify that younger children (ages 5–9) exposed to higher-quality bullying prevention education had lower levels of bullying offending and victimization.[13] However, it did not find reduced offending and victimization among those ages ten to seventeen even with higher-quality anti-bullying programming.

Other recent high profile reviews of bullying initiatives in schools came to the conclusion that many of the efforts failed to significantly reduce bullying.[14] The problem with these analyses is that they did not differentiate between the quality of the programs. For example, a study published in 2013 controversially concluded that "students attending schools in which bullying prevention programs are implemented are more likely to have experienced peer victimization, compared to those attending schools without bullying prevention."[15] While this might be an accurate statement, it belies the fact that the "bullying prevention program" measure was extremely unsophisticated (it was one question asked to the school administrator: "Does your school have a bullying prevention program?"). We know that not all programs are created equal. The previously mentioned 2014 study did find that older youth did make more disclosures to adults about victimization following good-quality programming, perhaps demonstrating some value in the messages they received (even if actual offending and victimization did not decrease).[13] The study also identified that effective programs need to comprise multiple presentations, information to send home for parents and youth, and opportunities for youth to practice what they've learned. The point is, educators should consider these findings and review all available evidence before choosing and implementing an anti-bullying program.

The bottom line is that little is currently known about what curriculum works best to educate youth about cyberbullying and online safety. Even less is known about what works in dealing with cyberbullying. At this stage, it is important to try a variety of different approaches, starting with those that have demonstrated *at least some success* at preventing traditional bullying (e.g., the Olweus Bullying Prevention Program).[16] This curriculum can be supplemented with netiquette lessons covering the unique features of online communication and responsibility, and even resources and activities found on various respected online safety websites (such as those available at www .cyberbullying.us/resources). While a detailed review of the literature concerning the effectiveness of various programs is beyond the scope of this book, below we offer a couple of avenues to explore further.

For starters, emerging evidence points to the effectiveness of social-emotional learning curricula, such as Committee for Children's "Steps to Respect" and "Second Step" in preventing bullying. In brief, these programs teach "children skills for coping with bullying, including recognizing bullying, using assertive behaviors to respond to bullying, and reporting bullying to adults."[17] University of Illinois psychologist Dorothy Espelage has been evaluating the effects of socioemotional learning programs in schools for several years. Initial results of this research show strong results with respect to reducing physical aggression, with less support for reductions in verbal or relational aggression.[18]

In addition, many schools are tackling bullying and other problematic behaviors in their schools using the Positive Behavioral Interventions and Supports (PBIS) framework.[19] PBIS isn't a curriculum per se, but rather a three-tiered system designed to help educators approach problem behaviors from the perspective of teaching, modeling, rewarding, and promoting positive behaviors instead of focusing on restrictions, discipline, and punishment. According to its website, PBIS "guides selection, integration, and implementation of the best evidence-based academic and behavioral practices for improving important academic and behavior outcomes for all students."[20] PBIS principles help educators work toward developing a positive school climate and can be customized and integrated into just about any school.

As a final suggestion, we encourage you to check out our book for teens titled *Words Wound: Delete Cyberbullying and Make Kindness Go Viral*.[21] We wrote this book to give teens a roadmap that they could use to be a part of the solution to cyberbullying. Not only does the book provide practical suggestions for those who are involved in cyberbullying (as a target, aggressor, or witness), it also discusses strategies modeled off of the experiences of teens who have used technology to make kindness and compassion go viral in their schools and communities. We also wrote the accompanying *A Leader's Guide to Words Wound*,[22] which is free to download (just visit www.wordswound.org), that you can use to teach these concepts in a classroom or other small group setting. In addition, student leaders could use this guide to inform younger students about the importance of using technology safely and responsibly.

Whatever approach you decide to take, make sure you conduct a formal and systematic evaluation of its merits so that you can tell whether it mattered and so that others can learn from your experience. A thoughtful and well-designed evaluation is crucial for demonstrating value, securing funding for more anti-bullying initiatives, and for convincing others of the utility of the program—especially given the fiscal and organizational constraints currently facing most schools and districts. Remember that a program is only as good as the quality of its evaluation.

Be a Trustee

Schools should designate one or more staff members to serve as *trustees*. These point persons—teachers, guidance counselors, or other staff members who work directly with students—must be specifically trained to deal with online aggression and be staff members whom students feel comfortable approaching for help. We recommend that each trustee post a sign on his or her door (such as the sample provided in Resource F) indicating to students that this staff member has been specially taught how best to help them with any problems related to online aggression. That way, students know who really understands the phenomenon on their campus and where they can turn for assistance. We find that so many teens are surveying the landscape of adults in their life and looking to identify someone who will not freak out on them but instead be calm, reasonable, receptive, and understanding. They do want to get help, and they do want their problem to go away. But a number choose to suffer in silence instead of going to the wrong adult who may be clueless and make their situation so much worse. This must not happen any longer, because adults are ideally positioned to assist youth and bring resolution to the problem! And so we must encourage more kids to reach out and give the adults in their life a chance to help them.

You (yes, you!) can and should become a trustee. Ask yourself, "If I were in their shoes, would I feel comfortable coming and talking to a person like me?" Better yet, specifically ask your students if they have experienced cyberbullying and whether they would be comfortable talking about it with you (or another adult). Do what it takes so that they know you are available for them and that you will work with them to improve the situation. Become someone they can trust with these types of issues. If you do, word will spread quickly around the student body that you can be trusted and that you provide a safe place to discuss and work through difficult matters. And in time, you will honestly save lives.

Educate Parents

Apart from connecting with and instructing students, educators have a unique platform from which to reach the parents of their students about

BREAKOUT BOX

Should Schools Monitor Students' Social Media Accounts?

There has been much discussion over the last few years about whether it is appropriate for schools to actively monitor the social media activities of students. Interest in this issue was sparked in September of 2013 when it was revealed that Glendale (California) Unified School District contracted with Geo Listening (a Hermosa Beach, California-based tech company founded in January of 2013) to monitor and keep track of the various things their student body says, posts, shares, and does online (at a cost of $40,500 for the school year). The company reportedly looks for anything online that could threaten the safety and well-being of students in the district, including cyberbullying and threats of self-harm. These could be posts that are initiated from school or not; using school-owned technology or not. The technology also allows for the flagging and reporting of drug use or class-cutting—or really anything publicly posted by a student that could be viewed as problematic to the school. Should schools be in the business of actively monitoring what their students are saying online?

Some argue that schools monitoring social media amounts to a violation of a student's privacy. We are not particularly convinced of that. Most students we speak with are savvy enough to realize that what they post in public spaces online is open for anyone to see. And they know that schools are looking. Counselors, principals, and school resource officers have been looking for years. The only thing new about this is that a school is contracting with a third party to do the looking. Moreover, most students say that they have their social media accounts (e.g., Facebook, Instagram, Twitter) set to private.[23] Indeed, in our early research into the social media behaviors of students on MySpace, we found that in 2006 less than 40 percent of students had set their profiles to private. By 2009, 85 percent of the active users had their profiles restricted.[24] And this was not a survey of students where we asked them to report what they were doing. We randomly selected profiles to carefully review to see how much information was publicly visible. So very early on—over four years ago—students recognized the need to avoid having their profiles open for the whole world to see. Further, more and more teens are moving to ephemeral communication apps like those referred to earlier in this book (e.g., Snapchat) that make it more difficult to watch over and track what they are saying.

From our perspective, schools (along with parents, of course) have an obligation to keep track of what students are doing online. We don't feel, however, that schools should need to go on fishing expeditions where they scour the web and social media for inappropriate behaviors. Schools should work to develop a culture where everyone looks out for everyone else and if something of concern arises, someone will step up and take appropriate action. Most of the time, when there is a threat to cause harm—either to one's self or others—someone sees or hears about it. What do they do at that moment? Are they empowered to take action themselves? Do students feel comfortable talking with an adult at school about what they witnessed or heard about? Do they feel that telling an adult at school or at home would resolve the situation? There is also the added benefit in that by encouraging and empowering students to come forward with concerns, schools have many more people on the lookout for trouble and are able to access much more potentially problematic information since even private profiles (not accessible to a 3rd party monitoring company) are visible to at least some students.

Consider this contradiction: When you ask a student what they should do if they are being cyberbullied or if they see it happen, more often than not they will respond with "tell an adult." Yet, when you ask them if telling an adult will help, they often say no! According to the Youth Voice Project, a survey of nearly 12,000 students from twelve different US states conducted by Stan Davis and Charisse Nixon, only about one-third of the students who were significantly impacted by bullying said that telling an adult made things better (29 percent said it made things worse!).[25] So perhaps the main problem isn't so much that schools need to do a better job of paying attention to what is going on online, but instead they need to do a better job thinking about how best to respond. If schools are able to respond to bullying and cyberbullying in a way that quickly stops the harassment without further harming or humiliating any of the parties involved, then students will feel much more comfortable going to them for help when problems arise in the future. And the word will spread, encouraging others to also do so. As we've shared, many are afraid that the school, or their parents, will just make things worse.

these important issues. As such, it is important for you to pass along information to parents regarding their children's use of electronic devices. In this way, you are partnering with them in promoting positive online experiences and behaviors among their kids.

By way of example, Montgomery County (Maryland) Superintendent Joshua Starr released an open letter to all parents in the district after receiving threats and other obscene messages through his Twitter account in December of 2013. The letter encouraged parents to take an active role in educating their children about the responsible use of technology: "I don't have all the answers in my home or in our schools. But I know it takes deliberate and tough conversations within families and communities to help kids understand how to use technology and social media appropriately."[26] Similarly, several principals in Chicago-area schools sent letters home to parents in March of 2014, warning them about an emerging cell phone application that was creating all sorts of problems in the schools (Yik Yak). Barry Rodgers of Lake Forest High School (Illinois) was one of the principals who communicated with parents: "A significant way that we can deal with the app is to promote digital citizenship at home and at school. This is a learning opportunity for students on how their behavior and the choices that they make can impact others and their own future in a digital world."[27] This is something you can easily do to demonstrate to parents that this is a priority area for the school, and to enlist their help (see Box 6.4 for a template).

An electronic newsletter can also be distributed to parents on a regular basis, updating them on new developments in the way kids are using and abusing technology. For example, the newsletter might make parents aware of new websites that teens are frequenting or innovative ways that youth are circumventing Internet safeguards on home computers. In addition, we recommend sponsoring regular community events to discuss issues related to Internet safety and cyberbullying. While it is tricky sometimes to get parents to attend these events, you must figure out a creative way to encourage or even mandate their attendance. Getting them on board to assist you on the front lines of this problem by learning about and then doing *their* part to educate and discipline will preempt many issues from surfacing in the first place. Through these initiatives, school personnel and parents can work together in addressing the inappropriate behaviors that will inevitably arise. After reading this book, you (we mean it!) should consider giving a presentation to parents after school or at a PTA meeting (or even online, through a Google+ Hangout or group Skype session). You are now much better informed than the majority of adults out there, and your efforts to educate those around you can be so incredibly valuable.

Box 6.4

Sample Letter From School to Parents

Dear Parents:

We wanted to send this brief letter home to let you know about some of the activities that students are involved in when using computers, cell phones, and other electronic devices. As you may have heard, many adolescents have reported experiencing "cyberbullying." Cyberbullying is when students use computers, cell phones, or other electronic devices to repeatedly harass or mistreat another person.

We have no reason to believe that this is a greater problem in our district than others, and we want to keep it that way. We are taking a number of important steps to help prevent cyberbullying, including educating the school community about its harmful nature. We have also recently updated our district policy and Student Handbook to reflect the changing nature of adolescent aggression. We have informed students and are now letting you know that we will discipline any cyberbullying that negatively affects the school environment or infringes upon the rights of others.

We encourage you to talk with your children about these issues. It is also important that you monitor their behavior to make sure they are responsibly using computers and cell phones. We are doing our part at school and trust that you will do your part at home so that we can jointly reduce the likelihood that cyberbullying will become a problem in our community.

Feel free to contact us if you have any questions or concerns.

Sincerely,

As a final point (and as alluded to earlier), an increasing amount of information is available across the Internet about cyberbullying. On our website (www.cyberbullying.us), we provide a large number of free, regularly updated downloadable resources that you can distribute in electronic or hard-copy format to fellow administrators, staff, teachers, counselors, parents, and youth as needed. There are no restrictions on their dissemination, and we are frequently creating and uploading new resources as we study the problem and work with those affected. For quick reference, some are included in Resources Section of this book; however, they are cleanly formatted and suitable for distribution as PDF files on our website (and if you obtain them from—or link to them at—our website, you will always have the latest version!). We also have a very active blog in which we dig deep into the most relevant issues that teens, parents, educators, and other youth-serving professionals have to face in this area. We now explore more specific and individualized strategies for parents to assist in a coordinated community approach to preventing cyberbullying.

> This school is an elementary school (K–5), so our prevention has been educating the parents about cyberbullying and encouraging them to be involved with their child's web page access and content. We have also asked students to come forward if they experience cyberbullying that would have an impact on the school community.
>
> —Principal, Florida

THE PARENT'S ROLE IN PREVENTING CYBERBULLYING

The following anecdote underscores the fact that parents cannot protect their children from everything wrong, bad, or evil in this world. However, there is much that they *can* do. They can engage their kids in a dialogue about the relevant issues, venture online with them, and informally or formally monitor their electronic activities. Cumulatively, these efforts should demonstrate to youth that the adults in their life actively care about their online safety.

> It was an argument with my two best friends. I had fallen out with both of them for many reasons. Since we had been best mates, I put up with lots of rubbish. I was sick of it and wanted to get out of the pain and trouble I had been through. So once I had got out of it I thought I would be free. But no. They continued to harass me. Via e-mail, MSN, text messages. Made me feel very lonely and depressed. They had turned everyone against me you see. So I got into depression and it was absolutely horrid. My parents were extremely supportive and helpful, I can't thank them enough. But no matter how great they can be, there is always the fact that you're on your own in the rest of the world—that is saddening.
>
> —Mallory, 15, UK

Communication Is Key

Above and beyond everything else, it is important for parents to develop an open dialogue with their children so they feel comfortable approaching them if confronted with an unpleasant online experience. It's often difficult to talk about these issues at first, but it is essential. As discussed earlier, our research suggests that only a minority of teens who experience cyberbullying tell their parents (or other adults). Much of this lack of openness relates to the youth's perception that they will be blamed or will lose their device, access to social media, or gaming privileges. Parents need to convey to their kids that they will patiently listen to their problem or situation and respond in a nonjudgmental and responsible manner. That is essential in cultivating and preserving an open line of communication.

> Bullying boils down to communication. Teach your kids to communicate with you about the small stuff and they'll tell you about the big stuff too.
>
> —Lydia, mother, Minnesota

Research in this area has consistently identified the utility of ongoing discussions by parents, caregivers, or teachers with youth about their online interactions and activities.[28] Essentially, there must exist a crystal-clear understanding about what is appropriate and what is not with respect to online activities. Toward that end, we have created a "Technology Use Contract," which can be used as is or as a template to create your own custom contract (Resource B). Its purpose is to promote a trusting relationship between parents and children when it comes to the latter's use of cell phones, electronic devices, and the Internet. Both parties agree to abide by certain mutually acceptable rules of engagement and indicate their acceptance and understanding of those rules with their signatures at the bottom of the form. To pique their conscience and jog the child's memory of this pledged commitment, we recommend that this contract be posted in a highly visible place. Just as in the "Rules for School-Owned Technology Use by Students" detailed on page 154, a parent should also specify which sites, games, apps, and networks are allowed (and, by extension, those that are not). The point to emphasize is that having Internet access or a cell phone is a privilege (and not a right!) that can be revoked for misbehavior.

That said, it is also important for parents to realize that they need to give their kids some space with respect to their communications with others. Parents should resist constantly hovering over their child when that child is texting friends and should not go through the phone's text message archives or camera roll when it is unattended (unless there is a serious cause for concern).

Instead, they should focus on developing a trusting relationship with their children and only invade privacy as a last resort.

Go Online

We also believe it is crucial that parents go online with their children. Many adults are intimidated by certain new technologies or apps, which is completely understandable given that they have not grown up with these devices like adolescents today have. Nonetheless, this should not prevent parents from exploring the mediums and venues through which youth communicate and interact in cyberspace. In fact, parents who are unfamiliar with online activities can enlist the assistance of their children in getting acclimated with them. Parents should ask their children to show them where they go online and why they like certain sites or apps. Some youth will be immediately open to this while others may resist. Parents should be patient and slowly work their way into the socially networked lives of their children. It may take time, but it will pay dividends down the road.

Once online with their kids, parents can casually inquire further about the technologies: What do you love about this app? What makes it more (or less) popular than other apps? Can everyone see the messages you send or post? Do you really "know" everyone with whom you are communicating? What sort of pictures or video have you posted online? Parents must remember to keep an open mind and resist knee-jerk reactions of a condemning or criticizing nature. Once parents have a trusting relationship with their children, they will be able to influence their Internet behaviors accordingly.

Box 6.5 provides several additional questions to help get the proverbial ball rolling. Expressing interest in their cyberspace experiences without criticizing or condemning their activities online paves the way for a long-term positive relationship with the adolescents in your life. Responses to these questions should serve to bring about deeper discussion about issues

---

Box 6.5

Questions to Ask Youth

General Tech Use

- What are a couple of sites that you and your friends go on most often?
- Why do you like them so much? How do they make your life better?
- What are the most popular sites used by kids younger than you?

- What are the most popular sites used by kids older than you?
- Are you ever contacted by someone online that you don't know? If yes, what did they want? What did you do? How did you respond?
- Have you ever received a text message from someone that made you upset? How did you respond?
- Do random people ever contact you? Are they strangers? People from school? Do you ever have to deal with creepers?
- How do you keep yourself safe online?
- Do you get concerned that people will read what others have written about you online that is not true but think it's true?

Cyberbullying

- Do you ever argue or post hurtful updates on your Instagram, Facebook, Twitter, or other social media site? Why?
- Have you ever gone off on someone online and posted something you probably shouldn't have?
- Have you ever had to delete a post or comment on your page that was written by someone else?
- Does cyberbullying happen a lot? Would you feel comfortable telling me if you were being cyberbullied?
- Do you think your school takes cyberbullying seriously? Have you ever had to contact a teacher or someone else at school because of a cyber threat? If so, did they do something about it and did it help?
- Does your school have a way to anonymously report bullying and cyberbullying?
- Do you feel like your friends would be supportive of you if you told them you were being cyberbullied?
- Do you ever get verbally attacked during online games? Have you ever had to leave an online game because someone was bothering you online?
- Have rumors ever started about you in school, based on something said online?
- Did you ever find out who started the rumor? What did you do when you found out?

(Continued)

(Continued)

- Have you ever blocked somebody online because you felt harassed? If so, did that make it stop?

Safe Online Social Networking

- What social media sites do you use most frequently?
- How many friends or followers do you have?
- What kind of people are you meeting on Instagram, Facebook, and Twitter? Are you connecting with people that you know? Or are you meeting people around the world?
- Do you get a lot of friend or follow requests from strangers? Do you accept all of them? How do you make decisions about who to accept and who to ignore or reject?
- Do you use Twitter? What for? Who do you follow and who follows you?
- Do you know how to use the privacy settings on Instagram, Facebook, and Twitter?
- Do you have them set so that only those you accept as friends can see what you post? How do you know who can see your information?
- What kind of personal information are you posting online? Have you ever posted your full name? Age?
- School? Phone number? Current location?
- Have you ever been tagged in a picture in a way that made you upset?
- Do you know how to edit your privacy settings so that if somebody wants to tag you in a post or photo, you have to approve it?
- Do you know how to untag yourself in pictures?
- Do you feel like social networking sites should be used to vent your frustrations? Do your friends vent on social media?
- Do people comment? What do they say?
- What kind of videos are you watching on YouTube? Do you ever post videos?
- Have you ever reported inappropriate videos that you have seen on YouTube? Or any other website?
- Does anyone else know your password or passcode for any site or social media app? What about for your laptop or cell phone?

related to cyberbullying and online harassment and will open the door for parents to the new connected worlds in which their kids are living.

At some point, further probing may be warranted. For example, parents might seek to determine the tendency of their child to rationalize cyberbullying given a specific circumstance or situation. Then, they can point out the faulty reasoning in those decision-making processes so that the youth's behavioral choices are not swayed by emotion or opportunity. To be sure, it is impossible for parents to protect and watch over their children at all hours of the day and night. Still, it is possible through a combination of these efforts to instill in them safe Internet practices that will guide their online (and consequently even offline) activities.

> Developing safe Internet practices very early on in the lives of children is essential to ensure that they internalize those habits as their computer and Internet proficiency grows.

The Earlier the Better

One of the most commonly asked questions we get from parents is, "When is the right time to get my preteen a phone or a Facebook account?" First of all, we are not the right persons to answer that question. Parents know their children better than anyone. And the appropriate time to introduce various technologies into their lives depends on a number of factors. As parents, we know that there will come a time when we need to give our children privacy, privileges, freedoms, and responsibility in amounts that are appropriate for *their* development. And that is different for everyone.

The bottom line about when to introduce technology really boils down to this: It is best when it is *the parent* that brings the technology to their child. It shouldn't be one of their friends. If a parent gives them access to technology it allows them to also introduce appropriate and reasonable rules. Say, for example, parents give their eleven-year-old a phone at the start of the school year. They can specify that the child is only allowed to call mom or dad for the first month. After that month, parents can show their child the phone bill and explain how much they are paying and that they can see everyone who was called. If they didn't get into too much trouble that first month, then the parent can open up the acceptable call list to a few more trusted individuals—then maybe texting. Then perhaps a social media app. If they make a mistake, parents might have to take a step back, and continue to negotiate this give and take scenario accordingly.

Developing safe Internet practices very early on in the lives of children is essential to ensure that they internalize those habits as their computer and Internet proficiency grows. Kids these days become technologically adept at a very early age, and parental guidance is of the utmost importance in teaching them to use electronic devices in responsible ways. Moreover, it will be much easier for parents to insist upon going online with their children at eight or nine years of age than when they are fifteen or sixteen. Good habits instilled will hopefully bear much fruit in their decision-making processes later in life. To be sure, developing appropriate value systems and decision-making frameworks is a much more valuable and enduring approach than simply threatening them with punishments for particular rule violations.

Monitor Their Activities

> I would never bully online because it hurts. Also, if the kids had half a brain they would consider that a parent is monitoring it like mine do.
>
> —Libby, 13, Massachusetts

We also feel that it is important for parents to monitor their children closely when they are online. This is especially true when younger children are new to technology and still figuring out the rules of the road. Traditional Internet safety practices in the household (such as keeping the family computer in an open, well-trafficked room) are completely irrelevant now with every kid having their Internet-connected devices, and Wi-Fi or cellular access practically everywhere. Parents are in search of a "silver bullet"—the perfect app or program to install on their kid's phone, tablet, or laptop to magically to reduce the chances of victimization. Unfortunately, there aren't any that are useful and user-friendly enough for us to recommend (yet) for phones and tablets of every operating system. And while there are some great products for laptops and desktop computers which can record various online activities including chats, instant messages, social media participation, online searches, and even every keystroke, the reality is that more youth access the Internet from their mobile device instead.

> Many parents use parental controls at home, which is a great first step. But relying solely on parental controls can provide a false sense of security since many children access the Internet from various locations [such as their phone]. It is crucial that children, parents and educators are informed and well-versed as to potential risks our children may face online.
>
> —Jace Galloway, Internet safety advocate, Illinois

Furthermore, parents should be advised that if their children are using electronic devices during all hours of the night, they may be using them for inappropriate activities. Parents should put reasonable restrictions on usage and determine exactly what their kids are doing online all night. If youth get unusually upset when their usage is limited, they are likely using it too much. Again, parents should be reasonable. They should listen to their children when they tell them what they are doing online and rationally assess whether further restrictions are necessary. Give them the benefit of the doubt but check up on them to make sure they are keeping up their end of the bargain.

As another point, parents should be encouraged to learn their children's e-mail addresses and social media usernames and make clear that the children are not allowed to create multiple online profiles or accounts. They should inquire further if they see that a youth is logged onto what seems to be a different e-mail address or social media account. A few kids to whom we have spoken admit to that they have a "parent-friendly" Facebook page that they don't regularly use and a completely separate one that they constantly use when interacting with their friends. Obviously, a level of trust must exist so that such outright deception does not occur. Not only does it make it difficult for parents to prevent their child's victimization and assist if something does happen, it also subverts any efforts to create the open line of communication indispensable for a healthy, functional parent-child relationship.

Use Discretion When Spying

To be honest, some parents with whom we speak are adamant that it is perfectly acceptable—if not demanded—that they covertly and surreptitiously spy on their children's Internet activities. Of course, parents ultimately decide what they think is appropriate in monitoring the online behaviors of the youth in their household. However, if parents do this without informing their children, there is a significant risk of damaging any positive relationship that exists between them. At that point, children may no longer trust their parents at all, which means they will not confide in them about problems they are having—online or offline. We strongly believe that parents should be honest and upfront with their children at all times. Plus, letting them know *why* you have chosen to monitor their online activities can open up an opportunity for productive dialogue in this area and demonstrate to kids that their online lives matter to you as much as their offline lives.

THE STUDENT'S ROLE IN PREVENTING CYBERBULLYING

Responsibility for youth safety online should largely be shared among the adults that serve this population because it appears that the problem of cyberbullying would quickly grow out of hand if kids were left to their own *devices* (pun intended). That said, adolescents can take a number of steps to help protect themselves from victimization. Safeguarding personally identifiable information (rather than heedlessly posting it in public spheres) and being careful with the passwords to their online accounts are the two most vital practices for avoiding victimization at the hands of bullies on the Internet.

Protecting Personal Information

While it seems like common sense, adolescents often need to be reminded that they should never give out their personal information anywhere on the Internet—especially to those they don't know in real life. They may think that the person on the other side of the online interaction is a friend, but how can they ever know for sure? Even if that person is a friend, there is no way of knowing if someone else is looking over that person's shoulder. Youth should know that anything they reveal about themselves online can (and likely will) be used against them. Cyberbullies can use the personal information to cause a significant amount of emotional and reputational harm.

> I was talking to my friend about something that was bothering me on an e-mail, I sent it to her then the next day another friend of mine had hacked onto my e-mail and took it, and she was the friend that was bothering me, saw it and printed it out, she took it to school with her the next day and showed every one, and it had personal stuff on it, it wasn't just about the person, that was only about 1 line of it. Everyone saw the personal information and teased me for a few days.
>
> — Bella, 12, undisclosed location outside the US

Along these same lines, youth should be careful in posting anything that they wouldn't want the entire world to see. We discussed this initially in Chapter 2 when we considered social media. Many youth today enjoy posting pictures or videos on sites like Facebook, Instagram, YouTube, or Vine for their friends or family members to check out. They need to understand fully that individuals with malicious motives may also access this content and decide to exploit it. For instance, pictures can be downloaded and then manipulated to make it look as though something inappropriate is occurring. Similarly, there have been numerous stories in the news detailing how predators and pedophiles have been able to contact minors based on personal data and digital photos posted on social media pages. Cyberbullies are also easily able to use such content to screw up the lives of those who unwittingly, naively, or carelessly shared something they shouldn't have.

Finally, adolescents must remember that photos, videos, and text cannot be easily deleted from the Internet because of the ease and speed with which digital content is reproduced and archived. Search engines or websites like www.archive.org regularly index (i.e., add to their databases) the contents of web pages (including social media posts) across the Internet. After being indexed, the content is retrievable and viewable by others who look for it—*even after it is removed from the original site.* Did you know that the Library of Congress is saving every single tweet ever sent? We are sure there is so much more saving and recording of our online activities by the government and third parties than we can even fathom, and perhaps one day we will understand the consequences. Apart from that, though, others you know directly or indirectly may have saved the pictures, videos, and text on their own devices and can repost the material or send it around to others at any time. Suffice it to say that the permanence factor of anything on the Internet can have significant and long-lasting repercussions for youth who have not been careful with what they've decided to share with others in cyberspace.

Password Protection

Passwords are necessary to access personal accounts on a computer network. They serve as authentication mechanisms, and uniquely identify someone as being who they claim to be. Of course, correct authentication prevents others from accessing or altering your personal data. In our current Information Age, passwords are a part of everyday life. However, some users inadvertently make themselves vulnerable to cyberbullying by exposing or carelessly distributing their password.

> A guy from school changed my MSN e-mail password, I still can't get into my account. He also threatens to beat me up if don't break up with my girlfriend.
>
> —Will, 16, Kentucky

Many youth simply don't see the risk in telling others their password. In our school assemblies to students, we ask how many of them know at least one other person's online password or device passcode, and (perhaps not surprisingly) a majority of the hands are raised every single time (so far). To be honest, this is very alarming to us. Even if youth are responsible enough not to distribute their passwords deliberately, they might inadvertently expose them to others. Many users leave their passwords on a sticky note on their computer desk (in case they forget it!) or in their Notes on their phone.

> As a guidance counselor in my present setting, I have experienced students telling me of problems mentioned over AOL Instant Messenger. Students get on other students' accounts due to the sharing of passwords and then say mean or horrible things as a joke or as intimidation. This can leave a student feeling highly scared to come to school, or even more distraught than normal as a teenager with his or her peer relationships.
>
> —Meredith, school counselor, Florida

Even if adolescents are extremely careful in never writing down their passwords in insecure locations or disclosing them to others, a password might still be discovered through other means. For instance, some sites have "password hint questions," which allow users to retrieve forgotten passwords to online accounts by responding correctly to the questions presented. If the response is successful, an e-mail is sent to the address associated with the account. Within this e-mail, the current password or a new password is given. One of these password hint questions might be "What is my pet's name?" If someone knows your pet's name and you've used it as a password hint, an e-mail with password information would be sent to the relevant e-mail account. If a person knows how to access that e-mail account, access to other accounts may then be possible. Through this procedure, a person can change the passwords of all of your other online accounts simply by having access to your e-mail and knowing a few facts about you.

Finally, some people use the same password for multiple purposes—school and personal e-mail, social media, online banking, gaming networks, eBay, PayPal, and many others. As such, finding out the password to one account can lead to simple access to other accounts. While we are considering cyberbullying in this text, there are obvious risks associated with identity theft when someone commandeers another person's password.

WARNING SIGNS: WHAT TO LOOK FOR

Our final topic in this chapter has to do with warning signs that are directly or indirectly given by youth. To be sure, it is often difficult to determine whether behavioral or attitudinal changes in youth are signals of distress or simply the usual "adolescent angst" commonly associated with this difficult transitional period in their lives. Nevertheless, it is important for educators, parents, and other adults to learn to read the behavior of their students and children so that real problems can be detected, diagnosed, and promptly handled. A number of red flags may suggest that a child is experiencing some type of distressing event while online (see Box 6.6). Identifying these indicators may help to minimize the negative emotional and psychological effects of Internet-based harm.

Box 6.6

A Child May Be a Target of Cyberbullying If He or She . . .

- unexpectedly stops using their device(s)
- appears nervous or jumpy when using their device(s)
- appears uneasy about going to school or outside in general
- appears to be angry, depressed, or frustrated after going online (including gaming)
- is oversleeping or not sleeping enough
- becomes abnormally withdrawn from usual friends and family members
- shows increase or decrease in eating
- seems regularly depressed
- makes passing statements about suicide or the meaninglessness of life
- loses interest in the things that mattered most to them
- avoids discussions about what they are doing online
- frequently calls or texts from school requesting to go home ill
- desires to spend much more time with parents rather than peers
- becomes unusually secretive, especially when it comes to online activities

---

The most obvious sign that something is wrong involves a marked change in the adolescent's electronic device habits. Students may suddenly stop using the computer or overtly refuse when asked to do something online. If a child has been known to go online every day at school but then unexpectedly goes several days without logging on, this change of behavior may signal an underlying problem. In addition, if a student appears nervous when a new message or social media notification arrives or is constantly looking over his shoulder when using his device, this behavior may indicate that something is amiss. If a student seems extraordinarily angry, upset, or depressed, especially when interacting in cyberspace, those emotions may signal a cyberbullying incident. And if youth try to avoid discussions about what they are doing online or put up emotional walls when questioned about harassment or bullying, a serious problem may be at hand.

At the same time, adults know that many youth try to avoid having to go to school for a variety of reasons. If a teenager adamantly refuses to go and will not discuss why, further probing is essential. From our discussions with victims, we know how difficult it can be to face cyberbullies at school—as well as face the rest of the student body who may know about the online harassment.

There are also a number of warning signs that may indicate that a child is mistreating others in cyberspace (see Box 6.7). If a teen quickly switches or closes screens or programs when you walk by, she is probably trying to hide something. If a group of kids is gathered around a computer laughing or giggling, and then appear jumpy, nervous, or unwilling to share the humor with you, they are probably doing something they shouldn't be doing. However, there are many appropriate humorous pieces of content on the Internet, so don't jump to conclusions. We all appreciate a hilarious comic or funny video; just ask them to show you what is so funny. In general, avoiding discussions or becoming defensive about what they are doing online is a clear sign that they are engaging in activities that likely don't align with your standards of appropriate behavior, thus meriting further inquiry. In these situations, it may be important for you to re-stress the rules and let the student know that if she gives you reason to be concerned about online activities, you will install tracking software (if you haven't already done so) or restrict Internet or device access to times when you will be able to supervise and monitor online behavior.

Box 6.7

A Child May Be Cyberbullying Others If He or She . . .

- quickly switches screens or hides their device when you are close by
- uses their device(s) at all hours of the night
- gets unusually upset if they cannot use their device(s)
- laughs excessively while using their device(s) and won't show you what is so funny

- avoids discussions about what they are doing online
- seems to be using multiple online accounts or an account that is not their own
- is dealing with increased behavioral issues or disciplinary actions at school (or elsewhere)
- appears overly concerned with popularity or continued presence in a particular social circle or status
- demonstrates increasing insensitivity or callousness toward other teens
- starts to hang out with the "wrong" crowd
- demonstrates violent tendencies
- appears overly conceited as to their technological skills and abilities
- the parent-child relationship is deteriorating

SUMMARY

Educators, parents, students, and other community leaders are all important pieces of the cyberbullying prevention puzzle, as shown in Figure 6.1. Individually, it is difficult for any one person to stop cyberbullying from occurring; together, however, adults can present a formidable force against online cruelty. As this chapter has discussed, teachers must supervise students who are using computers, tablets, and phones in their classrooms (and outside of class!) and educate the school community about responsible Internet use and netiquette. School administrators must take online aggression seriously and ensure that policies are in place that allows the school to take action against cyberbullies when their actions substantially and materially affect the learning environment or infringe upon the rights of others (as discussed in Chapter 5).

It is also clear that parents must be educated about and encouraged to participate in their child's online experiences—which also involves disciplining unacceptable online behaviors when necessary. Youth need to exercise care when it comes to the personal information they post online and should carefully protect their passwords. With all of this said, though, prevention efforts can only do so much, and unfortunately, even the best prevention strategies are not 100 percent effective. The next chapter provides guidance and direction on when and how to respond to cyberbullying incidents when they do occur—and they will in time.

Figure 6.1 Pieces of the Cyberbullying Prevention Puzzle

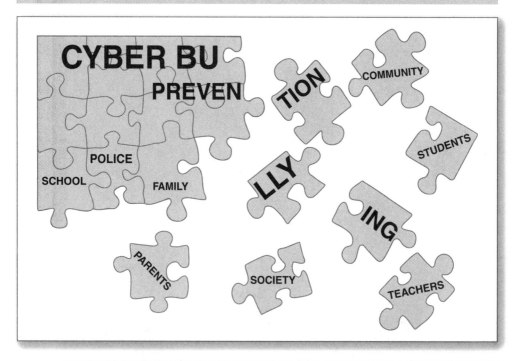

QUESTIONS FOR REFLECTION

1. Whose responsibility is it to prevent cyberbullying? What role does each play?

2. How can students be used to help prevent cyberbullying?

3. Do you think schools should formally monitor the online activities of students? Should parents put software on their devices to track where their kids are going?

4. At what age do you think it is appropriate for a youth to have Internet access? How about a smart phone?

5. What signs would you look for to tell if someone is being cyberbullied or cyberbullying someone else?

NOTES

1. *Ladies Home Journal*. "'I Couldn't Get Them to Stop.'" Polk County Public Schools. http://www.polk-fl.net/parents/generalinformation/documents/bullying_jeffreyjohnstonstory.pdf.

2. Sameer Hinduja and Justin W. Patchin. *School Climate 2.0: Preventing Cyberbullying and Sexting One Classroom at a Time*. Thousand Oaks, CA: Corwin, 2012.

3. Federal Communications Commission. "Consumer's Guide: Children's Internet Protection Act (CIPA)." Washington, DC: Author, 2012. http://transition.fcc .gov/cgb/consumerfacts/cipa.pdf.

4. Matthew Stucker. "Girl Costs Father $80,000 With 'SUCK IT' Facebook Post." CNN.com. http://www.cnn.com/2014/03/02/us/facebook-post-costs-father/ index.html.

5. Paul Levy. "Crowd at Elk River School Board Weighs in on Teen's Suspension." *Star Tribune*. http://www.startribune.com/local/west/246990421.html.

6. Jim Suhr. "Father of Bullied Student Who Committed Suicide Sues Illinois District and Producers of Anti-Bullying Video." http://legalclips.nsba. org/2014/07/08/father-of-bullied-student-who-committed-suicide-sues-illinois-district-and-producers-of-anti-bullying-video/#sthash.88rTq3dn.dpuf.

7. Amanda Lenhart, Rich Ling, Scott Campbell, and Kristin Purcell. "Teens and Mobile Phones." http://pewinternet.org/~/media//Files/Reports/2010/PIP-Teens-and-Mobile-2010-with-topline.pdf.

8. Helen Cowie. "Perspectives of Teachers and Pupils on the Experience of Peer Support Against Bullying." *Educational Research and Evaluation* 4 (1998): 108–125; Siwan Price and Raya A. Jones. "Reflections on Anti-Bullying Peer Counseling in a Comprehensive School." *Educational Psychology in Practice* 17, no. 1 (2001): 35–40; Ersilia Menesini, Elena Codecasa, Beatrice Benelli, and Helen Cowie. "Enhancing Children's Responsibility to Take Action Against Bullying: Evaluation of a Befriending Intervention in Italian Middle Schools." *Aggressive Behavior* 29 (2003): 1–14; Andrew Miller. *Mentoring Students and Young People: A Handbook of Effective Practice*. London: Kogan Page, 2002; Robin Banerjee, Carol Robinson, and David Smalley. "Evaluation of the Beatbullying Peer Mentoring Programme." http://mashup.sussex.ac.uk/ Users/robinb/bbreportsummary.pdf.

9. Helen Cowie and Ragnar Olafsson. "The Role of Peer Support in Helping the Victims of Bullying in a School With High Levels of Aggression." *School Psychology International* 21, no. 1 (2000): 79–95; Helen Cowie, Paul Naylor, Lorenzo Talamelli, Peter K. Smith, and Preeti Chauhan. "Knowledge, Use of and Attutudes Towards Peer Support: A Two Year Follow-Up to the Prince's Trust Survey." *Journal of Adolescence* 25, no. 5 (2002): 453–467; Peter K. Smith, Katerina Ananiadou, and Helen Cowie. "Interventions to Reduce School Bullying." *Canadian Journal of Psychiatry* 48, no. 9 (2003): 591–599.

10. ASCD. "School Culture and Climate." *ASCD's A Lexicon of Learning Online Dictionary*. http://www.ascd.org/research-a-topic/school-culture-and-climate-resources.aspx.

11. Eau Claire (WI) Area School District. "North High School Respect Policy" (2011). http://www.ecasd.k12.wi.us/cms_files/resources/nhs_respectpolicydoc.pdf.

12. Nancy E. Willard. "Safe and Responsible Use of the Internet: A Guide for Educators" (2003). http://www.ntia.doc.gov/legacy/ntiahome/ntiageneral/ cipacomments/comments/willard/Chapters.htm.

13. David Finkelhor, Jennifer Vanderminden, Heather Turner, Anne Shattuck, and Sherry Hamby. "Youth Exposure to Violence Prevention Programs in a National Sample." *Child Abuse & Neglect* 38, no. 4 (2014): 677–686.

14. Kenneth W. Merrell, Barbara A. Gueldner, Scott W. Ross, and Duane M. Isava. "How Effective Are School Bullying Intervention Programs? A Meta-Analysis of Intervention Research." *School Psychology Quarterly* 23, no. 1 (2008): 26–42.

15. Seokjin Jeong and Byung Hyun Lee. "A Multilevel Examination of Peer Victimization and Bullying Preventions in Schools" (Article ID 735397). *Journal of Criminology* Volume 2013 (2013). http://dx.doi.org/10.1155/2013/735397.

16. Dan Olweus, Susan P. Limber, and Sharon Mihalic. "Bullying Prevention Program." In *Fight Crime: Invest in Kids. Blueprints for Violence Prevention: Book Nine*, edited by Delbert S. Elliott. Boulder, CO: Center for the Study and Prevention of Violence, 1999.

17. Committee for Children. "Steps to Respect Program Guide" (2005). http://www.cfchildren.org/Portals/0/STR/STR_DOC/Research_Review_STR.pdf.

18. Dorothy Espelage, Sabina Low, Joshua R. Polanin, and Eric C. Brown. "The Impact of a Middle School Program to Reduce Aggression, Victimization, and Sexual Violence." *Journal of Adolescent Health* 53, no. 2 (2013): 180–186.

19. Catherine P. Bradshaw. "Preventing Bullying Through Positive Behavioral Interventions and Supports (PBIS): A Multitiered Approach to Prevention and Integration." *Theory Into Practice* 52, no. 4 (2013).

20. George Sugai. "What is School-Wide Positive Behavioral Interventions & Supports?" (2009). http://www.pbis.org/common/cms/files/pbisresources/What_is_SWPBS.pdf.

21. Justin W. Patchin and Sameer Hinduja. *Words Wound: Delete Cyberbullying and Make Kindness Go Viral*. Minneapolis, MN: Free Spirit Press, 2014.

22. Justin W. Patchin and Sameer Hinduja. *A Leader's Guide to Words Wound: Delete Cyberbullying and Make Kindness Go Viral* (2014). http://cyberbullying.us/leaders-guide-words-wound.

23. Mary Madden, Amanda Lenhart, Sandra Cortesi, and Urs Gasser. "Teens and Mobile Apps Privacy" (2013). http://www.pewinternet.org/files/old-media//Files/Reports/2013/PIP_Teens%20and%20Mobile%20Apps%20Privacy.pdf.

24. Justin W. Patchin and Sameer Hinduja. "Trends in Online Social Networking: Adolescent Use of MySpace Over Time." *New Media & Society* 12, no. 2 (2010): 197–216.

25. Stan Davis and Cherisse Nixon. *Youth Voice Project: Student Insights into Bullying and Peer Mistreatment*. Champaign, IL: Research Press, 2014.

26. Valerie Strauss. "MoCo Supt. Starr Calls for Online Civility After Being Targeted by Obscene Tweets." http://www.washingtonpost.com/blogs/answer-sheet/wp/2013/12/13/moco-supt-starr-calls-for-online-civility-after-being-targeted-by-obscene-tweets.

27. "'Yik Yak' App Causes Concern for Bullying at Lake Forest High School." *Lake Forrester.* http://lakeforest.suntimes.com/2014/03/06/yik-yak-app-causes-concern-for-bullying-at-lake-forest-high-school.

28. Claire P. Monks, Susanne Robinson, and Penny Worlidge. "The Emergence of Cyberbullying: A Survey of Primary School Pupils' Perceptions and Experiences." *School Psychology International* 33 (2012): 477–491; Ken Rigby. *Children and Bullying: How Parents and Educators Can Reduce Bullying at School.* Boston, MA: Wiley-Blackwell, 2008; Wanda Cassidy, Karen Brown, and Margaret Jackson. "'Making Kind Cool': Parents' Suggestions for Preventing Cyber-Bullying and Fostering Cyber-Kindness." *Journal of Educational Computing Research* 46, no. 4 (2012): 415–436; Jacques F. Richard, Barry H. Schneider, and Pascal Mallet. "Revisiting the Whole-School Approach to Bullying: Really Looking at the Whole School." *School Psychology International* 33 (2012): 263–284; Justin W. Patchin and Sameer Hinduja. "Traditional and Nontraditional Bullying Among Youth: A Test of General Strain Theory." *Youth and Society* 43, no. 2 (2011): 727–751. doi: 10.1177/0044118X10366951.

CHAPTER SEVEN

Responding to Cyberbullying

Seventeen-year-old David Knight from Burlington, Ontario, had been the target of bullies for years. Primarily at his high school, he was assaulted both physically and emotionally by classmates on a regular basis. Unfortunately, it didn't take long for the taunts to move online. One day, someone from his school sent him an e-mail inviting him to check out a particular website. He clicked on the link and it took him to a page that seemed to have been created for the sole purpose of humiliating him. The page—labeled as "THE PAGE THAT MAKES FUN OF DAVE KNIGHT"—was chock full of rumors, gossip, and numerous offensive comments. "I was accused of being a pedophile. I was accused of using the date rape drug on little boys," David told CBC News.[1]

In order to get help, he decided that it might be useful to tell his parents and see what they could do. His mom and dad printed out the website and took it to the school and asked them to help. But school officials said that there was nothing they could do because the site was not made or even accessed from the school. Not to be deterred, the parents then contacted the police for assistance. However, here again they were turned away with the remark that the site held neither evidence of a threat nor any other violation of the law. They then decided to get in touch with Yahoo, who was hosting the site, and implored them to intervene. "I waited a couple of weeks and checked the web page and found that it was still there and so I called them again and asked them to take it down again, and again the same thing," recalled David's mother. When she eventually reached someone from the company, they stated that they were not the Internet Police and that it wasn't their place to restrict free speech.

At the end of their proverbial rope, and as a last-ditch effort, they contacted an attorney and threatened legal action against the hosting company. This finally led to the site being taken down, more than seven months after David first learned of it. Amidst all of this stress and emotional suffering, David withdrew from school and finished his senior year at home. "Rather than just some people, say 30 in a cafeteria, hearing them all yell insults at you, it's up there for 6 billion people to see. Anyone with a computer can see it. And you can't get away from it. It doesn't go away when you come home from school. It made me feel even more trapped,[1]" he expressed when interviewed by the media.

Nobody that David and his parents contacted was able or willing to help. This wasn't "their problem." But it was. And is. *Cyberbullying is everyone's problem.* Everyone has a moral (and in some cases legal) responsibility to do *something* about these kinds of problems. This chapter will guide you through exactly what it is you can and should do.

A lot has changed since David's experience occurred more than a decade ago, and most individuals and even technology companies (such as Yahoo) have generally become more helpful, realizing that online bullying can be just as detrimental to the development of adolescents as traditional schoolyard bullying. That said, even though most adults recognize their obligation to do something, many still struggle to identify suitable courses of action. In this chapter, we explore appropriate responses from several different perspectives. Obviously, *educators* play a critical role in responding to cyberbullying incidents that negatively affect the school environment and infringe upon the rights of others. *Parents* who are made aware of cyberbullying activities must discipline their children. *Bystanders* need to step up and do something about peers being victimized instead of tacitly condoning it through inaction. *Students* must be equipped with strategies they can employ if they experience cyberbullying. And *law enforcement* should become involved in those cases when cyberbullying involves threats to someone's physical safety or when a criminal law violation may have occurred.

> Cyberbullying is everyone's problem.

> When I was being cyberbullied, I was called a dork, unpopular, and other cruel things. The cyberbully said that the school rules don't apply online, because they are home and friend problems. I couldn't sleep the entire night. I wondered whether people actually thought of me that way. I felt so miserable, so I called two of my friends over, and we found out that the school has rules about cyberbullying. They helped me print out a hard copy of the evidence, and we showed it to the principal the next day. When you are being cyberbullied, make sure to tell someone you trust. It will only make things worse if you are trying to deal with this alone.
>
> —Jess, 12, US

In many ways, we feel it is the educator who serves as the linchpin to connect all of these stakeholders together in a comprehensive response strategy. We believe that school personnel have the power to positively (and powerfully!) influence the thought processes and behaviors of youth (and the parents of those youth), interface with law enforcement when necessary, and appreciably reduce the occurrence of cyberbullying. Before we delve into a discussion of practical responses for all stakeholders involved, we'd first like to begin with an oft-invoked solution that, to be honest, drives us crazy. It may be well intentioned, but as we will point out, it is completely off-base.

JUST TURN IT OFF!

We have spoken to many parents, teachers, and youth about cyberbullying over the last decade. Those who do not completely understand the phenomenon often wonder, "What's the big deal? Why don't kids just turn off their computers?" In fact, here are some examples of recent tweets that express this perspective:

"If you're being cyberbullied, just close the damn laptop and go outside."

"There's no such thing as cyberbullying!!! Just close ur computer!!"

"Solution to #cyberbullying: Turn. Off. Your. Computer."

"No one is forcing you to go on Facebook. U can't be cyberbullied if you're not on the site."

We feel these comments are flippant, dismissive, and naive, to say the least. There are a number of reasons why "delete the app" or "shut down your phone" simply aren't viable options for those being cyberbullied.

First, why should a victim be required to give up something positive and beneficial in their lives simply because of someone else's maliciousness? Since when is it appropriate to blame the victim or essentially punish them for another's aggressive actions? In fact, this is one of the main reasons many kids don't tell adults about their negative online experiences: They don't want to be blamed and, as a consequence, lose their social media privileges or otherwise be forced to miss out on all of the fun and useful interaction that goes on online. Krista, a thirteen-year-old from Virginia expressed this, stating, "I wanted to tell my parents but I was afraid that they would never let me chat again, and I know that's how a lot of other kids feel."

Another reason that this suggestion is not viable is because cyberbullying can continue whether or not the target is online. For example, a bully could set up a fake account on Instagram or spread rumors via e-mail among classmates.

A bully could also circulate information through Facebook posts or even create a defamatory website (like in David Knight's case) to harass and embarrass the victim. In these examples, the mistreatment continues and the victimization still occurs (as others see and even share the hurtful content), even when the victim is offline. Finally, when we counsel youth just to turn off their devices, we are sending the wrong message. What do you tell them if they are being bullied at school? Do you suggest that they simply stop going? While schools are among the safest places for kids to be, many harmful, uncomfortable, and at times violent behaviors do happen there. That potential should not (and cannot) cause children to miss out on all of the educational and social benefits that accompany going to school because, as we know, victimization actually can happen anywhere. Plus, if you think through all of the relevant factors, you do realize that the Internet is not the problem. Social media is not the problem. Smartphones are not the problem. Bullying was around long before Twitter and iPhones. Instead, it is the underlying issues of peer conflict, immaturity, insecurity, ethics, socioemotional dysfunctions, and behavioral issues that foster cyberbullying among individuals.

So if we still want to encourage kids to embrace technology and use it to meet their educational, social, and relational goals, what should be done when youth are harassed or mistreated with those devices? We now turn our attention to specific guidance for educators. These strategies revolve around determining an *appropriate* response, using creative methods to discipline the inappropriate use of technology and teach about its acceptable use, becoming someone whom students can approach and trust, being sensitive to the concerns of cyberbullying victims, creating an anonymous reporting system, recognizing special circumstances of an incident that warrant enhanced penalties, and contacting relevant Internet and cell phone service providers as necessary.

I was always a misfit growing up. At the end of 5th grade I was 64 pounds. Well I had some problems and went to seek help. I got put on an anti-depressant which made me gain a lot of weight. At the beginning of my 6th grade year I was 186 pounds . . . People didn't even notice it was me. I started getting bullied a little at a time. I'd get shoved and called names but I just acted like it didn't affect me but it did. I started getting bullied every day. People called me Twinkie. They pointed at the bus and said go catch the Twinkie. I came home and cried and slept. Then out of nowhere it started happening on Facebook. I finally lost the weight and people started to stop bullying me. Nothing was done about these bullies. I reported them to the

> principal and counselor nearly 100 times (no exaggeration) nothing was done. Why? I want to know why was nothing done? Well now I am a Jr. in high school. I really want answers.
>
> —Ryan, 17, Indiana

SCHOOL'S RESPONSE TO CYBERBULLYING

As discussed in Chapter 5, liability concerns arise when technology provided at school (or brought to school) is used to cause harm. If a student reports being cyberbullied, the school is obligated to intervene. Harassment and discrimination in general is a violation of the Civil Rights Act of 1964[2] and other state and federal legislation. School district personnel who fail to respond to it when it is brought to their attention can be held legally responsible. While it is not expected that teachers and other school employees actively police the Internet and social media to make sure youth are not involved in inappropriate online behaviors, they must move to action when they become aware of a cyberbullying situation that affects students under their care (see Box 7.1).

Box 7.1

**What Schools Should Do When Made
Aware of a Cyberbullying Incident**

- Assess the immediate threat.
- Ensure the safety of the target.
- Demonstrate compassion and empathy to the target.
- Restrain the bully if necessary (separate from target; closely monitor).
- Investigate and gather evidence.
- Contact parents.
- Contact the site, social media company, gaming network, Internet service provider, or cell phone service provider as needed.
- Contact the police when physical threats, stalking, coercion, blackmail, or sexually explicit pictures or videos of minors are involved.
- Enforce disciplinary policy.
- Contact legal counsel if considering serious disciplinary action (e.g., suspension or expulsion) to make sure you don't overstep your bounds.

To review briefly what was covered in Chapter 5, the common theme woven throughout the decisions of courts is that school officials can place educationally based restrictions on student speech and behavior necessary to maintain an appropriate school climate. This can involve content created and disseminated through the school's network or through personally owned phone use that occurs at school. It also involves incidents where students bring printouts of cyberbullying to school or encourage others to visit or see specific online environments (websites, profile pages, pictures or videos on phones, etc.) where cyberbullying is occurring or when this content is accessed at school. Finally, we have stressed that restrictions on student speech can be made on content created and disseminated away from school when it results in a substantial and material disruption on campus or infringes upon the rights of others to attend a safe and nonthreatening environment.

Intervening does not necessarily mandate student suspension or expulsion or some other *formal* sanction. In fact, most often, it does not. Zero-tolerance policies that thoughtlessly dictate particular responses can be problematic because they are inflexible when dealing with situations that may require discretion and creativity on the part of the educator. Many cyberbullying incidents can readily be addressed using a variety of informal mechanisms (see below). Simply approaching the student and having a quick talk about the issue may be enough. In fact, teachers engage in this kind of activity just about every single day. If this doesn't work and the behavior continues, perhaps the student's parents need to be called or the principal needs to meet with them. Parents often wield immense power in dictating the behaviors of their children, and are usually quick to take action when informed of wrongdoing.

> School officials can place educationally based restrictions on student speech and behavior necessary to maintain an appropriate school climate.

Along these lines, educators should defer to parental authority when possible. Hopefully the parents of the offending student are willing to work with you to resolve the situation. Addressing cyberbullying informally and working closely with parents keeps the school district reasonably safe from any accusations of inappropriate discipline. Indeed, Pima County, Arizona, attorney Mike Tully—an expert on school law and bullying legislation—argues that the wisest course of action for educators frequently may be to limit or forego formal discipline. He clarified this by recently telling us that "educators should proceed with caution and not resort to discipline as a knee-jerk fix when a simple conversation with a parent or guardian might be more effective, both in terms of addressing the bullying behavior as well as leaving room for restorative justice and similar nonpunitive but effective interventions." Not only does an informal or restorative approach preempt litigation, but it avoids subsequent negative fallout to the district and community. This latter fact is underappreciated but tremendously vital, as you cannot put a price on the value of positive morale and a peaceable environment among school staff, students, and parents.

It also deserves comment that some disciplinarians in schools may be inclined to make emotionally laden, overly punitive decisions when one of their administrators, teachers, or students is victimized. The school is presented with an affront to the sanctity of the educational environment, sees digital content that is offending, and immediately becomes defensive and exacts a severe sanction. Sometimes this is clearly warranted. Other times, it is disproportionate, done in haste, and may even overstep the bounds of acceptable corrective action against a student. Overstepping disciplinary bounds is an open invitation for lawsuits because of the First and Fourth Amendment rights of students. The factors that accompany cyberbullying incidents are obviously complex and multifaceted, which makes a proper response even more challenging.

Overall, school district policy should clearly spell out a range of penalties based on the severity of the incident. The type of response should be proportionate to the weight of the offense and convey the extent of its gravity and severity (and go no further). Feel free to use our basic model as a starting point to develop your own comprehensive continuum of strategies for responding to cyberbullying (see Table 7.1). The measure of an effective response is that the offender comes away knowing that the behavior is clearly inappropriate and will not be tolerated and that subsequent refusal to follow the rules will result in future disciplinary action.

Since they can foster a hostile school climate and escalate into more serious behaviors if left unchecked, even minor forms of harassment should not be ignored. We believe that *every* cyberbullying incident should be investigated and documented (see Resource D, the sample "Cyberbullying Incident Tracking Form"). Many times, bullying behaviors intensify because nothing is done to stop them, and perhaps cyberbullying is attractive to students because it is perceived to be overlooked by adults.

Generally speaking, cyberbullying incidents should be addressed using many of the same strategies that the school uses to deal with traditional bullying. The vast majority of schools by now have policies that cover online behaviors in conjunction with their prohibitions about bullying offline. But outlining what is acceptable and specifying sanctions for what is not is not enough. We don't want you to just do the bare minimum. Even though educators are typically overextended and underresourced, much more is required above and beyond good policy implementations.

Table 7.1 Continuum of Cyberbullying Behaviors and Appropriate Responses

Behaviors		
Minor	**Moderate**	**Serious**
Teasing	Identity theft	True physical threats
Ignoring	Spreading rumors	Stalking
Name-calling	Posting pictures online without permission	Intimidation
Taunting	Recording a video of bullying to hurt someone (rather than to help someone)	Death threats
Flaming		Extortion or blackmail related to private pictures or videos

Responses		
Minor	**Moderate**	**Serious**
Meeting with parents	Meeting with principal	Restorative practices
Meeting with counselor	Behavior plan	Legal/criminal punishment
Creative sanction (e.g., research paper or anti-cyberbullying posters)	Civility education	Change of placement
	Extracurricular consequences	Civil punishment
	Detention	Suspension
		Expulsion

Be Creative in Your Response

Educators should be encouraged to be creative in addressing cyberbullying situations when they arise. This can occur in a number of ways. For example, many like to capitalize on teachable moments that present themselves throughout the school year, and an instance of cyberbullying could serve to promote quality dialogue and discussion about the topic. As another suggestion, cyberbullies (or all students) might be required to write a research paper on the effects of harassment from the perspective of the victim—perhaps even in "the old-fashioned way"—using the library and a pen (no Internet or laptop!). Through this process, they will learn what it feels like not to be able to use technology, which should promote a greater respect for those valuable tools—which are a privilege, not a right. We have previously covered how targets of cyberbullying may not feel comfortable using technology and, therefore, may miss out on all of the advantages it affords. Those who engage in cyberbullying need to understand the effect their harmful behavior can have, and hopefully this assignment will make that point.

Well, I started a website about the principal and saying how much we hated him. No one ever threatened him but it hurt his feelings. Needless to say, even though I did no wrong, I got in trouble for making the website. Needless to say I don't regret making the website because everything on it was true. He really is a jerk. I do however wish the things that were said about him were said in a nicer way. Now instead of getting expelled I have to write a stupid paper on cyber-bullying.

—James, high schooler, US

As another suggestion, online aggressors could be required to create informative posters to be displayed throughout school hallways or classrooms about the nature of online bullying. Or they might be assigned to create a public service announcement (PSA) in the form of a digital video to educate the school or broader community on the subject. Not only can this help on an individual level to convey and inculcate standards of appropriate behavior toward others, but it can serve as a broad messaging strategy for the rest of the student body (and beyond). When others see these projects, they will be reminded about the campuswide focus on these issues—which can help them more readily lean in the direction of kindness and peer respect.

Be Sensitive to the Concerns of Those Who Are Bullied

Why is there so little sympathy toward people who are bullied? It's like, it's gotten to the point online where you either take it, or get off-line. Why did it ever get to this point, and what can I do that I haven't already done?

—Anonymous

When cyberbullied, many youth will try to avoid conversations about their experiences, be dismissive about the extent of their impact, or shun offers for assistance in responding to the problem. Well, we can tell you that they do want help. They just don't think adults can really do anything to improve their situation. In fact, they fear the opposite—that any action taken by teachers or parents will only make matters worse.

As an adult, you should begin very early in laying the groundwork for youth to feel comfortable approaching you to discuss these and other issues they are confronting. Adolescence is a painfully difficult journey on hazardous terrain that should not be traveled alone. Technology has increased the number of land mines youth can stumble upon, and they need trustees in their lives to help them avoid those pitfalls and pick them up when one takes its toll.

Then, if a student comes to you to talk about an experience with cyberbullying, you must take certain steps to address the situation. In fact, a swift and appropriate response is important so that the victim knows that the school is doing *something* to alleviate the problem. If it is not taken seriously, schools risk alienating students who might then continue to suffer from victimization or attempt to take matters into their own hands through misguided retaliation or revenge.

Educators can start by asking the student what she would like to see happen—what would make things better. Regardless of whether you implement the suggestion(s) of the student, you are validating her experience and giving credence to her voice. This itself is often so helpful in the restorative process, but something which some adults may disregard by quickly acting on their own impulses and ideas for a forceful response. Outside of hearing what they have to say, one measure might be as basic as discretely separating the bully from the victim at school (to the extent possible). Along these same lines, all staff (including cafeteria workers, bus drivers, coaches, and other support staff) should be briefed on any harassment incidents so that they can quickly identify and respond to any future situations that may flare up.

> It seems like I can't ever get anyone to take me seriously. I know how important it is to report cyberbullies, but peer pressure says "it's the Internet, take it, get over it, stop being a you know what" kind of thing. I WANT to do something but I'm told not to, I'm told I will be marked for direct attacks if I do.
>
> —Willie, 16, unknown location

Recently, we spoke with a school counselor at a local middle school who described the ways that she deals with relatively minor forms of harassment when they come to her attention. After speaking with the victim, she calls the accused party into her office to discuss the allegations. The very first thing she tells the student is, "Right now, you are not in trouble. But I've been made aware that you are engaging in bullying, and if this behavior continues, or you discuss our meeting with anyone other than your parents, you *will be* in trouble." She then reminds the student about the school's conduct policy and refers to the section in that policy that defines bullying. Next, she points out the listed consequences for violations of the policy. She then covers the specific disciplinary action that will be taken if the behaviors continue. Finally, she reiterates the importance of not talking to other students about their office meeting. And she (like most counselors) doesn't disclose the identity of the person who reported the behavior. This also makes retaliation less likely.

We believe this last point is particularly important. As mentioned, many targets of harassment fail to tell adults about their experiences because they are concerned about retribution. The counselor with whom we spoke preemptively alleviated this concern by conveying separately to the target and the bully that discussion of the incident(s) will not occur outside of her office. In most cases, the inappropriate behavior has been identified and addressed, which will hopefully be the end of the problem. If not, all parties clearly understand the progression of steps that will follow.

Create an Anonymous Reporting System

You understand by now that students are very reluctant to discuss their cyberbullying experiences with adults for a number of reasons. Moreover, victims or others who *witness* bullying may be disinclined to report their experiences for fear of fallout. Therefore, every school should have a system in place that allows students who experience or observe cyberbullying (or any inappropriate behavior) to report it anonymously. Being able to broach the subject without being forced to reveal one's identity may prove valuable in alerting faculty and staff to harmful student experiences and help promote an informed response to bring positive change.

The reporting system could be as simple as a box located near the office labeled "Report Inappropriate Behavior Here." The challenge is placing the box in a location that is visible and easily accessible, but where students can discreetly submit information. Alternatively, the school might set up a method where students can anonymously send their concerns via text or through a web form on the school or district website (see Figure 7.1). That way, concerned students can contact the school from the privacy of their own homes on their own time, without the anxiety associated with another student seeing them dropping something in the reporting box. Of course, if you provide such a resource, every complaint should be taken seriously and thoroughly investigated.

Figure 7.1 Example of an Anonymous Web-Based Reporting System

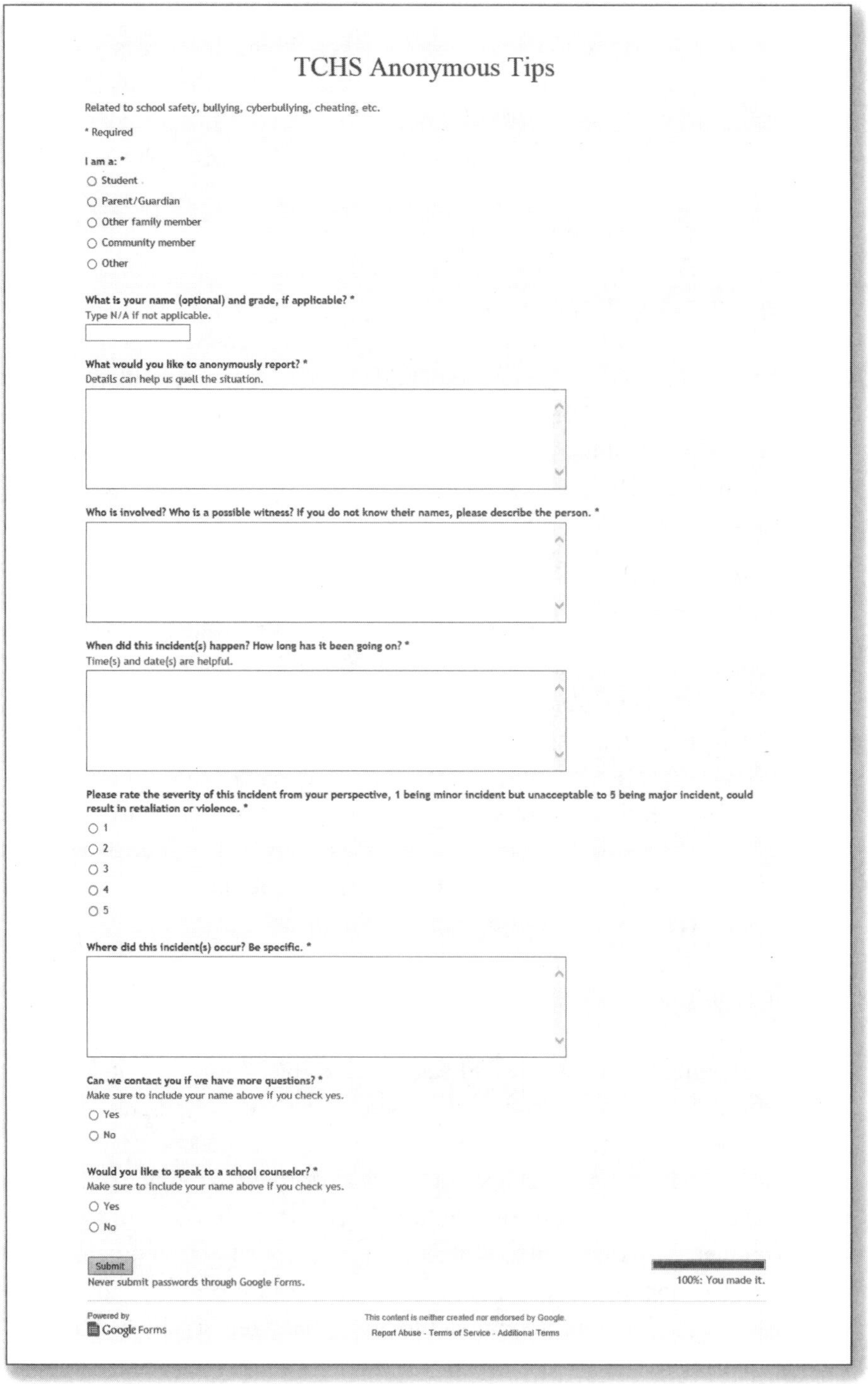

TCHS Anonymous Tips

Related to school safety, bullying, cyberbullying, cheating, etc.

* Required

I am a: *
○ Student
○ Parent/Guardian
○ Other family member
○ Community member
○ Other

What is your name (optional) and grade, if applicable? *
Type N/A if not applicable.

What would you like to anonymously report? *
Details can help us quell the situation.

Who is involved? Who is a possible witness? If you do not know their names, please describe the person. *

When did this incident(s) happen? How long has it been going on? *
Time(s) and date(s) are helpful.

Please rate the severity of this incident from your perspective, 1 being minor incident but unacceptable to 5 being major incident, could result in retaliation or violence. *
○ 1
○ 2
○ 3
○ 4
○ 5

Where did this incident(s) occur? Be specific. *

Can we contact you if we have more questions? *
Make sure to include your name above if you check yes.
○ Yes
○ No

Would you like to speak to a school counselor? *
Make sure to include your name above if you check yes.
○ Yes
○ No

Submit
Never submit passwords through Google Forms.

100%: You made it.

Powered by
Google Forms

This content is neither created nor endorsed by Google.
Report Abuse - Terms of Service - Additional Terms

Source: Used with permission of Temple City (California) High School.

Aggravating Circumstances

Cyberbullying incidents vary in seriousness from relatively minor teasing and name-calling to very serious threats to a person's physical safety. While we argue that educators have the ability and responsibility to intervene (at least informally) in *all* cases, administrative sanctions should escalate in accordance with the severity of behaviors or if there are aggravating circumstances surrounding the incident. Below we discuss several factors that may warrant increased or more serious repercussions to the offender.

Substantial Disruption of the Learning Environment

As we discussed at length in Chapter 5, educators have the ability to discipline students for behavior or speech that results in a substantial disruption of the learning environment. While most cyberbullying incidents will not have this effect (at least if they are dealt with quickly before they have a chance to intensify), those that do warrant firm penalties. If school administrators, for instance, are forced to spend inordinate amounts of time dealing with an incident, clearly the order and workings of the school have been disrupted. If the school network needs to be shut down for a significant period of time because students are accessing and disseminating hurtful content, the delivery of some curriculum and the provision of electronic resources to all will be greatly hindered. Or if it becomes the topic of conversation during the school day, forcing teachers to repeatedly rein in the attention of students, instruction has been negatively impacted. Please remember that it is critical to articulate and document the substantial disruption as thoroughly as possible so that if a student challenges a disciplinary action, the school's procedure will hold up in court.

Cyberbullying Based on Race, Class, Gender, Sexual Orientation, or Any Other Protected Status

Any cyberbullying incident that appears to be motivated by race, class, gender, or sexual orientation must be taken more seriously than those that are not. While it may be directed solely at one person, it reflects malice and bias toward an entire group of people who share the same distinguishing demographic feature. This has the potential to inflame the emotions of multiple individuals and to incite further violence due to its extremely sensitive nature. What is more, society widely agrees that such conduct is completely intolerable and, when combined with behavior such as a threat, becomes a hate crime. The school has an absolute responsibility to take strong action any time staff witness or are made aware of electronic harassment that discriminates against a particular group of people. This is what we believe should have been done in the David Knight case summarized at the onset of this chapter. We stated in Chapter 5 that Title IX prohibits discrimination related to a failure to

BREAKOUT BOX

Anonymous Reporting

Our school, like every school is heartbroken by the all-too-often accounts given by children who say that aid came too late or that they felt compelled to change schools rather than deal with what felt like an impossible situation. In many cases, these middle school students do not have the background experiences to know how to handle a difficult situation and, in a few cases, do not have a support system at home.

It became clear that it was necessary to provide an anonymous means for students to report an incident, one that was available and accessible to them when *they* needed it. We found the "Bully Report" drop boxes in the school had been ineffective. The solution we chose was an online form on our school website. The form is not exactly anonymous, meaning that it does record the sender's IP address, but from a student's perspective, this does not seem to be a deterrent and no student has ever asked about that aspect of the submission process.

The form we use has provided a simple and effective means for students to report incidents that they are not comfortable reporting in person. We designed it to be simple but include the critical questions that would allow for documentation of a crime as well as remain comfortable for a student to complete. We shared the form via our weekly announcements, through a message sent home to parents, and through assemblies. It has also become a common occurrence to redirect students to take their verbal account of an incident and use the online tool. This allows for thoughtful reflection and documentation.

In the year since implementation of the form, we have had around 144 submissions with around three false reports. While this has been a tremendous number of reports for a school of 1,100 kids, we believe that the time spent in follow up and investigation is well worth the payoff of having students feel safe at school. In fact, the number of reports has been manageable and has also led to more prevention rather than punitive action.

These reports range from online harassment in cases where students have sent threatening messages on Facebook to cases of students asking for money during our lunch period on a daily basis. The most typical submissions are reports of name-calling or "he kicked me" during class time in which the student does not report the issue to the teacher. The majority of submissions have been legitimate instances where a student needed support in dealing with a difficult situation and required only a small amount of time to investigate and provide support. These forms of support include mediation between students who have had a disagreement, increased supervision during lunch periods to deter other students from demanding money, changing the direction of on-campus cameras to observe acts of bullying during lunch, or parent contact to notify families that their student has been sending threatening messages via Facebook.

I would say that this approach is not only important but I believe that it is completely necessary. We have all been in situations where we were caught between the consequences of calling for help and the consequences of suffering in silence. In most cases, this simple online tool offers a path to safety and resolution that does not include the consequences from either path previously available. As educators, we enter this profession motivated by our love for young people and our desire to see them succeed.

—Ryan Brock, Assistant Principal,
Lewis Middle School, San Diego, CA

conform to stereotypical notions of masculinity and femininity, and regardless of actual or perceived sexual orientation or gender identity of the harasser or target.[3] Since the bullying implied homosexuality in a denigrating manner, it can be argued that his civil rights were violated.

Digital Video Recordings

We are seeing more and more situations where students are making video recordings of bullying or cyberbullying incidents. In some cases, these incidents are documented for the purpose of gathering information to take to the authorities so the offending party can be appropriately disciplined. In others, they are recorded and posted online or distributed to classmates to further the humiliation of the target. We've covered the repetitive aspect of victimization in these situations, as the content is viewed by hundreds, thousands, and even millions of people and continually shared, discussed, and mocked among them. Students need to be made aware that any bullying that is digitally recorded will be dealt with more seriously than other forms and that *everyone* who is involved will be disciplined. This includes the student behind the recording device, any others who are filmed participating in the mistreatment, those who upload it to the Internet, and those who disseminate it (or link to it) through text, e-mail, instant messages, or social media (see the discussion of *Requa v. Kent School District* [2007][4] in Chapter 5 for a real-life example). Criminal law may also be implicated in these situations, as some states (e.g., California, Connecticut, Florida, Maryland, Massachusetts, Montana, New Hampshire, Pennsylvania, and Washington)[5] require consent of both parties whenever an audio recording is made of a telephone conversation. Courts in these states appear likely to extend this rule of law when evaluating cases involving covert digital video because, of course, the audio component is also recorded without both parties' consent.

Repeated Cyberbullying Following Intervention

Ideally, students who engage in cyberbullying behaviors will stop after an initial intervention. From our research, we find that most teens who cyberbully others just made a mistake—and got caught up their emotions and acted spontaneously and without forethought, and actually do deserve a second chance if they demonstrate true remorse and guilt. Some, however, may continue to hassle others as if this behavior were perfectly acceptable. In these cases, it is imperative that educators step up and intervene again—but with enhanced severity. In your initial meeting with the perpetrator, you hopefully outlined what would happen if the online mistreatment continued. Now, you have to follow through. Not only must you avoid appearing as a pushover to the student you are disciplining, but you should remember that others in the student body will probably hear how you (and the school) responded. The goal is for them, in part, to be deterred as well from engaging in a similar behavior in the future.

Informing Service Providers

Many victims with whom we speak tell us that they don't want their parent or school administrator to punish the bully, or even to confront them. Rather, *they just want the problem to go away so that they can get back to living their life.* How can you help make this happen? It may turn out to be simple: Educators can contact an Internet service provider, cell phone service provider, or social media site, inform the company of the cyberbullying, request the service to check for itself (or provide the company with electronic evidence in the form of screenshots, account names, URLs, or logs), and consequently close the account or delete the problematic image or post. We have a regularly updated list of specific contact information for the most popular websites, social media apps, gaming networks, and service providers on our website (www.cyberbullying.us/report).

Each of these providers has formal agreements that a user agrees to abide by when signing up. For example, Facebook's "Terms of Service" (revised November 15, 2013) includes the following conditions:

- You will not solicit login information or access an account belonging to someone else.
- You will not bully, intimidate, or harass any user.
- You will not post content that is hate speech, threatening, or pornographic, incites violence, or contains nudity or graphic or gratuitous violence.
- You will not use Facebook to do anything unlawful, misleading, malicious, or discriminatory.
- You will not post content or take any action on Facebook that infringes or violates someone else's rights or otherwise violates the law.

Other service providers include similar language. For example, AT&T's Acceptable Use Policy states the following:

IP Services shall not be used to host, post, transmit, or re-transmit any content or material (or to create a domain name or operate from a domain name), that harasses, or threatens the health or safety of others. In addition, for those IP Services that utilize AT&T provided web hosting, AT&T reserves the right to decline to provide such services if the content is determined by AT&T to be obscene, indecent, hateful, malicious, racist, defamatory, fraudulent, libelous, treasonous, excessively violent or promoting the use of violence or otherwise harmful to others.[6]

Accounts that violate these terms or policies by engaging in cyberbullying can be terminated. As we explained in Chapter 3, the companies are not legally responsible to proactively police all of the accounts created by users of their services, as they are considered third-party providers instead of content creators. However, they *are* obligated to investigate whenever you let them know that their formal terms or policy have been violated through harassing behavior by one of their users. But *you* have to let them know! Also, please convey to teens that no one gets "outed" when they file reports against the problematic accounts or content of others—they are confidential and kept as such. Otherwise, use of the reporting features across these sites would fade away as users realized that it only led to more abuse.

Your Response Must Be Effective to Matter

We likely can all agree that the purpose of any response to bullying (whether it be an informal response such as a conversation with a counselor or a formal response such as suspension) should be to get the bullying to stop. If you respond in a particular way but the bullying continues, then you need to take additional measures to ensure that it does cease. This point was exemplified in the Anthony Zeno case discussed in Chapter 5, about the mixed-race teen who received threats and was subject to racial hatred from some of his high school peers. You will recall that a jury awarded Anthony $1.25 million (reduced on appeal to $1 million plus attorney's fees) after agreeing that his civil rights under Title IX had indeed been violated. What educators need to take away from this ruling is that once they learn of harassment taking place, they have an obligation to do everything in their power to ensure that it stops. Simply disciplining the student who did the bullying, *without following up to make sure that it actually stops and that the person targeted is safe*, is not enough. Applying discipline and implementing new programming is only sufficient to the extent that the behaviors desist. Citing *Wills v. Brown University* (1999)[7] the court stated, "[E]vidence of an inadequate response is pertinent to show fault and causation where the plaintiff is claiming that she was harassed or continued to be harassed after the inadequate response."[8] The jury in Anthony's case found, and the appellate court agreed, that "the District's additional remedial actions were little more than half-hearted measures."[8]

> The purpose of any response to bullying should be to get the bullying to stop.

Implementing a particular response without concern for its effectiveness evidently is not enough to protect a school from a claim of deliberate indifference. This is a crucial point to remember! Responses to bullying need to be *targeted* (focusing on the nature of the harassment), *comprehensive* (long-term recurring programming vs. a one-time brief presentation), and *effective* (the bullying has to stop or at least be reduced significantly in frequency and seriousness). Due diligence involves more than just applying an immediate response—it demands that the response move behaviors in the desired direction (away from harassment and toward respectful behavior).

RECOMMENDATIONS FOR PARENTS

Apart from their important work with students at their school, educators must also take the time to reach parents about these issues. While we know this might feel like one more responsibility that perhaps shouldn't be on your plate to deal with, doing so will hopefully save your school from having to deal with major incidents down the road. The bottom line is that you need the support and cooperation of parents to help instill the positive messages that you want to convey!

Parents who are contacted because their child was involved in a cyber-bullying incident may immediately be defensive, emotional, panic stricken, or otherwise freaked out. School personnel should try to demonstrate that they are on the same side as parents, with the goal of helping kids navigate the difficult terrain of adolescence and grow up to be productive, healthy, and compassionate people. Calmly explain your role as an educator and as a representative of the school district. Articulate that your primary objective is to ensure a safe school environment so that all students feel supported and free to get the most out of their educational experience. Point to the formal policy that prohibits bullying and discuss the various response options moving forward. The key is to empower parents to help resolve the situation by giving them specific strategies that they can employ, whether their child is the target or the aggressor.

Many parents are inclined to respond to their children's victimization by immediately banning access to their phones, social media, their gaming console, or the Internet in general. This may be the easiest short-term solution, but it obviously does not address the underlying problem of interpersonal conflict. Moreover, it fails to eliminate current or future instances of cyber-bullying victimization because—as we mentioned—it can still go on even if their child isn't seeing it. Additionally, knee-jerk, defensive reactions will probably close off any lines of communication the parent has tried to open and maintain over the years. Apart from crippling that connection between the parent and child, such a response may also promote overt rebellion, as kids so inclined will find a way to use the technologies at different times and in different places. As we have discussed throughout this book, they are indispensable components of 21st century adolescence.

The best tack parents can take when their child is cyberbullied is to convey unconditional support (see Box 7.2). They should do this at a time when their children seem really open to them (parents know how teenagers are—one minute they are your best friend, the next they "hate" you). Similar to what we suggested when educators sit down with cyberbullying victims, parents should solicit the child's perspective as to what might be done to improve the situation. Consider their emotional state, and how much harm has taken place, and determine whether their prospective response is sufficient or if more should occur.

Box 7.2

What Parents Should Do If Their Child Is Cyberbullied

- Make sure their child is, and remains, safe.
- Solicit their perspective as to what they would like to see happen.
- Collect evidence.
- Keep detailed records of what happened, where it happened, and who else might have witnessed the incident.
- Contact the school to make them aware of the situation.
- Contact the service provider or content provider.
- Contact the police when physical threats, stalking, coercion, blackmail, or sexually explicit pictures or videos of minors are involved.
- Express to the child how important it is *not* to retaliate.

If necessary, parents should explain the importance of scheduling a meeting with school administrators (or a particular teacher they trust) to discuss the matter. Informing the administration can also ensure they monitor the interactions at school to make sure there is no retaliation. Bringing counselors into the loop is also beneficial, as these professionals are often among the best at handling relationship problems and can offer advice on how to deal with the situation. They are often willing to intervene quietly in a way that stops the harassment without unduly instigating the bully or her family. Overall, parents must demonstrate to their children through words and actions that they both desire the same end result: that the cyberbullying stop and that life does not become even *more* difficult. This can be accomplished by working together to arrive at a mutually agreeable course of action.

Someone made an Instagram account claiming it was my account like me as the owner but it was not. Pictures kept getting posted of my friends with horrible comments and pornography was posted too. But then the owner of the account deleted those pictures and decided to start fresh. The final posting they threatened to shoot my two friends. Somehow my school got involved with it and the day after it was posted I was called down to the office. Obviously the policeman was just finishing up his report which meant that the owner of the account had confessed. My parents went to the office the next day after that asking to speak with my assistant principal. They had told my parents that the owner of the account confessed and was suspended. The owner of the account was one of the girls that were my friends. She is smart to make herself seem like she wasn't the one but she was pointing the finger at me claiming I have a hacking device which I don't. All along she was out for me to have no friends now it's her with no friends. My parents are working on pressing charges.

—Kendra, 11, Florida

Talking to the Parent of the Bully

A question that is occasionally asked of us by educators is whether it is advisable to recommend that the parents of cyberbullying victims contact the parents of the students doing the cyberbullying to try to resolve the situation. This can be a very tricky proposition. In theory, this seems like a very good approach and for some parents can be an effective strategy. However, victims of any form of bullying are usually terrified by the prospects of this idea. They believe that confronting the parents of the bully will only make matters worse. And it certainly can, if the conversation is not approached delicately.

The problem is that some parents confronted with accusations that their child is a bully or cyberbully may become defensive and therefore may not be receptive to the other parent's thoughts, ideas, or any formal or informal intervention. They might immediately put up a wall and even become antagonistic. The key here really is to protect the safety of the bullied child. A parent who is considering this approach must first carefully weigh the various factors at hand and take into consideration the "totality of circumstances" as the courts like to say. Do the parents know each other? Based on what is known about them, how receptive do you think they would be? Is the bully a former friend of the victim? Have there been problems in the past? Will the parents have to deal with collateral damage in other social situations, if they have to interact in other environments? We have heard of at least one instance where the father of a bully "got back" at the father of a victim by embarrassing him and picking on him in front of their other friends during their weekly softball games.

Because each situation is different and clearly complicated, it is difficult to say with any certainty that confronting the parents of the bully is a good idea. Parents that choose this approach should tread lightly and keep in mind what life was like when they were teens. They should also consider how they would feel if someone confronted them about the behavior of their child. It is easy to say that you would listen calmly and respond appropriately, but would you? That crazy "do onto others" rule might apply to our behaviors as adults just as much as it does to what our children are doing.

Working With Parents of Children Who Bully

Parents also need to understand that if their child is the perpetrator, they have an obligation to do something about it (see Box 7.3). This ties into the groundwork laid in Chapter 6; part of a preventive strategy is informing parents that cyberbullying is a violation of school policy and is subject to discipline (and, of course, the behavior must be corrected). Parents of the aggressor sometimes need to be briefed on the facts of the case in as nonthreatening a manner as possible. It is critical here to explain calmly to parents that such misbehavior interferes with the mission and mandate of the school, and that parents and educators must work side by side when these situations arise.

Box 7.3

What Parents Should Do If Their Child Is the Cyberbully

- Talk about the hurtful nature of bullying.
- Apply reasonable consequences.
- Set firm limits and stick to them.
- Consider installing tracking software.
- Closely monitor technology use.
- Convey additional consequences if the behavior continues.

I need to remember that they might not always be the victim but the perpetrator. That is the true test of parenting. Defending your child because you want to believe everything they tell you when there could be little bits and pieces left out to avoid the wrath of Mom or Dad.

—Shannon, mother, Minnesota

Parents can start by discussing how cyberbullying (and all forms of bullying) affects others and by working to cultivate empathy. Many teens simply don't fully comprehend how actions in cyberspace have significant real-world ramifications. Depending on the level of seriousness of the incident, and whether it seems that the child has realized the inappropriate and regrettable nature of his behavior, reasonable and logical consequences should be applied. If parents were proactive and had their child sign the "Technology Use Contract" discussed in Chapter 6 (see Resource B), this process is going to be much easier. The child knew the rules and knew that there would be repercussions for violations of the contract. Parents may revoke their child's Internet or phone use for a period of time or temporarily revoke other privileges (remember to be sensible and proportional with your discipline; the "time" should fit the "crime"). If the behavior was particularly serious, parents may consider installing tracking or monitoring software as a consequence as well (though tech-savvy and unrepentant teens can quickly circumvent these). Moving forward, it is essential that parents pay even greater attention to the technology use of their kids to make sure that they have internalized the lesson and are acting in appropriate and responsible ways.

EMPOWERING TEENS TO TACKLE CYBERBULLYING

> Don't let yourself just be a victim thinking nobody can do anything because it's online, don't do nothing in hopes it will go away. Don't give them the satisfaction of getting upset and yelling at them. Solve the problem in the real world. Don't give them the satisfaction by responding to what they say.
>
> —Kevin, 17, Canada

Adolescents who are cyberbullied are often overwhelmed by the emotional and psychological pain, and so responding to the problem in a healthy and productive way is usually not their first inclination. In fact, level-headed youth who do confide in a parent or teacher sometimes react with concern and panic when that adult suggests certain steps be taken to reduce or stop the problem. And as we've discussed extensively, their anxiety revolves around several things: the desire to avoid being labeled a tattletale; not being strong enough to handle the harassment on their own, by not capably defending themselves against the cyberbully or simply ignoring the cyberbullying; the impact the response might have on how their peers perceive or treat them; the actual utility that such steps will have in stopping the problem and preventing future victimization; and the possibility that the aggressor (and perhaps others) might increase the intensity and frequency of harm to get back at the victim for telling an adult and trying to get them in trouble.

Targeted youth first need to realize that they are not to blame for the way they have been treated. They need to be reminded that no one deserves to be harassed in any environment. Then, they need strategies to help them fend off cyberbullies (see Box 7.4). As a rule, the most effective response to minor forms of cyberbullying is simply no response at all (they shouldn't give the bully the satisfaction of knowing they've been provoked to respond!). Similarly, we also recommend that youth try not to wallow in posts, messages, and content they know (or expect) to be of a harassing or upsetting nature, and to take a break from social media environments in which they are continually being cyberbullied. They might feel like they need to always be on Instagram to stay in the social loop, but the fact is that they are not going to die if they don't receive constant updates on what everyone is posting. However, if they hear that it is continuing even after a while, it is bad advice to ask youth to keep trying to shrug it off or ignore it. Teens should know that you are not dismissive of what they are experiencing and how they are being harmed.

Box 7.4

What Youth Should Do If They Are Being Cyberbullied

- Ignore minor teasing or name-calling.
- Block messages from unknown people.
- Don't respond to the bully—especially don't retaliate.
- Keep a log or journal of attacks.
- Keep all evidence of bullying.
- Once you collect the evidence (screenshots, printouts, etc.), report the content or the account user to the website as abusive.
- Talk to a trusted adult.

If the behaviors escalate in seriousness, then swift action must be taken. If adolescents are threatened with physical harm, please remember that such threats are criminal offenses, and the police should get involved. Such statements from cyberbullies cannot be taken lightly or casually dismissed as frivolous. All threats to another's well-being must be thoroughly investigated.

Apart from these response options, youth must learn strategies to help reduce their vulnerability to online aggression. For example, targets of cyberbullying may consider adjusting their Account or Privacy settings to block or regulate the content they receive (or are exposed to). Remind them that they should be in control of their online experience. They don't need to accept every friend or follower on social media. And they shouldn't feel socially obligated to keep from unfriending or unfollowing those that they simply don't have a peace about. They might say it is because they want to avoid drama and conflict with others, but it is better to deal with that than keep giving people that they really don't trust and don't fully like access to their online life. Those are the individuals who are most likely to use that content against them. It does take time to read "Help Files" and "Frequently Asked Questions" documents within the app or on the associated website to learn how to apply the proper settings to delete, block, filter, and report certain people and content. However, we believe it is well worth the time spent.

It remains critical that all targets of cyberbullying document those instances so they can be used as evidence against the person doing the bullying when working with the school or content and service providers. Victims must be encouraged to *save all evidence* without internalizing or becoming otherwise consumed by the mistreatment. Along these same lines, youth who are harassed online should be encouraged to keep a log or journal of their experiences. They should note specific incidents with as much detail as possible, including who was involved, where and when it happened, how they responded, who witnessed the incident, and what was done to prevent its reoccurrence. This will become powerful evidence if disciplinary action is to be taken against the bully. Moreover, writing the experiences down may help youth reconcile, heal, and then expel the experiences from their mind, much like sitting down with a close friend and sharing a difficult time.

> People choose to use the Internet for this because they're too cowardly to say it in front of you so they do it anonymously. If someone's going out of their way to do this, it's because something about you or something you have that they don't is making them so angry that they can't stand to see you happy, they're just compensating for something they don't have by trying to destroy it. Website administrators can track IP addresses which can be used to locate the computer used to post that message. Keep log files of their offenses as evidence and report it to someone (parent, teacher, police). Nobody will just stand by and allow this to happen and these people can be found and will be dealt with seriously.
>
> —Scott, 17, Canada

A final point: We certainly do not want to trivialize any instance of cyberbullying and would encourage teens to seek help in addressing those they perceive as serious. However, it bears repeating that they should do all they can to keep from dwelling on hurtful words they know are false and only said to inflame emotions and promote controversy, conflict, and drama. This is an acquired skill, to be sure, and even as adults we do not always perceive and respond to sarcastic, mean, or hateful comments in the most productive way. Cultivating *resiliency* is vital to relational success in adulthood—which is chock full of interpersonal challenges, and perhaps youth (with the help of involved teachers and parents) can use the more minor instances of cyberbullying as life lessons in that regard.

Bystanders: Encouraging Teens to Step Up for Others

Bystanders—those who witness cyberbullying and its fallout among their classmates—are admittedly in a tough position. They generally do not want to get involved because of the hassle and problems they fear it might bring upon them, yet they often recognize that what they are seeing is not right and should stop. But we need to always remember that by doing *nothing,* bystanders are doing *something.* As members of a peer group and of society, we have a responsibility to look out for the best interests of each other. Humans are relational beings, and relationships continue and thrive because of this willingness to dismiss the cost to oneself temporarily and come to the aid of those who are in distress. In fact, we argue that bystanders can make a huge difference in improving the situation for cyberbullying victims, who often feel helpless and hopeless and need someone to come to their rescue. Yet many times no one is willing to step up to help.

Some might interpret the failure to act as a function of the *bystander effect.*[9] The theory behind this idea is that oftentimes even good and caring people refuse to take action when confronted with someone in need of help. Perhaps they don't think it is any of their business, or maybe they think others will step in. Maybe they feel it isn't their place to intervene and behave differently from the social group around them, which gets them to think "no one else is doing anything, why should I?" We don't believe that the majority of people fail to act when they see bullying because they are apathetic or uncaring. They may simply not know what to do or could legitimately be afraid for their own safety (especially when it comes to physical bullying or threats of physical harm).

In general, we don't think it is a good idea to *compel* someone to intervene in a physical bullying incident. If the person feels physically and socially capable, then by all means he or she should. But the truth is that many just don't. It is true that most who witness bullying *do* want to do *something.* So we believe it is crucial to equip teens with a variety of tools they can use should they confront a situation like this. It is important to remember that most teen bullying happens between, and in view of, people who are known. That is, typically witnesses to bullying either know the one doing the bullying or the one being targeted, or both. If they are not comfortable stepping in at the moment when it occurs, they still have other options for responding (see Box 7.5).

It is true that many instances of cyberbullying occur outside of the watch of third parties—such as through e-mail and instant messages. However, those who observe cyberbullying on social media, or in a chat room, or on an online discussion board should be moved to some type of action. That action might simply be anonymously reporting the incident to an adult or to the owners, administrators, or moderators of a particular Internet-based environment. More bold and assertive steps would include communicating with the victim and encouraging her to talk to someone who can help. Bystanders must feel equipped and empowered to do something about injustices they witness and must believe that positive outcomes will result from their efforts—or they will simply be discouraged and much more hesitant to step up in the future. Along these lines, educators must convey to students that if they see or receive electronic content that mistreats or makes fun of another person, they should immediately contact an adult. As we've discussed in the previous chapter, they should have the option to remain anonymous in their reporting.

Box 7.5

What Youth Should Do If They Witness Cyberbullying

- Document what you see and when.
- Don't encourage the behavior.
- Don't forward hurtful messages.
- Don't laugh at inappropriate jokes.
- Don't condone the act just to fit in.
- Don't silently allow it to continue.
- Stand up for the victim.
- Talk to the one who was being bullied after the fact and offer your support.
- Anonymously report the incident and persons involved to the school.
- Report cyberbullying to the website it appears on.
- Enlist friends to help resolve the conflict.
- Tell a trusted adult.

CIVIL REMEDIES

When school-based responses handed down by administration leave victims without a sense of equity or justice, US civil law can be applied as a remedy to interpersonal wrongdoing between private citizens. These remedies exist in cyberbullying cases where the victim (whether student or staff) can seek monetary damages from the offender and possibly the offender's parents, or a formal injunction against the harmful behavior. Often the simple initiation of legal action against an aggressor is enough to end the malicious behavior immediately and permanently. Of course, continuing on to trial can be a significant financial burden to all parties involved—so most individuals would seek to avoid such an outcome. A complete discussion of the many possible civil responses is well beyond the scope of this book, but we thought it would be important to briefly highlight some of the most common actions that meet the standard for an intentional tort (or wrongdoing). Some examples include defamation, invasion of privacy, intentional infliction of emotional distress, and negligence. Those so inclined should consult with legal counsel for more information as it relates to their own situation.

Defamation

Defamation involves "an intentional false communication, either published or publicly spoken, that injures another's reputation or good name."[10] Defamation originates in the torts of slander (spoken defamation) and libel (written defamation). Online communications would be considered libelous since they are not fleeting and have a measure of permanence associated with them. In order for cyberbullying to be defamatory, in a legal sense, the one doing the cyberbullying needs to post a "false statement of fact." That is, they would need to say something that could be true, but isn't, such as "Jenny has herpes!" or "Robert is gay!" Calling someone a *tool* or a *douche bag* would not be grounds for defamation because those are not statements of fact (one cannot actually be a tool).

> I started getting flamed and harassed, and I became afraid to go outside . . . I told my mother and showed her the page. We couldn't do anything. We tried about everything. I got sick from all the stress and ended up in the hospital, but I became a bit better now that the harassing has let down a bit. My friends in my neighborhood found the page on that site, and thought those lies were all true so I have lost about all of my friends under their false words. And I have changed my e-mail address multiple times, and I am being flamed again for that page with false, imprudent and horrible words.
>
> —Anonymous

Invasion of Privacy

Invasion of privacy involves "the unwarranted appropriation or exploitation of one's personality, publicizing one's private affairs with which public has no legitimate concern, or wrongful intrusion into one's private activities, in such a manner as to cause mental suffering, shame or humiliation to person of ordinary sensibilities."[10] So if, for example, someone posts private pictures of another online for the purposes of humiliating them, that may be grounds for an invasion of privacy lawsuit.

> My sisters were being cyberbullied online for the past 3 weeks. They were teased because of their sexual behavior. One told her guy friend that she was sexually active and sent pictures of herself. He screenshotted the pictures she sent to him, and put them on Facebook. She was embarrassed the next day she came to school. She didn't come to school after that, she was homeschooled, and still got bullied.
>
> —Audrey, 12, Virginia

Intentional Infliction of Emotional Distress

Intentional infliction of emotional distress involves deliberately or recklessly causing "severe emotional distress to another" by "extreme and outrageous conduct."[11] It is not necessary that the act be meant to cause distress; reckless disregard for the potential of distress occurring is enough. Furthermore, the conduct must be beyond a certain established standard of decency or civility. We've spoken to a few lawyers over the years about the viability of this particular civil action and most say that it is difficult to be successful in these kinds of cases because "extreme and outrageous" is a pretty high standard to meet.

> It's one thing for freedom of speech, but it's another when you're actually harming the person where they can't even eat anymore without feeling horrible all the time.
>
> —Anonymous

Negligence

Negligence involves "the omission to do something which a reasonable man, guided by those ordinary considerations which ordinarily regulate human affairs, would do, or the doing of something which a reasonable and prudent man would not do."[10] A claim of negligence can also be brought against a school, seeking to make the institution liable for harm. In these cases, the plaintiff must prove that the school had a duty of reasonable care to prevent harm in a situation, that the harm was foreseeable, that harm occurred, and that the breach of duty led to the harm. To be sure, this is not limited to physical harm but also covers emotional, psychological, or mental forms, which are amply present in most cyberbullying situations.

RECOMMENDATIONS FOR WORKING WITH LAW ENFORCEMENT

While it would be nice to live in a society where law enforcement never had reason to be at school, preserving the safety and security of students often requires their presence. Recent data are hard to come by, but thousands of officers work in schools every day across the United States. They are mostly responsible for the well-being of the students, staff, and visitors but are often utilized in a variety of other roles. These officers are either stationed at a specific school or are dispatched to schools within a particular district when the need presents itself. In areas where this is not the case, an administrator at each school should interface with the local police department to provide for continual discourse concerning safety issues, threats and vulnerabilities, and formal response plans.

It is important that school districts develop official relationships with the local police so they have a point of contact in the event of a serious cyberbullying incident (or any other incident requiring their assistance). Schools that have a dedicated school resource (or liaison) officer (SRO) assigned to their building are at an advantage when it comes to dealing with student issues that may implicate law enforcement. These officers generally have more training and experience in dealing with students and schools and their unique issues than their counterparts assigned to general patrol functions. Since SROs are in the schools on a continual basis, they are usually more attuned to student interpersonal relationships and the concerns of educators. The best officers know the students personally and interact with them in a relatable way. As a result, students come to respect the police and better understand that they do more than just show up at their house when there is a domestic disturbance or issue them a citation for driving 5 miles-per-hour over the speed limit.

Unfortunately, this model has been disappearing in many schools across the country as both school and municipal budgets have contracted. Historically, SROs were often funded through a combination of money from schools and cities or counties, but when one partner pulls the financial plug, the other rarely has the resources to make up the difference and the position is usually lost. As a result, police are often called to the school only in situations where a significant (and possibly criminal) incident has occurred. Sometimes it is the same officer that responds throughout the school year, but often the call will be directed to whoever is on duty at the time. Having a consistent contact is important from a procedural stand-point (making sure the officer is aware of the issues related to schools and students), but it also helps to have a familiar face—both from the perspective of the staff and students.

Different Roles and Responsibilities

When it comes to responding to bullying (or any incident, really), school administrators and law enforcement officers play different, yet complementing roles. Usually law enforcement is only pulled into the discussion when the incident appears to rise to the level of a violation of criminal law. Assaults or serious substantiated threats of violence would be the most common examples where the police should be brought in. Law enforcement can also assist in investigating incidents. They often have more training in interviewing and evidence collection and would be able to evaluate the evidence to determine if a crime has been committed. That said, schools should be careful when including law enforcement officers in an interview because it changes the dynamic considerably. Having an officer stand over the shoulder of the principal while she is asking the student about school behaviors is intimidating under any circumstance, but especially so if the officer is not one who is regularly seen in the school.

Technically speaking, when administrators are investigating an incident, they are doing so as a representative of the school, for possible *school discipline*. If the police is involved (whether it is a SRO or other officer), the investigation may become one where the focus is on uncovering evidence of a crime for possible *criminal punishment*. When that happens, the procedural rules change. For instance, when a school official is interviewing a student or searching his property, that official typically only needs a reasonable belief that the student has engaged in, or possesses evidence of, a behavior that violates school policy. Very few constitutional protections are afforded to students in these cases because the school is acting *in loco parentis* (in place of parents) and not as a government official for the purpose of formal punishment. When the police are involved in investigating a crime, however, citizens (including minors) do have certain rights.

In *Miranda v. Arizona* (1966), the US Supreme Court ruled that, prior to "custodial interrogations," law enforcement officers must inform individuals who are suspected of committing a crime that they have many constitutional rights.[12] We've all heard this statement before on crime shows: "You have the right to remain silent, anything you say can be used against you in a court of law . . . You have the right to an attorney . . . If you can't afford one, one will be provided. . . ." This standard also generally applies when officers are interviewing minors in the community, but the question was recently raised in the Supreme Court of Kentucky about whether students should be informed of their rights when being questioned by an officer at school or by a school administrator in the presence of an officer.[13] In the decision, the court reaffirmed the ability of school officials to interview students for the purpose of a possible school sanction without being required to inform them of their rights but ruled that in circumstances where criminal charges are possible, *Miranda* warnings are required. This deviates from previous interpretations which basically held that if a law enforcement officer was assisting in a *school investigation*, the officer was beholden to the rules that applied to school officials. No doubt this issue is headed to the US Supreme Court for clarification.

There are also different issues associated with whether an educator or a law enforcement officer can search the contents of a student cell phone. *New Jersey v. T.L.O.* (1985), for example, states that students are protected by the Fourth Amendment to the US Constitution which protects citizens against unreasonable searches and seizures.[14] In *T.L.O.*, the Supreme Court also made it clear that the standard that law enforcement officers must reach to conduct a search (probable cause that *a crime has been committed*), is not required of educators. The standard applied to school officials is whether the search is "justified at its inception and whether, as conducted, it was reasonably related in scope to the circumstances that justified the interference in the first place."[14] Of course, there is a bit of subjectivity to this standard and what appears to be reasonable for one person may not be for another. In *T.L.O.*, the Court ruled that for a search of student property to be justified, there must exist "reasonable grounds for suspecting that the search will turn up evidence that the student has violated or is violating either the law or the rules of the school."[14] That would be the standard that gives you the go-ahead if you are an administrator with the opportunity to search a student's personal device(s).

In *Riley v. California* (2014), the US Supreme Court ruled on whether law enforcement officers can search the contents of cell phones confiscated in conjunction with an arrest. The law allows the police to conduct a basic search of any property possessed by someone who is arrested. The purpose here is to identify weapons or evidence of a crime that may have been stashed by the accused upon hearing that the police were at hand. Some have argued that a cell phone is in essence no different than a bag: it contains "stuff," including possible evidence of a crime (though admittedly no weapons). And the rules, therefore, should be the same. The Court disagreed with this interpretation, reasoning that cell phones have the potential to contain so much information, both locally on the device, but also remotely through cloud storage and Internet access, and that the risk of invading one's personal privacy is too great to allow a search without reasonable justification. Nothing included in the language of the ruling suggests a change in law or policy concerning the circumstances under which it is appropriate for *educators* to search the contents of student-owned cell phones (or other portable electronic devices, for that matter) that are brought to school. That said, it is advised that educators discuss these issues with their school resource/liaison officer and school district attorney so that everyone is more or less on the same page. Don't wait until you are confronting a student who is believed to have contraband content on their phone before you develop appropriate procedures.[15]

These are just some of the issues, and as you can probably tell, many of the important questions have not been fully settled. Overall, officers and educators need to use their judgment about situations that might benefit from, or necessitate, law enforcement involvement. As long as there is no immediate threat of harm, it is usually best for school administrators to interview students involved in misbehavior without a law enforcement officer present. Under these circumstances, they have a lot more freedom and leeway to gather the necessary information. As soon as the administrator reaches the conclusion that a crime may have been committed, the investigation should be turned over to the police.

When Cyberbullying Becomes a Crime

In some (rare) situations, cyberbullying rises to the level of criminal behavior. As explained earlier, the most common factor in these cases is a threat to the physical safety or personal property of oneself or one's family. Threats are often made by youth involved in interpersonal squabbles and adolescent drama, and most have limited potential to escalate into real-world violence. Still, some require deeper inquiry and demand a formal response. Discerning which threats are viable is difficult, to say the least. The matter is complicated when reviewing texts or social media content, as it is largely devoid of socioemotional cues (such as tone of voice or body language) that can indicate the seriousness of ostensibly threatening words.

The criminal law may also be implicated when the behavior involves stalking, can be characterized as a hate or bias crime (against protected populations), or involves sexually explicit images or the sexual exploitation of youth. In situations where a student is threatening another student or a staff member and an attempt at informal resolution does not immediately end the problem, law enforcement should (and must) get involved. In our post-Columbine era, no threat—regardless of how trivial or humorous it might seem—should be taken lightly or rationalized away. That said, we don't advocate that educators frivolously devote significant resources toward each threat unless there is an articulable and verifiable cause for concern. We do, however, recommend that they always inform law enforcement of situations which may cross the criminal line and let *them* investigate the matter.

SUMMARY

As an adult who is reading this book, you will eventually—if you haven't yet already—face a cyberbullying incident that affects a child under your care or supervision. It is crucial to have a solid idea of possible courses of action to pursue after evaluating the circumstances of every unique situation. Clearly, victims and witnesses of cyberbullying need to be supported and empowered, while cyberbullies need to be disciplined and inspired to demonstrate positive choices and behaviors in the future. We have sought to provide you with a variety of ways in which these goals can be accomplished; it is up to you to determine which to implement when the time comes.

To assess where your school stands in terms of meaningful efforts to address cyberbullying, we've created a "Cyberbullying Report Card for Schools" (Resource E). This will be useful in identifying the areas in which you are prepared and those that require more attention. We hope that you are able to answer yes to each of the statements; if not, create a plan to correct the deficiencies. By now you've understood the severity of the problem, and it's time to be part of the solution. When you have conscientiously engaged in all of the prevention and response strategies provided, you should be in great shape to deal with any instances of cyberbullying that arise.

QUESTIONS FOR REFLECTION

1. Why is the suggestion to "turn off your device" not an appropriate response to cyberbullying?

2. What are some creative punishments for students who engage in cyberbullying?

3. Why is cyberbullying based on gender, race, or sexual orientation more serious than other forms of cyberbullying?

4. What should you do if a teen comes up to you and tells you he or she has been cyberbullied?

5. What specific things can be done to help bystanders at your school stand up for those victimized?

NOTES

1. Joan Leishman. "Cyber-bullying" (2005). CBC News Online. http://www.njbullying.org/CBCNewsIndepthBullying.htm.
2. *The Civil Rights Act of 1964*. Pub. L. 88–352, 78 Stat. 241 (1964).

3. Russlynn Ali. "Dear Colleague Letter: Harassment and Bullying" (2010). http://www2.ed.gov/about/offices/list/ocr/docs/dcl-factsheet-201010.pdf.

4. Requa v. Kent School District No. 415. 2007 WL 1531670 (W.D. Wash. May 24, 2007).

5. Digital Media Law Project. "Recording Phone Calls and Conversations" (2014). http://www.dmlp.org/legal-guide/recording-phone-calls-and-conversations.

6. AT&T. "Acceptable Use Policy" (2014). http://www.corp.att.com/aup/.

7. Wills v. Brown University. 184 F.3d 20 (1st Cir. 1999).

8. Zeno v. Pine Plains Central School District. 10–3604-CV (2d Cir. Dec. 3, 2012).

9. John M. Darley and Bibb Latané. "Bystander Intervention in Emergencies: Diffusion of Responsibility." *Journal of Personality and Social Psychology* 8 (1968): 377–383.

10. Henry C. Black. *Black's Law Dictionary*. 6th ed. St. Paul, MN: West Publishing, 1990.

11. American Law Institute. *Restatement of the Law, Second, Torts, § 46*. Washington, DC: American Law Institute, 1965.

12. Miranda v. Arizona. 384 U.S. 436 (1966).

13. N.C., a Child Under Eighteen v. Com. 396 S.W.3d 852 (2013).

14. New Jersey v. T.L.O. 469 U.S. 325 (1985).

15. Riley v. California. No. 13–132, reversed and remanded; No. 13–212, 728 F. 3d 1, affirmed (2014). http://www.supremecourt.gov/opinion.

Concluding Thoughts

As adolescents communicate via text and social media, interpersonal conflict will continue to transcend cyberspace and affect youth academically, emotionally, psychologically, behaviorally, and physically. While some responsibility to oversee and intervene must be shouldered by the parents of adolescents, other adults in supervisory roles are not exempt from doing their part. The blurring of boundaries and distinctions between online and offline interaction among adolescents underscores the need for all youth professionals to pay attention to both venues with equal attention. It is likely that the school in particular will serve as the front-line institution for prevention and response, as interpersonal conflict continually moves from the real world to the virtual and back again.

We have definitely made some progress over the last six years since the first edition of this book was released. There still exists a bit of a disconnect, however, between what youth are doing in cyberspace and what adults know about what youth are doing in cyberspace. Both parties, to be sure, share some responsibility. Youth are hesitant to talk to most adults for fear of judgmental and overly harsh responses, and adults are hesitant to discuss these issues with youth because of unfamiliarity, busyness, or indifference. This book brought you up to speed with respect to the ways many teens are using and misusing their electronic devices and social media access and sought to encourage you to approach the issue with a calm perspective, a level head, and an informed action plan. And believe it or not, *your* role as someone who cares about kids is absolutely instrumental in helping us make further headway in safeguarding, equipping, and empowering our kids as they navigate the difficult waters of adolescence and technology use.

If you have made it this far, you are clearly very committed to helping your students and children avoid the landmines on the landscape of new technology. And, you now have a solid foundation from which to operate and a wealth of resources at your disposal to assist you along the way. Start with our website (www.cyberbullying.us) to which we have regularly referred throughout this book. There you will find the latest research, a frequently updated blog, and an ever-expanding list of free resources that will likely provide the answers to many of your questions. Next, spread the word about cyberbullying. With your help, we hope to continue making strides in educating the general public and enlisting their active support. Finally, keep us informed with regard to your struggles and successes on the front lines of this issue. You can e-mail us at connect@cyberbullying.us. Knowing that bullying has moved beyond the schoolyard, we will help in any way we can.

SCENARIO 1

> James is frustrated and saddened by the comments his high school peers are making about his sexuality. Furthermore, it appears a group of male students has created an imposter account to impersonate him on an online dating site. Posing as James and using his contact information, they start sending out very provocative and sexually bold messages to other guys on the site. When James starts receiving e-mails from members of this site in his inbox, he is mortified and devastated.

If you were a school guidance counselor or administrator within the school, what would you do if James approached you with the problem? What about if you were James's mom or dad? What can James do to deal with the embarrassment? What would be some incorrect and unacceptable ways that James might try to deal with this problem?

SCENARIO 2

Two female sixth-graders, Katie and Sarah, are exchanging malicious texts back and forth because of a misunderstanding involving a boy named Jacob. The statements escalate in viciousness from trivial name-calling to very vicious and inflammatory statements, including death threats. Both girls have come to speak to the school counselor in tears, both angry at what is going on, and emotionally wrecked about the things being said online—that so many other students in their classes are seeing. In fact, other girls at school are getting involved and starting to take sides, which is leading to additional drama and even some minor physical violence at school.

Should the police be contacted? Are both girls wrong? What should the kids do in this instance? What would you do as a parent if you discovered this problem? What might a school counselor or administrator do to keep this situation from further deteriorating?

SCENARIO 3

A mother is walking by her son Jonathan while he is on his iPhone and notices that he keeps hiding the screen and pretending that he isn't doing anything when she walks by or gets close to him. Upon further observation, the mother sees that Jonathan is sending out hateful tweets via what seems to be a Twitter account he has set up to impersonate someone else.

What should the mother do first? Should Twitter get involved? How should Jonathan be allowed to use his phone moving forward? How can things be made "right," as it relates to those he hurt and humiliated with his online posts?

SCENARIO 4

Lindsay has just moved to town from Oregon and enrolls in the local middle school. Very pretty, outgoing, and funny, she quickly wins the attention of a number of the school's football players—much to the chagrin of the school's cheerleaders. Bonnie, the head cheerleader, is concerned about Lindsay stealing away her boyfriend Johnny, the quarterback. With the help of her cheerleader friends, Bonnie decides to create a "We Hate Lindsay" website, where girls can post reasons why they hate Lindsay and why they think she should move back to Oregon. Soon, the entire school becomes aware of the site's web address, and many others begin to post hurtful sentiments about Lindsay. Desperately wanting to make friends in a new town, Lindsay is crushed and begins to suffer from depression and a lack of desire to do anything aside from crying in bed.

If you were her mom or dad, what would you do? What might the school do to help Lindsay? If you were Lindsay's teacher, what would you do? If you were her best friend, what might you say or do to help?

SCENARIO 5

Chester, a tall, skinny teenager who excels in math and science classes, feels embarrassed when he has to change into gym clothes in the boy's locker room at school because he lacks muscularity and size. Other, more athletic, and well-built teens notice Chester's shyness and decide to exploit it. Using their phones, they covertly take pictures of Chester without his shirt on and in his boxer shorts. These pictures are then circulated among the rest of the student body via Instagram. Soon enough, boys and girls are pointing, snickering, and laughing at Chester as he walks down the school hallways. He overhears comments such as "There goes Bird-Chested Chester," "Big Wus," and "Pansy." These words cut him deeply, and the perception that his classmates have of him begins to affect his math and science grades.

If you were his teacher, what would you do? If you were his parent, what would you do? What can Chester do to deal with the harassment—now and in the future? How can his harassing classmates really understand how much pain they are causing with their words and actions? What would you do if you were a bystander?

SCENARIO 6

Heather is a fourth-grader who is extremely proficient at using the Internet. On Monday, she receives an e-mail from someone named "stalker2015@hotmail.com." The subject and body of the e-mail state, "I'm watching you. Be afraid." Heather immediately deletes it and thinks nothing of it. On Tuesday, she receives another e-mail from stalker2015@hotmail.com, and this time, the subject and body of the e-mail are, "I am getting closer, and I see you on the computer right now as you read this." Heather starts to get worried but doesn't want to tell her parents because she is concerned they will take away her Internet privileges. On Wednesday, she awakens to a new e-mail from stalker2015@hotmail.com that reads, "Be very afraid. Today may be your last." Definitely frightened and concerned now, she makes up her mind to tell her parents about the e-mails when she returns from school that day. She is unable to concentrate in any of her classes because of intense fear as to what the e-mail meant when it said, "Today may be your last." She rushes home after school, bent on bringing it up to her mom and dad as soon as she sees them. To her dismay, she finds a note on the table stating her mom went grocery shopping and her dad will be home late. Her palms begin to sweat and her heart begins to race. She goes to her bedroom, throws her backpack on her bed, and checks her e-mail. Twenty-five new e-mails pop up. Each one is from the same sender: stalker2015@hotmail.com. They all say the same thing: "I am in your house. I am on a wireless Internet connection. You don't know where I am, but I know where you are!" Heather grabs her house key, rushes out of the front door, locks it, runs to her friend's house, and tells her friend's mom about her situation.

What would you do if you were her friend's mom? What can Heather do to ensure her safety now and in the future? To whom else should she turn for help?

SCENARIO 7

Stan is an eighth-grader who is physically abused by his alcoholic uncle when he visits him on weekends. Additionally, Stan is being pushed around by some of his peers in middle school because he wears black all the time and is basically a loner. Recently, Stan has realized that on the Internet—on sites like Ask.fm and messaging apps like Kik—he can freely become a person who seems much more attractive and fun and lighthearted than he is in real life. By taking on a different persona, he is finding social interaction with others much easier and more rewarding. Nonetheless, he still harbors much anger and bitterness within due to the treatment by his uncle and some of his classmates. He decides to get back at his uncle and some of his classmates by posting personal information about them—along with some true stories about his negative experiences with them—on an anonymous confessions page he created on Ask.fm. This information includes their cell phone numbers, home phone numbers, and home addresses. Because Stan has made many friends on Ask.fm, they rally around him in support and decide to exact some vigilante justice on their own to help Stan get revenge. A large number of his online friends use the phone numbers and addresses to make repeated prank calls, to order hundreds of pizzas to the victims' doors, and to sign them up for many, many pornographic magazines and Sears catalogs. Stan is extremely pleased at the harassment that his uncle and mean classmates are now experiencing.

What would you do if you were a parent or school administrator and the police alerted you, themselves contacted by Stan's Internet service provider after an online complaint was filed by Stan's uncle about these incidents? How might Stan learn that such vengeful behavior is inappropriate? How might Stan get help for the abuse he suffers and the way he feels?

SCENARIO 8

Karen is a very devout teenager who leads a prayer meeting every morning by the high school flag pole. Many boys and girls are simply drawn to Karen as a friend because of her sweet nature and hopeful innocence. Other girls in her school, however, feel threatened by Karen's piety and commitment to holy living, and they begin to drum up ideas to expose her as a fraud. Specifically, they begin to spread rumors via Instagram that Karen is sleeping around with the boy's track team. Karen is alerted to the online rumors by a close friend and is heartbroken. She tells her teachers and pastor, who then contact the school administration.

What would you do if you were the principal in this situation? What would you do if you were Karen? What would you do if you were Karen's close friend and really wanted to help? How could those who spread the rumors understand how hurtful their actions were?

SCENARIO 9

Casey loves playing games on his Xbox console, especially since it allows him to link up to and compete with other players across the world on Xbox Live. He recently met one teenager in Russia named Boris while playing Call of Duty: Advanced Warfare, and they became fast friends because both enjoyed and excelled at it. Together, they became almost unbeatable whenever they competed as a team against other teams online. At some point, though, Casey told Boris he had found a better gaming partner and didn't want to play with Boris anymore. Boris was outraged that he was being "dumped" as a gaming partner for someone else, and he began to tell other people on the gaming network that Casey "sucked" at all video games and no one should ever be his partner unless they wanted to lose really badly. Soon after these statements started circulating, Casey's new gaming partner dumped him, and everyone else on the network started to reject him (which was particularly crushing because online gaming was a safe haven in his difficult life). When coupled with recollections of other instances of rejection in his life, this experience began to make Casey feel completely hopeless. He then started to express suicidal intentions to his sister.

Can this example really be characterized as cyberbullying? How would you handle this as a school administrator? What should his sister do and how can schools equip her to respond effectively to Casey's problems?

SCENARIO 10

Trevor is sixteen and into drag racing. He and his friends often go down to the local drag strip and race other sixteen- and seventeen-year-olds in their souped-up cars. Because drag racing is a testosterone-heavy event, egos get involved quickly. Speed is often equated to masculinity and strength, and physical fights sometimes break out when winners gloat too much over losers of races. Local police have had to report to the drag strip often in recent weeks and have threatened to shut down the strip completely if any more fights occur. Therefore, the aggression has been transferred from the real world to cyberspace, and winners are gloating over and making fun of losers online through texts and public forum posts at the local racing scene's Facebook page. Trevor is undefeated in his racing exploits, and this has given him a very inflated self-conception. His success has gotten to his head, and he has been getting his kicks by insulting and humiliating online those who lose against him. Some guys he has defeated are sick of how he's been acting, and are organizing a group to go over to his house, trash his hot rod with shovels and sledgehammers, and beat him up. Trevor gets tipped off about this plan the day before it is supposed to happen.

What should Trevor do? Who should be involved, and what should be done about this problem—in order of priority?

Technology Use Contract

Child Expectations:

I understand that using electronic devices and the Internet is a privilege and not a right and that it is subject to the following rules:

1. Mom/Dad will pay for my devices, Internet, and cell phone access, unless otherwise agreed upon, but I will pay for any charges above and beyond the usual monthly fees (repairs due to carelessness, if my device is stolen, etc.).

2. I will respect the privacy of others online and on all devices I access or use. I will not touch any content or file that is not mine.

3. I will not download anything or install apps, games, or other programs on any of my devices without first asking Mom/Dad.

4. I will never give out private information while online. At no time will I ever give out my last name, phone number, address, or school name—even if I know the person with whom I am communicating—unless approved.

5. I will never agree to meet an online friend in person without first asking Mom/Dad.

6. I understand that I can use electronic devices for approved purposes only, and I understand that what I do reflects my character, upbringing, and family name—and affects my reputation and future opportunities.

7. I will not send hurtful, harassing, or threatening texts or inappropriate photos and videos, or make such posts on social media, gaming networks, or elsewhere online.

8. I will not say or send anything to anyone using my device(s) that I wouldn't be *completely* comfortable with Mom/Dad hearing, seeing, or knowing about. This includes profanity and any offensive language.

9. I will not take and/or send a picture or video of anyone without that person's permission.

10. I will not be disruptive in my device use. If Mom/Dad or another adult asks me to end a call, stop texting, or finish playing a game, I will.

11. I will always respond to calls and texts from Mom/Dad and not ignore their desire to ask me a question or otherwise check in to ensure my safety. If I miss a text or call from them, I will respond to it as soon as I possibly can.

12. I will not use my electronic devices for any purpose after _____ AM/PM on a school night or after _____ AM/PM on a nonschool night, unless approved.

13. I will abide by all the rules my school has put in place regarding students' phones.

14. I understand that Mom/Dad have the right to look through the contents of my device(s) at any time if/when they have a reasonable concern and will do so in my presence.

15. If I ever feel uncomfortable about an experience online, I will immediately tell Mom/Dad. I understand that Mom/Dad are willing to help me and will not punish me as long as these rules are followed.

16. My online account usernames and accounts are as follows:

Signed: _____

Parent Expectations:

I understand that it is my responsibility to protect my family and to help them receive the best of what electronic devices and the Internet have to offer. In that spirit, I agree to the following:

1. I will pay for their devices and their Internet and cell phone plans, unless otherwise agreed upon.

2. I will listen calmly. If my child comes to me with a problem related to online experiences, I promise not to get angry but to do my best to help my child resolve the situation.

3. I will be reasonable. I will set reasonable rules and expectations for Internet usage. I will establish appropriate consequences for lapses in judgment on the part of my child.

4. I will treat my child with dignity. I will respect the friendships that my child may make online as I would offline friends.

5. I will not unnecessarily invade my child's privacy, and I will respect it. I promise not to go further than necessary to ensure my child's safety. I will not look through the contents of my child's device(s) unless there is a reasonable concern, and I will do so in their presence.

6. I will be reasonable with consequences for violations of this contract. Consequences will start at loss of device privileges for 24 hours and progress according to the seriousness of the violation.

7. I will not take drastic measures. No matter what happens, I understand that these technologies are important tools which are essential to my child's success in school or business, and I promise not to ban it entirely.

8. I will be involved. I will spend time with my child and be a positive part of my child's online activities and relationships—just as I am offline.

Signed: _____

Cyberbullying Victimization

Cyberbullying is when someone <u>repeatedly</u> harasses, mistreats, or makes fun of another person online or while using cell phones or other electronic devices.

	Never	Once	A Few Times	Several Times	Many Times
I have seen other people being cyberbullied.					
In my lifetime, I have been cyberbullied.					
In the last 30 days, I have been cyberbullied.					
In the last 30 days, I have been cyberbullied in these ways:					
Someone posted mean or hurtful comments about me online					
Someone posted a mean or hurtful picture of me online					
Someone posted a mean or hurtful video of me online					
Someone created a mean or hurtful web page about me					
Someone spread rumors about me online					
Someone threatened to hurt me through a cell phone text message					

(Continued)

(Continued)

	Never	Once	A Few Times	Several Times	Many Times
Someone threatened to hurt me online					
Someone pretended to be me online and acted in a way that was mean or hurtful to me					
In the last 30 days, I have been cyberbullied in these online environments:					
In a chat room					
Through e-mail					
Through computer instant messages					
Through cell phone text messages					
Through cell phone					
PictureMail or VideoMail					
On Facebook					
On a different social networking website (other than Facebook)					
On Twitter					
On YouTube					
On Instagram					
In virtual worlds such as Second Life, Gaia, or Habbo Hotel					
While playing a massive multiplayer online game such as World of Warcraft, EverQuest, Guild Wars, or RuneScape					
While playing online with Xbox, Playstation, Wii, PSP or similar device					

Cyberbullying Offending

Cyberbullying is when someone <u>repeatedly</u> harasses, mistreats, or makes fun of another person online or while using cell phones or other electronic devices.

	Never	Once	A Few Times	Several Times	Many Times
In my lifetime, I have cyberbullied others.					
In the last 30 days, I have cyberbullied others.					
In the last 30 days, I have cyberbullied others in these ways:					
I posted mean or hurtful comments about someone online					
I posted a mean or hurtful picture of someone online					
I posted a mean or hurtful video of someone online					
I spread rumors about someone online					
I threatened to hurt someone online					
I threatened to hurt someone through a cell phone text message					
I created a mean or hurtful web page about someone					
I pretended to be someone else online and acted in a way that was mean or hurtful to them					
In the last 30 days, I have cyberbullied others in these online environments:					
In a chat room					
Through e-mail					

(Continued)

(Continued)

	Never	Once	A Few Times	Several Times	Many Times
Through computer instant messages					
Through cell phone text messages					
Through cell phone					
PictureMail or VideoMail					
On Facebook					
On a different social networking website (other than Facebook)					
On Twitter					
On YouTube					
On Instagram					
In virtual worlds such as Second Life, Gaia, or Habbo Hotel					
While playing a massive multiplayer online game such as World of Warcraft, EverQuest, Guild Wars, or RuneScape					
While playing online with Xbox, Playstation, Wii, PSP or similar device					

PSYCHOMETRIC PROPERTIES

Utilized in 6 different studies (2007–2014)
(also pilot-tested and refined in 4 studies from 2003–2007)
Approximately 15,000 11- to 18-year-old students; over 90 schools
Coefficients represent range across the most recent 6 studies

Internal Reliability

Cyberbullying Victimization Scale—previous 30 days

(Cronbach's Alpha range 0.892–0.935)

1. I have been cyberbullied
2. Someone posted mean or hurtful comments about me online
3. Someone posted a mean or hurtful picture of me online
4. Someone posted a mean or hurtful video of me online
5. Someone created a mean or hurtful web page about me
6. Someone spread rumors about me online
7. Someone threatened to hurt me through a cell phone text message
8. Someone threatened to hurt me online
9. Someone pretended to be me online and acted in a way that was mean or hurtful

Cyberbullying Offending Scale—previous 30 days

(Cronbach's Alpha range 0.935–0.969)

1. I cyberbullied others
2. I posted mean or hurtful comments about someone online
3. I posted a mean or hurtful picture online of someone
4. I posted a mean or hurtful video online of someone
5. I spread rumors about someone online
6. I threatened to hurt someone online
7. I threatened to hurt someone through a cell phone text message
8. I created a mean or hurtful web page about someone
9. I pretended to be someone else online and acted in a way that was mean or hurtful to them

Factor Analysis

Cyberbullying Victimization Scale	Loadings
1. I have been cyberbullied	.686–.744
2. Someone posted mean or hurtful comments about me online	.765–.813
3. Someone posted a mean or hurtful picture of me online	.793–.861
4. Someone posted a mean or hurtful video of me online	.753–.900
5. Someone created a mean or hurtful web page about me	.688–.910
6. Someone spread rumors about me online	.717–.802
7. Someone threatened to hurt me through a cell phone text message	.764–.855
8. Someone threatened to hurt me online	.784–.870
9. Someone pretended to be me online and acted in a way that was mean or hurtful	.700–.866

All loaded onto 1 component; Eigenvalue range 5.51–6.40 (61.22–71.52% of variance)

Cyberbullying Offending Scale	Loadings
1. I cyberbullied others	.537–.776
2. I posted mean or hurtful comments about someone online	.780–.857
3. I posted a mean or hurtful picture of someone online	.919–.949
4. I posted a mean or hurtful video of someone online	.910–.968
5. I spread rumors about someone online	.742–.916
6. I threatened to hurt someone online	.853–.923
7. I threatened to hurt someone through a cell phone text message	.910–.930
8. I created a mean or hurtful web page about someone	.910–.942
9. I pretended to be someone else online and acted in a way that was mean or hurtful to them	.877–.938

All loaded onto 1 component; Eigenvalue range 5.13–7.34 (57.08–81.57% of variance)

Inter-Item Correlations

Cyberbullying Victimization Scale	1	2	3	4	5	6	7	8
1. I have been cyberbullied								
2. Someone posted mean or hurtful comments about me online	.43–.64							
3. Someone posted a mean or hurtful picture of me online	.36–.57	.62–.67						
4. Someone posted a mean or hurtful video of me online	.30–.58	.49–.67	.70–.89					
5. Someone created a mean or hurtful web page about me	.37–.59	.59–.62	.80–.87	.83–.92				
6. Someone spread rumors about me online	.35–.51	.63–.72	.55–.63	.44–.62	.29–.69			
7. Someone threatened to hurt me through a cell phone text message	.35–.54	.50–.68	.47–.69	.48–.72	.39–.73	.65–.70		
8. Someone threatened to hurt me online	.42–.60	.57–.70	.58–.71	.54–.73	.44–.75	.61–.66	.75–.80	
9. Someone pretended to be me online and acted in a way that was mean or hurtful	.35–.55	.35–.64	.41–.77	.50–.77	.60–.78	.53–.66	.53–.70	.53–.73

Cyberbullying Victimization Scale	1	2	3	4	5	6	7	8
1. I cyberbullied others								
2. I posted mean or hurtful comments about someone online	.52–.68							
3. I posted a mean or hurtful picture online of someone	.45–.70	.72–.83						
4. I posted a mean or hurtful video online of someone	.53–.67	.69–.75	.85–.94					
5. I spread rumors about someone online	.49–.63	.56–.78	.77–.83	.80–.86				
6. I threatened to hurt someone online	.51–.66	.67–.78	.74–.83	.83–.85	.71–.84			
7. I threatened to hurt someone through a cell phone text message	.48–.64	.56–.75	.74–.84	.77–.84	.71–.83	.77–.88		
8. I created a mean or hurtful web page about someone	.51–.66	.62–.72	.81–.92	.88–.94	.70–.82	.79–.83	.79–.85	
9. I pretended to be someone else online and acted in a way that was mean or hurtful to them	.46–.64	.65–.74	.79–.86	.86–.89	.74–.85	.78–.82	.82–.85	.79–.89

Scale Construction

Cyberbullying Victimization Scale

Variety scale: recode to dichotomy (never and once = 0; a few times, many times, every day = 1); range = 0–9

Summary scale: never = 0; once = 1; a few times = 2; many times = 3; every day = 4. Sum responses with higher values representing more involvement in cyberbullying; range = 0–36

Cyberbullying Offending Scale

Variety scale: recode to dichotomy (never and once = 0; a few times, many times, every day = 1); range = 0–9

Summary scale: never = 0; once = 1; a few times = 2; many times = 3; every day = 4. Sum responses with higher values representing more involvement in cyberbullying; range = 0–36

Dichotomy

Recode *summary scale* for victimization and offending so that 0 and 1 = 0 and 2 or above = 1.

RESOURCE D

Cyberbullying Incident
Tracking Form

Report taken by: _____ **Date of report:** _____

Complainant Information

Name:		❑ Student ❑ Staff ❑ Other
Age: Sex:	School:	Grade:

Target Information

Name:		❑ Student ❑ Staff ❑ Other
Age: Sex:	School:	Grade:

Offender 1 Information

Name:		❑ Student ❑ Staff ❑ Other
Age: Sex:	School:	Grade:

CYBERBULLYING INCIDENT TRACKING FORM

(page 2 of 4)

Offender 2 Information

Name:	❏ Student ❏ Staff ❏ Other
Age: Sex:	School:	Grade:

Offender 3 Information

Name:	❏ Student ❏ Staff ❏ Other
Age: Sex:	School:	Grade:

Other Party Information (witnesses and those with indirect knowledge)

Name:	❏ Student ❏ Staff ❏ Other
Age: Sex:	School:	Grade:

Other Party Information (witness, bystander, other)

Name:	❏ Student ❏ Staff ❏ Other
Age: Sex:	School:	Grade:

Other Party Information (witness, bystander, other)

Name:	❏ Student ❏ Staff ❏ Other
Age: Sex:	School:	Grade:

CYBERBULLYING INCIDENT TRACKING FORM

(page 3 of 4)

Location of Incident: _____

Description of Incident (use additional sheets if necessary):

	Yes
Threat to someone's physical safety	
Sexual harassment	
Discrimination based on race, class, gender, perceived or actual sexual orientation, or other protected status	
Repeated cyberbullying after previous intervention	
Image or video or audio recording or evidence of harassment	
Other notable feature (please list)	

Did the incident involve any of the following features?
Did the incident result in a substantial disruption of the school environment or infringe on the rights of other students or staff?   Yes   No
(If yes, please describe in as much detail as possible)

Attach printouts of all evidence and additional sheets with statements by individuals listed earlier.

CYBERBULLYING INCIDENT TRACKING FORM

(page 4 of 4)

Description of Action Plan:
What sanctions are being applied and what steps are being taken to ensure behavior does not continue? What additional consequences will be applied if offender fails to comply with action plan?

Comments by principal or other administrator:

Other comments:

I have been made aware of this incident and will discuss this issue further with my child.

Parent's signature: _____ Date: _____

Case closed date: _____ Reason for closure: _____

Cyberbullying Report Card for Schools

CYBERBULLYING REPORT CARD

Is your school adequately addressing or prepared for cyberbullying concerns? Fill out this Report Card to find out. How much do you agree with the following statements?

General Assessment	Strongly Disagree	Disagree	Unknown	Agree	Strongly Agree
We know how many students at our school have been victims of cyberbullying.					
We know how many students at our school have cyberbullied others.					
We know how many students at our school have observed cyberbullying among their classmates.					
We know what web environments and apps are most popular among our students and how they can be misused.					
School Climate/Culture	Strongly Disagree	Disagree	Unknown	Agree	Strongly Agree
Students who witness cyberbullying are empowered to step up and inform a trusted adult rather than remain silent bystanders.					

(Continued)

(Continued)

School Climate/Culture	Strongly Disagree	Disagree	Unknown	Agree	Strongly Agree
Teachers regularly remind students to approach them for help if they are dealing with an issue related to cyberbullying or online safety.					
It is clear to students that the inappropriate use of technology will not be tolerated by school administration.					
We work to create a school climate in which bullying and cyberbullying is not considered "cool" among the student population.					
Students feel that teachers are fair and equitable in their treatment of all students.					
Teachers are trusted and respected by students.					
Students generally feel that teachers care about them.					
School staff generally know all students by name.					
Students feel safe at our school.					
Curriculum and Education	**Strongly Disagree**	**Disagree**	**Unknown**	**Agree**	**Strongly Agree**
Students are taught about acceptable device, social media, and Internet use during the school year through in-class presentations, assemblies, and other regular instructive programming.					

Curriculum and Education	Strongly Disagree	Disagree	Unknown	Agree	Strongly Agree
Students are taught about safe password practices and the protection of personal information.					
Students are taught about how to recognize cyberbullying and threats to their online safety.					
Students are taught about how to respond to cyberbullying in an appropriate manner.					
Teachers know how to recognize cyberbullying issues and how to intervene in an appropriate manner.					
We distribute materials to students and parents to educate them about cyberbullying.					
We hold afterschool meetings and events during the school year for parents and community members to help them care for youth.					
We use older students to educate younger students about identification and prevention of bullying and cyberbullying and how to respond to it.					
We are (and stay) familiar with the relevant major court decisions related to student speech using electronic devices and the Internet.					
We are familiar with the ways in which the school district might be financially liable for negligently preventing or improperly responding to cyberbullying incidents, and we work to avoid them.					

(Continued)

(Continued)

Cyberbullying Response	Strongly Disagree	Disagree	Unknown	Agree	Strongly Agree
Students know to whom to report if they experience or witness cyberbullying.					
We take all incidents of cyberbullying seriously at our school.					
We have developed and made known a continuum of disciplinary consequences for cyberbullying incidents.					
We know when we can intervene in cyberbullying incidents that originated off campus.					
We have developed a formal procedure for investigating incidents of cyberbullying.					
We have an anonymous reporting system to allow students and teachers to report instances of cyberbullying without fear of reprisal.					
We have a formal relationship with a local law enforcement department capable of conducting computer and network forensic examinations should the need arise.					
Policies	Strongly Disagree	Disagree	Unknown	Agree	Strongly Agree
Our school has a clear bullying policy that includes cyberbullying.					
Our cyberbullying policy includes language about off-campus behaviors being subject to discipline when the behaviors disrupt the learning environment at school.					

Policies	Strongly Disagree	Disagree	Unknown	Agree	Strongly Agree
Our school has a clear policy regarding phones and other student-owned portable electronic devices.					
Students know our policy regarding technology.					
Parents know our policy regarding technology.					
Signage about acceptable device, social media, and Internet use is posted in various places throughout the school.					
Technology	**Strongly Disagree**	**Disagree**	**Unknown**	**Agree**	**Strongly Agree**
We have website-blocking and content-monitoring software/ hardware installed on our network to ensure age-appropriate web browsing and communications.					
We avoid putting student personal information on the school website.					
We use an online platform to provide educational interactivity among staff and students.					
Teachers are trained in how to handle technology distractions that compromise student learning.					
We utilize online environments or software to provide scenario-based learning for students.					

DESIGNATED CYBERBULLYING TRUSTEE

Talk to me if you or someone you know
is being electronically harassed or threatened!
I care about your online experience and can help!

RESOURCE G

Supplemental Staff Development Questions

CHAPTER 1

1. How is *bullying* most commonly defined?

2. What are the most important elements of any bullying definition?

3. What distinction is usually made between harassment and bullying?

4. How is *cyberbullying* defined in the text?

5. Do you believe this definition effectively describes what cyberbullying is among the youth you care for? If not, how would you modify it?

6. How is cyberbullying similar to other forms of bullying?

7. What makes cyberbullying different from traditional bullying?

8. Why might many adolescents choose to cyberbully their victims as opposed to bullying them in person?

9. Why might some adults fail to take cyberbullying seriously? How might this affect the identification and prevention of cyberbullying incidents?

10. What types of harm may victims experience as a result of cyberbullying? In what ways are these similar to other forms of bullying?

11. What are some of the emotional and psychological consequences for victims of traditional bullying? How could these be potentially life threatening? Do you think victims of cyberbullying are at risk for experiencing the same consequences as victims of traditional bullying?

12. What are some of the behavioral problems associated with bullying victimization? Could these problems ultimately lead to physical violence at school? How?

CHAPTER 2

1. How do teens and adults differ in their use of the Internet?

2. How could keeping pace with new Internet-based technologies help educators address cyberbullying?

3. What are some of the popular social media sites in use today?

4. Which social media apps seem to be most popular among youth at your school?

5. Give two examples of the methods used by individuals to communicate with others on social media.

6. How might some youth measure their social success on these sites? Do you think youth equate this to social success outside the realm of cyberspace?

7. How do youth make their profiles and other posted content stand out from those of others? What might an adolescent do or use to accomplish this?

8. Why do you think many youth are willing to divulge personal information online?

9. Why might youth lie about their age when signing up to use various social media sites?

10. Which safety measures have been developed by social media sites to protect their users?

11. What makes Yik Yak and Ask.fm particularly problematic? Is there any redeeming value in sites and applications like these?

12. What is *geotagging*?

13. Do you think young people should avoid social media altogether? Should parents forbid their children to use these sites and apps?

14. What are some of the potential benefits of online interaction?

15. How are some schools currently using social media as instructional tools? What is your school doing?

16. How might an individual use a fictitious account to bully others online?

17. Why are social media sites often ideal environments for cyberbullying?

18. Why might an adolescent decide to post personal information on their profile page but not make this same information available to others in real life?

19. How do cyberbullies steal their targets' identities on social media sites?

20. What simple step can students take to control who views the content of their profile pages?

21. Aside from text messaging capabilities, what other common features of many tablets and phones can be used to cyberbully?

22. How might cyberbullies use technology to shield their true identities from their victims? Why does the ability to remain anonymous seem to encourage cyberbullying?

23. Why might many adolescents fail to make distinctions between their lives offline and their lives in cyberspace?

24. In what ways can online interaction be beneficial to youth?

CHAPTER 3

1. In what ways might cyberbullying cause recurring harm to the victim?

2. How might cyberbullies obtain a "position of power" over their victims in an online setting? How might this position of power change? How is this different than traditional bullying?

3. Which is easier to investigate—cyberbullying or traditional bullying? What are the differences?

4. Can cyberbullies be completely anonymous while online?

5. If bullies seem to have the ability to hide their identities from their targets, how can they ever be identified?

6. In what ways might the Internet remove inhibition for the bully? How could this lead to additional harm for the victim?

7. With regard to cyberbullying, what is meant by the term *viral*?

8. Why might cyberbullying seem to cause unending suffering for those targeted?

9. Why would attacks by multiple aggressors be easier to coordinate through the use of cyberbullying techniques?

10. How might teens use their phones to cyberbully peers while at school?

11. What is *photoshopping*? How do some adolescents use this to cyberbully others?

12. Why do electronic devices make attractive tools for those desiring to spread rumors about others?

13. Aside from computers and phones, what other electronic devices might be used to perpetrate cyberbullying?

14. Why do teens flock to confessions pages?

15. Why do you think a teen would self-cyberbully?

16. What does the term *flaming* mean?

17. How might cyberbullies use the hijacked accounts of their victims on social media?

18. What does it mean to "tag" someone online?

19. Give two examples of how technology could allow bullies to extend their reach of aggression beyond settings normally associated with traditional bullying. Are there any limits to this reach?

20. How does cyberstalking differ from cyberbullying?

CHAPTER 4

1. Why do girls seem to be equally as likely to participate in cyberbullying as boys? Is this different than traditional bullying?

2. How are females likely to express their aggression online toward their victims?

3. How do females tend to feel after becoming a victim of cyberbullying? How is this different than feelings experienced by male victims? What might explain these differences?

4. When does cyberbullying activity tend to peak for adolescents? How does this compare to traditional forms of bullying?

5. According to recent research, which grade seems to signify an important shift for students with regard to cyberbullying activity?

6. What does recent research tell us about the relationship between cyberbullies and their victims? Do victims usually believe they know the identity of their aggressors?

7. Why do we believe there is a connection between cyberbullying and traditional bullying?

8. Are victims of cyberbullying likely to experience other forms of bullying as well?

9. What does research tell us about cyberbullies and their involvement in more traditional forms of bullying? What do these findings mean for educators seeking to counsel students believed to be involved with one particular type of bullying or victimization?

10. What happens more frequently, bullying at school or bullying online? Why do you think that is?

11. Why do you think cyberbullying victims are unlikely to tell adults about their experiences?

12. With whom are female victims likely to share information about cyberbullying experiences? Does this differ from male victims of cyberbullying?

13. How do victims tend to deal with minor forms of cyberbullying? Are these techniques effective in dealing with aggressors? Why are these techniques simply short-term solutions?

14. What are some of the emotional consequences of cyberbullying victimization? Are these consequences similar to those experienced by victims of schoolyard bullying? Do you believe the emotional responses of cyberbullying victims are cause for concern?

15. How are cyberbullying victims and offenders generally related? Are teens more likely to be cyberbullied by someone they know or a stranger online?

16. What is the nature of the relationship between cyberbullying and suicide?

17. Give two examples of the behavioral consequences associated with being cyberbullied.

18. Give two examples of the behavioral consequences associated with being a cyberbully.

19. Why do you think adolescent victims of cyberbullying have an elevated risk of suicidal thoughts?

20. What explanation do youth often give for their acts of cyberbullying?

21. How might some victims of traditional bullying seek retribution? Why is this strategy attractive to those individuals?

22. Why do youth cyberbully others?

23. Why are cyberbullies able to easily rationalize their attacks on others?

24. How could educators help students understand the seriousness of cyberbullying?

CHAPTER 5

1. When do educators have the authority to discipline student behavior and restrict student speech on campus? According to the *Tinker* ruling, what must educators be able to do in order for this to be justified?

2. When are students' expressed views on campus not protected by the First Amendment? Does this mean individuals lose their constitutional rights regarding freedom of speech after stepping on school property? How has the Court made this distinction?

3. If the expressed views of students can be restricted on campus by school administrators, can students be disciplined for these same views when they express them off of school grounds? If so, when is such action appropriate? Can you think of any specific scenarios or situations?

4. With respect to *Morse v. Frederick,* what did the Court mean by "school speech"? What do you believe the ruling might have been if this incident had occurred outside the scope of a school-sponsored event?

5. What requirement has the Court set forth regarding the discipline of off-campus student speech? Do you believe off-campus acts of cyberbullying could warrant discipline by school administrators? Do you think disciplining students for cyberbullying would be supported by the courts? Why or why not?

6. Aside from the important need to protect students, what might happen if educators fail to address harassment based on sex or race?

7. How would you define *substantial disruption?*

8. Why would a formal school policy on cyberbullying help protect students, teachers, and school administrators?

9. What are some of the essential elements of an effective policy on cyberbullying? Can you think of any additional elements you believe should be added to the list found in the text?

10. Why is it important for administrators to properly define the terms contained in their policy?

11. Why is it necessary to investigate all known incidents of cyberbullying involving your students?

12. Would you encourage teachers to deal with acts of cyberbullying on their own? If not, who would you suggest they notify? What if the cyberbullying incident is thought to be relatively minor?

13. When students are involved in cyberbullying, do they have an expectation of privacy with respect to their personal property? What has the Court cited as a prerequisite to student searches? In your opinion, how might this be different than probable cause?

14. How can school districts help discourage acts of cyberbullying? What else can educators do to help protect students?

CHAPTER 6

1. Why do we believe forbidding youth from using electronic devices, social media, and the Internet is an inappropriate method of cyberbullying prevention?

2. When should teachers begin the process of educating students about safe Internet use? Who should be involved in this endeavor?

3. As an educator, what do you believe are your responsibilities regarding cyberbullying prevention?

4. How might educators make an assessment of online behavior at their school? What should be addressed during this assessment period?

5. If you were to develop a policy governing the use of technology in your classroom, what rules would you include?

6. Do you think student-owned phones should be completely banned at school? What rules should be included in a school policy concerning phones, tablets, and other portable devices?

7. Under what circumstances are educators allowed to confiscate student-owned devices? When would educators be allowed to search the contents of those devices? How do the rules differ between educators and law enforcement officers?

8. How could you use peer mentoring in your efforts to prevent cyberbullying?

9. What steps do you believe educators should take to help promote a safe and respectful school environment?

10. What is the underlying goal of developing an honor code?

11. How should an honor code be expressed?

12. How does "content monitoring" work?

13. With respect to the Internet, what is a *proxy*? How could a student use a proxy to access prohibited social media sites?

14. What can parents do to help prevent cyberbullying?

15. How would you help parents become more proactive in preventing their child's involvement with cyberbullying?

16. What questions would you suggest parents ask their children regarding their child's online experiences?

17. At what age range would a "Technology Use Contract" be appropriate?

18. What methods can parents use to monitor their child's online activities?

19. Why do we consider monitoring software to be insufficient by itself?

20. Is it a good idea for schools to monitor the online (off-campus) activities of minors?

21. What steps would you tell your students to take to help protect them while online?

22. What are some of the signs of cyberbullying victimization? What might lead you to believe your student could be involved in cyberbullying others?

23. Why should schools designate cyberbullying trustees?

CHAPTER 7

1. Why would *just turn it off* be an impractical solution to deal with cyberbullying?

2. What connection does cyberbullying have with civil rights legislation? What does this mean for educators and school officials?

3. What steps should schools take immediately following the discovery of a cyberbullying incident?

4. Why are zero-tolerance policies not the best option for dealing with cyberbullying?

5. Which informal mechanisms might you use to respond to cyberbullying among your students? How could these help protect your school district?

6. What are some creative ways schools could respond to cyberbullying?

7. What is the ultimate goal when disciplining a student for participating in cyberbullying?

8. Why do you think it is important to respond to varying levels of cyberbullying with varying levels of disciplinary action?

9. What is the importance of an anonymous reporting system? Why would this system be beneficial for students?

10. Why is it important to document the disruption caused by cyberbullying incidents?

11. Why should incidents centered on protected statuses be taken very seriously?

12. Why are incidents involving digital video especially harmful for those victimized?

13. How can educators go about working with Internet and cellular service providers when investigating acts of cyberbullying?

14. What would you tell parents to do if they suspect their child has been cyberbullied? What would you discourage them from doing? Why?

15. What should parents do if they suspect their child is cyberbullying others?

16. What are some of the steps children should take if they believe they are being cyberbullied?

17. When can we consider cyberbullying as a *civil* matter?

18. When can we consider cyberbullying as a *criminal* matter?

19. When should law enforcement become involved in cyberbullying incidents?

20. How does the role of law enforcement officers differ from the role of educators in responding to cyberbullying?

Index

A SAGE Company

Corwin is committed to improving education for all learners by publishing books and other professional development resources for those serving the field of PreK–12 education. By providing practical, hands-on materials, Corwin continues to carry out the promise of its motto: **"Helping Educators Do Their Work Better."**